PAUL SELIGSON
LEANNE GRAY
LUIZ OTÁVIO BARROS

2nd edition

English ID

Student's Book 3

ID Language map

	Question syllabus	Vocabulary	Grammar	Speaking & Skills
1 1.1	Do you know all your classmates?		Review of present tenses	Ask questions to get to know someone
1.2	How do couples meet?	Relationships Phrasal verbs		Talk about relationships Talk about how a couple met
1.3	How many Facebook friends do you have?	Types of friend	Review of question forms	Describe your relationships Talk about your friends
1.4	Do you have many social media profiles?	Personality adjectives	Emphatic forms	Describe your personality Express your opinions about social media
1.5	How much time do you spend online?			Read for main ideas and specific information
	Which do you do more: listen or speak?	Active listening phrases		Practice listening actively
Writing 1: A personal profile p. 16		**ID Café 1: He said, she said p. 17**		
2 2.1	How green are you?	Going green Adjectives from verbs and nouns		Discuss how you could be greener
2.2	How long have you been studying here?	Time / Frequency / Degree phrases	Present perfect continuous	Ask and answer about personal habits
2.3	How has the climate been changing?	The environment	Present perfect simple vs. Present perfect continuous	Talk about environmental problems in your city
2.4	What's the best ad you've seen recently?		Simple past vs. Present perfect simple / continuous	Interview your partner
2.5	Do you support any charities?	Endangered species		Expressing numerical information
	Have you made any lifestyle changes recently?			Encourage or discourage a friend
Writing 2: A report p. 28		**ID Café 2: Down to earth p. 29**		**Review 1 p. 30**
3 3.1	Which city would you most like to visit?	Cities		Describe a city
3.2	Was your last vacation as much fun as you'd hoped?	Social conventions	Past perfect	Talk about rules where you live Talk about a place you've been to
3.3	Do you ever want to get away from it all?	Urban problems		Conduct a survey and report on the findings about problems in your city
3.4	Have you ever missed any important dates?	Active listening phrases	Past perfect continuous	Share stories about missing an important event
3.5	Do you always follow the rules?	Common sign phrases		Talk about rules and regulations
	When did you last break a rule?	Phrases for explaining and questioning rules		Share stories about breaking a rule
Writing 3: A narrative p. 42		**ID Café 3: Global swarming p. 43**		
4 4.1	Does your school system work well?	School life do / get / make / take collocations		Describe an ideal school
4.2	What's the ideal age to go to college?	College life	too / enough	Debate educational issues Talk about choosing a career
4.3	What do you regret not having done?		should have	Talk about regrets
4.4	What would you do if you won a million dollars?		First and second conditional	Imagine what will / would happen Talk about a goal or aspiration
4.5	What makes someone a genius?			Make predictions
	How do you deal with criticism?			Sympathize and criticize
Writing 4: A blog p. 54		**ID Café 4: AIQ: Artificial Intelligence Quotient! p. 55**		**Review 2 p. 56**
5 5.1	Are you a shopaholic?	Shopping		Make a "shopping haul" video
5.2	What shouldn't you have spent money on?	Money collocations	Third conditional	Talk about a mistake or something you wish you had done differently Talk about ways to reduce personal debt
5.3	Have you ever borrowed money from a relative?		Modals of possibility / probability	Present a crowdfunding project Speculate about your partner's life
5.4	Have you ever bought a useless product?	Word formation	Adjective order	Share shopping experiences Create an infomercial
5.5	Do you often buy things on impulse?			Read for confirmation Talk about your experience with supermarkets
	When did you last complain in a store?	Shopping problems		Make complaints and ask for a refund
Writing 5: An advert p. 68		**ID Café 5: Shop around p. 69**		**Mid-term review: Game p. 70**

Question syllabus		Vocabulary	Grammar	Speaking & Skills
6	**6.1** What are you watching these days?	TV genres and expressions		Talk about TV habits
	6.2 What's your favorite TV show ever?		Restrictive relative clauses	Talk about first episodes of TV shows Write a quiz about movies / music
	6.3 What was the last movie you saw?		Non-restrictive relative clauses	Describe movies
	6.4 Where do you usually watch movies?	Movies		Create a story for a movie
	6.5 Who are the wildest celebrities you know?			Understand details
	When were you last surprised?			Express surprise
Writing 6: A movie / book review p. 82		**ID Café 6: Best in show p. 83**		**Review 3 p. 84**
7	**7.1** Does technology rule your life?	Phrasal verbs		Talk about your habits
	7.2 What was the last little lie you told?		Reported speech (1)	Share stories about being deceived
	7.3 How much of your day is screen time?	Using touch screens	Indirect questions	Present an invention to make life easier
	7.4 Are machines with personality a good idea?		Reported speech (2)	Talk about machines with personality Write a questionnaire about tech habits
	7.5 How often do you use a pen?			Take notes while listening Talk about a book
	Do you enjoy a good argument?	Phrases for expressing your views		Debate a topic
Writing 7: A complaint email p. 96		**ID Café 7: The road NOT taken p. 97**		
8	**8.1** How important are looks?	Photography and photos		Talk about appearance and the effect of Photoshopping images
	8.2 Do you like watching illusions?		Modal perfects – *must have, can't have, might have / may have*	Describe how an illusion is done
	8.3 Have you ever cut your own hair?		Causative form	Talk about the things you do and the things you have / get done
	8.4 Do you have a lot of furniture in your room?	Furniture	Tag questions	Check information
	8.5 Is your listening improving?			Make predictions
	What's the hardest part of language learning?			Express preferences
Writing 8: An opinion essay p. 108		**ID Café 8: Small talk and smart phones p. 109**		**Review 4 p. 110**
9	**9.1** Does crime worry you?	Crime and violence	Review of verb families	Talk about crime
	9.2 How could your city be improved?		Passive voice	Talk about a city's transformation
	9.3 Have you ever been to court?	Crime and punishment		Decide on the right punishment for crimes
	9.4 Where will you be living ten years from now?		Future perfect and continuous	Discuss ways to protect yourself from cyber crime
	9.5 Do you watch TV crime dramas?			Talk about stupid crimes Identify sarcasm
	Are you good at making excuses?	Phrases for giving excuses		Give excuses
Writing 9: A formal letter p. 122		**ID Café 9: A knight at the museum p. 123**		
10	**10.1** What drives you crazy?	Moods Binomials		Talk about temperament
	10.2 What do you love to hate?	Common expressions with *for* and *of*	Gerunds and infinitives	Talk about pet peeves Role-play an anger management session
	10.3 How assertive are you?		Verb + gerund or infinitive	Test your assertiveness
	10.4 How similar are you to your friends?	Phrasal verbs	Separable and inseparable phrasal verbs	Talk about toxic people Take a friendship test
	10.5 What do you find hardest about English?			Practice proofreading Talk about your mistakes in English
	Are you going to take an English exam?	Phrases for making recommendations		Make recommendations
Writing 10: A forum post p. 134		**ID Café 10: Mad men p. 135**		**Review 5 p. 136**

Grammar p. 138   Verbs p.158   Sounds and usual spelling p. 160   Audioscript p. 162

Welcome to English ID!

Finally, an English course you can understand!

Famous **song lines** illustrate language from lessons.

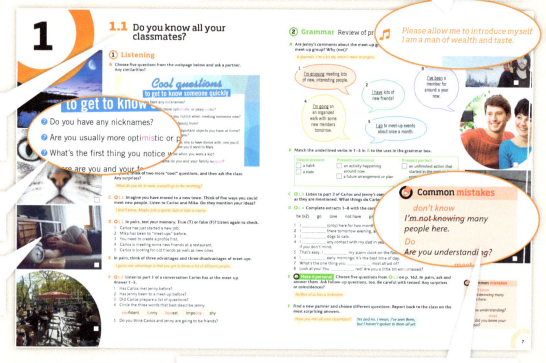

Lesson titles are questions to help you engage with the content.

Word stress in pink on new words.

Contextualized Picture Dictionary to present and review vocabulary.

Focus on **Common mistakes** accelerates accuracy.

ID Skills: extra reading and listening practice.

ID in Action: communication in common situations.

Authentic videos present topics in real contexts.

ID Café: sitcom videos to consolidate language.

Reviews systematically recycle language.

A complete **Grammar** reference with exercises.

Welcome

Stimulating **Grammar** practice.

Speech bubbles: models for speaking.

Make it personal: personalized speaking tasks to help you express your identity in English.

Audioscript activities to consolidate pronunciation.

Pictures to present and practice **Pronunciation**.

Workbook to practice and consolidate lessons.

Richmond Learning Platform
- Teachers and students can find all their resources in one place.
- **Richmond Test Manager** with interactive and printable tests.
- Activity types including pronunciation, common mistakes, and speaking.

Phrase Bank to practice common expressions.

Learn to express your identity in English!

1

1.1 Do you know all your classmates?

1 Listening

A Choose five questions from the webpage below and ask a partner. Any similarities?

Cool questions
to get to know someone quickly

- Do you have any nicknames?
- Are you usually more opti**mis**tic or pessi**mis**tic?
- What's the first thing you notice when meeting someone new?
- Where are you and your family from?
- What are the three most important objects you have at home? Why are they important to you?
- Choose three famous people: one to have dinner with, one you'd go on va**ca**tion with, and one you'd send to Mars.
- What did you want to be when you were a kid?
- Which sports teams do you and your family su**pport**?

B In pairs, think of two more "cool" questions, and then ask the class. Any surprises?

What do you do to wake yourself up in the morning?

C ▶1.1 Imagine you have moved to a new town. Think of five ways you could meet new people. Listen to Carlos and Mika. Do they mention your ideas?

I don't know. Maybe join a sports club or take a course.

D ▶1.1 In pairs, test your memory. True (T) or false (F)? Listen again to check.
1 Carlos has just started a new job.
2 Mika has been to "meet-ups" before.
3 You need to create a profile first.
4 Carlos is meeting some new friends at a restaurant.
5 Carlos is looking for old friends as well as new ones.

E In pairs, think of three advantages and three disadvantages of meet-ups.

I guess one advantage is that you get to know a lot of different people.

F ▶1.2 Listen to part 1 of a conversation Carlos has at the meet-up. Answer 1–5.
1 Has Carlos met Jenny before?
2 Has Jenny been to a meet-up before?
3 Did Carlos prepare a list of questions?
4 Circle the three words that best describe Jenny.

con**fi**dent   **fu**nny   **ho**nest   impo**lite**   shy

5 Do you think Carlos and Jenny are going to be friends?

2 Grammar Review of present tenses

🎵 *Please allow me to introduce myself. I am a man of wealth and taste.*   1.1

A Are Jenny's comments about the meet-up group all positive? Would you enjoy a meet-up group? Why (not)?

It depends. I'm a bit shy when I meet strangers.

1 I'm enjoying meeting lots of new, interesting people.
2 I have lots of new friends!
3 I've been a member for around a year now.
4 I'm going on an organized walk with some new members tomorrow.
5 I go to meet-up events about once a month.

B Match the underlined verbs in 1–5 in **A** to the uses in the grammar box.

Simple present	Present continuous	Present perfect
☐ a habit	☐ an activity happening around now	☐ an unfinished action that started in the past and continues to the present
☐ a state	☐ a future arrangement or plan	

➡ Grammar 1A p. 138

C ▶1.3 Listen to part 2 of Carlos and Jenny's conversation and number the photos 1–7 as they are mentioned. What things do Carlos and Jenny (not) have in common?

D ▶1.4 Complete extracts 1–8 with the correct form of these verbs. Listen to check.

be (x2)   go   love   not have   prefer   throw   turn   not want

1 I _____ (only) here for two months, so it's difficult to say.
2 I _____ there tomorrow evening, actually.
3 I _____ dogs to cats.
4 I _____ any contact with my dad in years. I _____ to talk about that if you don't mind.
5 That's easy. I _____ my alarm clock on the floor. I hate the noise it makes.
6 I _____ early mornings! It's the best time of day.
7 What's the one thing you _____ most afraid of?
8 Look at you! You _____ red! Are you a little bit em**ba**rrassed?

E 🗣 **Make it personal** Choose five questions from ▶1.3 on p. 162. In pairs, ask and answer them. Ask follow-up questions, too. Be careful with tenses! Any surprises or coincidences?

Neither of us has a nickname.

F Find a new partner and choose different questions. Report back to the class on the most surprising answers.

Have you met all your classmates?   *Yes and no. I mean, I've seen them, but I haven't spoken to them all yet.*

⚠ **Common mistakes**

don't know
I'm ~~not knowing~~ many people here.

Do
~~Are~~ you understanding?

          meet
How did you ~~know~~ your partner?

1.2 How do couples meet?

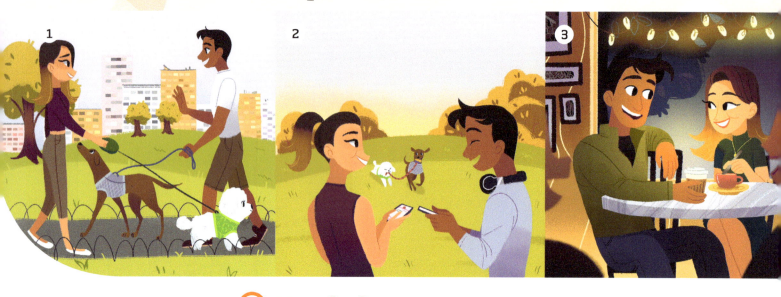

1 Vocabulary Relationships

A ▶1.5 Match the phrases to pictures 1–6. Listen to the story to check.
- ☐ be attracted to (someone)
- ☐ fall out (with someone)
- ☐ get along (well)
- ☐ get (back) together
- ☐ get to know someone
- ☐ break up

> ⚠ **Common mistakes**
> ~~fell~~ ~~with~~
> I instantly felt in love to him!
> ~~to~~
> Jack isn't married with Tina.

B In pairs, retell the story in **A**. Do you know anyone who broke up and then got back together?

> My sister broke up with her boyfriend last year, but they got back together after a week.

> Oh yeah? Are they still together?

C ▶1.6 Read the celebrity gossip article. Can you identify couples 1–3? Match the photos to the texts. Do you enjoy celebrity gossip?

FAMOUS 💔 EXES!

1 ☐ ☐ This couple broke up in 2017 after seven years of marriage. They originally fell for each other when they were working on the same movie. Their divorce came as a shock to fans who believed they had the perfect marriage. However, she recently admitted that the image they showed on social media wasn't real.

2 ☐ ☐ They have known each other since they were very young. They met when they worked on the Mickey Mouse Club together and used to hang out. They dated for a long time before they broke up. Some people say they fell out over her relationship with her choreographer.

3 ☐ ☐ This couple met when they both starred in the movie *Mr. & Mrs. Smith*. Their relationship became public after he broke up with his first wife. He moved in with her and her children soon after. They have six children. They say they began to drift apart and eventually got divorced in 2016.

D 🔘 **Make it personal** Do you know of any other famous break-ups? Or anyone who has fallen out with a boss, a friend, a family member, etc.?

> Taylor Swift and Calvin Harris broke up in 2016.

> But ooh, this time I'm telling you, I'm telling you, We are never ever ever getting back together.

1.2

E Reread the article and match the highlighted phrasal verbs from **C** to definitions 1–6.

1	_fall out_ (with so / over sth)	have an argument / fight	4	_____ (from so)	become emotionally distant
2	_____ (with so)	spend time together	5	_____ (so)	fall in love with someone
3	_____ (together / with so)	start living in the same place	6	_____ (with so)	end a relationship

F Complete the sentences with phrasal verbs from **E**.
1 My best friend and I started to _____ when we went to different colleges.
2 Do you want to _____ this weekend? We could go to the movies.
3 After two years of dating, my parents decided to _____ together. That was 20 years ago!
4 My brother and I _____ with each other over a stupid argument about money.
5 I _____ with my boyfriend because he hated my dog. Love me, love my dog!

> **Common mistakes**
> split up
> My son ~~terminated~~ with his first girlfriend.
> drifted apart
> They ~~distanced themselves~~ after ~~a discussion~~.
> an argument

G 🔵 Make it personal Complete 1–5 however you like. Compare with a partner. How many similar ideas?
1 If you fall out with someone you love, you should …
2 I like to hang out with people who …
3 I'd never fall for someone who …
4 In my opinion, couples drift apart if they …
5 Before you move in with someone, I think it's really important to …

> I'd never fall for someone who likes pop music – I can't stand it!

2 Listening

A ▶ 1.7 Listen to / Watch three couples who have been together for over 40 years. Check the items they consider most important.

What's most important for a lasting relationship?
☐ facing life's ups and downs   ☐ communication   ☐ shared interests
☐ being flexible   ☐ physical attraction   ☐ solving problems quickly

B Do you agree with their choices? Why (not)? What other advice can you think of?

C 🔵 Make it personal Think about a couple you know. How did they meet? How long were they / have they been together? In groups, share stories.

> Justin Bieber met Selena Gomez in 2009 after his manager called her mom to arrange a meeting. They dated on and off for years, but they finally broke up in 2018.

9

1.3 How many Facebook friends do you have?

1 Reading

A In pairs, how would you answer the question on the book cover? Define the differences between very close friends, good friends, friends and acquaintances.

I'd say everyone needs at least one really close friend to confide in. A good friend is someone who ...

B ▶1.8 Read and match the four paragraphs to the types of friendship in **A**. Can you guess the missing numbers (a–d)? Listen to check.

1 _____
These are people you know slightly, but they aren't really friends. It might be someone you know through work or sometimes talk to on the train. You can memorize their names, faces, and traits, and remember them when necessary. Basically, if circumstances force you to talk to each other, you are this type of friendship; if you really want to talk to each other, you are friends. According to Dr. Dunbar, a_____ is the maximum number of such connections your brain can manage.

2 _____
You might have hundreds of them on Facebook or other social media, but are they real friends? These are the people you're usually in contact with, though not necessarily on a weekly or monthly basis. You might socialize now and then and enjoy each other's company, but if times get tough, they won't hang around to help you. Maximum number: b_____

3 _____
These are people you may hang out with and probably get along with. You have fun together and can tease each other. You know you can call on them if you need some help. However, if you have a serious problem, they're not necessarily people that you can count on. Maximum number: c_____

4 _____
These are the people you can rely on. You would trust them with your secrets, and your problems, and to take care of your children. They'll be there beside you in good times and in bad. These are the people you can borrow money from when you need it. Marlene Dietrich used to call them the friends you can call at four o'clock in the morning. They're like family in a way. Maximum number: d_____

Common mistakes

I can only count ~~with~~ **on** my family.

These are the people ~~most close~~ **who are closest** to you.

C You are going to listen to a talk about Dunbar's theory of friendship. In pairs, guess what the signficance of these seven items will be.

primates   brain   small villages   social media
Christmas cards   Facebook friends   Oxford University

Dunbar probably went to Oxford University.

D ▶1.9 Listen to the talk and number the items 1–7 in the order you hear them. Were your ideas in **C** correct?

E **Make it personal** In pairs, use the infographic in **B** to explain Dunbar's theory. How well does it describe your relationships?

I'm not convinced. I have a lot of very close friends.

② Grammar Review of question forms

♫ *Have I made it obvious? Haven't I made it clear? Want me to spell it out for you? F-R-I-E-N-D-S.*

1.3

A ▶1.10 **Alison and her friend Jamie are looking at these photos on her phone. Listen and categorize the people according to Dunbar's theory.**

B **Match questions 1–7 to the four types of question in the grammar box. Then complete the rules with these words. There is one extra.**

auxiliary (x2)   object   subject   verb (x2)   beginning   end

1 Are they your colleagues?
2 When did you take that one?
3 Who's that?
4 Does she play professionally?

5 Can she play any other instruments?
6 Who took this one?
7 Who are you closest to?

---

yes / no questions ☐ ☐ ☐
When there is an auxiliary or a modal verb, the word order is:
_____ + subject + _____ + ?
When there is no auxiliary, use *do* to form the question.
When the main verb is *be*, invert the subject and the verb.

Questions ending in prepositions ☐
The preposition comes at the _____ of the sentence.

Wh-questions

Object questions ☐
Ask for information about the object, so the word order is:
question word + _____ + _____ + verb + ?

Subject questions ☐ ☐
Ask for information about the subject, so the word order is:
question word + _____ + _____ + ?

➜ **Grammar 1B** p. 138

C **Correct typical student question errors in 1–8. Which ones have you made?**

I used to make that mistake a lot.

1 With who do you live?
2 To which country you would really like to go?
3 Did you went out the last Saturday?
4 Who does help you with your homework?

5 With which three people do you spend the most time?
6 How many languages you can speak well?
7 How arrived you to class today?
8 Have you a best friend?

⏱ Common mistakes

does
Where ~~your~~ best friend lives?

said
Who did ~~say~~ that?

D **In pairs, take turns asking the questions in C. Any coincidences?**

E 👤 **Make it personal** **Write the names of a very close friend, a good friend, a friend, and an acquaintance.**

1 For each person, think about these questions.

How long have you known her / him?	What's he / she up to these days as far as you know?
How well do you get along with him / her?	How often are you in touch?
How much do you have in common?	Are you doing anything together any time soon?

2 In pairs, take turns describing each person and your relationship. Work out where on the infographic each one belongs. Ask follow-up questions, too. Any surprising answers?

We've known each other since elementary school. We used to be really close.

What's she like?

11

1.4 Do you have many social media profiles?

Selfies

Nature photos

Couple photos

Work photos

Group photos

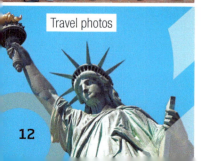
Travel photos

1 Reading

A Read the introduction to the article and the paragraph headings on the photos. What do you think each photo type says about the person?

> I think selfies show that someone cares a lot about what they look like.

B ▶1.11 Read the article and match the paragraph headings in A to 1–6. Listen to check.

Your INSTA PERSONALITY

Whether your social media posts are carefully planned or completely spontaneous, what you post reveals a lot more than you imagine. Psychological studies have found connections between personality, emotions, and the photos we post, showing Instagram can be a "window to your soul".

1 _____

Do you post a lot of these? If they are extreme images, e.g. taken while you are skydiving, it shows you have an adventure-seeking personality. If you enjoy posting funny ones, your followers can see that you are fun-loving and easygoing. But be aware that the need for "likes" reveals a desire for recognition and is often a sign that you are self-centered.

2 _____

If you often post images of yourself and your partner, it demonstrates a strong and stable relationship. We see two like-minded individuals who want to be together. Be careful about uploading too many of these. Ask yourself why you feel the need to prove yourself and your relationship to other people.

3 _____

If your profile has plenty of images of you with lots of people at parties, etc., sure, it sends the message that you're outgoing and sociable. However, it can also point to loneliness. Are you trying too hard to show everyone that you have plenty of friends?

4 _____

If you post photos of landscapes, it shows a thoughtful person who has the time to admire the beauty of his or her environment. On the other hand, it may also point to someone who is tired of the pace of life and needs some time off.

5 _____

Posting vacation images is a way of storing memories and emotions you felt while on your trip. A love of exploring the planet shows that you are open-minded and enjoy experiencing new places. Be aware that posting photos from a vacation is like posting an ad that you're not at home. Perhaps wait and post them when you're back home.

6 _____

If you post a lot of photos of your office, it shows your professional life is a priority for you. It can also mean that you want to portray yourself as a knowledgeable person with a high-status position. Or maybe you're just looking for promotion!

C True (T) or false (F)? Reread to check. Are you into Instagram?
1. Selfies show an adventurous, but sometimes fragile, personality.
2. Constantly posting couple photos is a sign of an insecure relationship.
3. Group photos can send both positive and negative messages.
4. Photos in a natural environment show someone who doesn't have much free time.
5. Posting travel photos can pose a security risk.
6. Workplace photos might mean you want to show people how important you are.

D **Make it personal** The article gives some advice about social media security. What other advice can you think of?

> Your friends may not always want you to tag them or show their locations.

♪ *Near, far, wherever you are, I believe that the heart does go on.* 1.4

2 Vocabulary Personality adjectives

A Match the highlighted adjectives to definitions 1–10. Notice the hyphens.

1	_____	prepared to listen to new ideas
2	_____	considering things very carefully and thinking about others
3	_____	intelligent; knows a lot about something
4	_____	with similar ideas and interests
5	_____	enjoys having a good time
6	_____	likes doing dangerous or unusual activities
7	_____	friendly; extroverted
8	_____	relaxed
9	_____	thinking only about yourself and not other people
10	_____	enjoying being with other people

B 🗨 Make it personal In pairs, discuss the questions. Any discoveries?
1 Which of the adjectives in **A** best describe you?
2 Which kinds of images do you post?
3 Are the descriptions in the article true for you and your posts?
4 What about the images posted by your friends / people you follow? Are the opinions in the text true about them?

> *I post a lot of group photos, but I definitely don't feel lonely!*

> *My brother is always posting selfies, and he's incredibly self-centered.*

3 Grammar Emphatic forms

A ▶ 1.12 Anna wants to find new Instagram accounts to follow. Listen to her talking to her friend Betty. What different types of accounts does she mention?

B ▶ 1.13 Listen and repeat sentences a–e in the grammar box. Notice the stress and cross out the wrong option in the rule.

Emphatic forms with adverbs
a Wow! They sure look like they're having an amazing time.
b They certainly are worth following, I think.
c That one's definitely for me.

With auxiliary *do*
d I do love this one.
e It does make perfect sense.

With emphatic forms, auxiliaries and adverbs are usually **stressed** / **unstressed**.

➔ Grammar 1C p.138

⚠ **Common mistakes**
It does sounds interesting.
                say
They did s̶a̶i̶d̶ they were going to Japan next.

C Complete Betty's comments with the words in parentheses and an appropriate verb.

1	ANNA	Look at this one. What a view! Imagine being on that beach!
	BETTY	Yes, it _____ like an amazing place. (does)
2	ANNA	"Life's a journey, not a race."
	BETTY	Yes, that _____ a good one to remember! (definitely)
3	ANNA	I love this one of the man and the tiger together.
	BETTY	They _____ to have a strong bond. (sure)
4	ANNA	Oh, goodness. What a cute little ball of fluff! I want one.
	BETTY	You _____ to get a kitten, don't you?! (do)
5	ANNA	Look at them! Skydiving together.
	BETTY	Hmm … They _____ braver than me. (certainly)

D 🗨 Make it personal Which of these views on social media do you agree with? Compare with a partner. Any interesting conclusions?

"Social media apps make us less sociable."
"Instagram is the best social media app there is."
"How many friends or followers I have matters to me."
"You should be over 16 to have a social media account."
"Running a social media account is a special skill."
"You can have too many social media accounts."

> *I do believe that …*   *I do agree that …*
> *People seem to …*   *I definitely think that …*

1.5 How much time do you spend online?

Skills Reading for main ideas and specific information

A What do you think is special about these four social media apps?

1   2   3   4

Maybe the first one helps gamers to play better?

B Read and match these descriptions to three of the apps in **A**.

A social media app for EVERYONE

Facebook is the world's largest social media network. In fact, it's so huge that it's easier to find distant relatives than someone who actually shares the same interests as you. Here are some interesting examples of niche* social networks where people with very specific tastes and hobbies can socialize.

☐ Unlike other social media apps, you don't check into locations, but into your favorite movies and TV shows. Your "friends" on this network see what you're watching right now, and it allows you to comment on and react to TV moments with other fans. You can also unlock digital stickers related to your favorite shows and bands.

☐ If you want something practical with your social networking app, then this app is perfect for you. It links people who are learning a particular language with others who are fluent. There are approximately 100 different languages available, including endangered ones. This is a brilliant way to learn a new language in a realistic setting and also learn about other cultures at the same time.

☐ This is a social media site for those who have a deep interest in gaming. With this app, you can connect and chat with other like-minded players and gaming friends. Create a gaming profile, then share your status updates, and photos, and stream live videos. There is also a group feature, so you can join and meet gamers who are into the same games as you. So, all you nerds out there, this is the place for you to network!

* *niche* exactly suitable for a small group of the same type

C ▶1.14 Cover the texts and listen to check. Which is harder, listening or reading? Why? Uncover, listen, and read. Any surprising pronunciation or spelling?

D Reread and match the apps to the descriptions.
1 It lets you chat about your favorite soap opera.
2 It helps you find members of your family.
3 It offers you the chance to hear a dying language.
4 It tells your friends what you're doing, but not where you are.
5 It combines social networking and learning a skill.
6 It introduces you to people who have a lot of computer knowledge.

E **Make it personal** In pairs, discuss 1–4. Which apps are most used by the class?
1 Which of the apps most appeals to you and why? And the least appealing?
2 Which app(s) would you recommend to the class?
3 Can you think of any other "niche" social media apps?
4 What kind of app do you think govloop might be?

Common mistake
It lets you / It allows you to
It's let you tell your friends ...

I'm interested in indigenous languages, so I'd go for italki.

The apps I use most are ..

Which do you do more: listen or speak?

1.5

ID in Action Listening actively

A ▶1.15 **Listen to two friends talking about a date and answer 1–3.**
1. Which app in **A** on p. 14 did Roberto use?
2. Did he like the woman?
3. Was the date successful?
4. Who was easier to understand?

B ▶1.15 **Listen again. True (T) or false (F)? Do you believe in blind dates?**
1. Roberto and the woman met at a coffee shop.
2. The woman arrived late.
3. Roberto had never met her before.
4. She left as soon as she saw Roberto.
5. Roberto has had other unsuccessful dates before.

C ▶1.15 **Complete the informal expressions. Listen again to check.**

Formal	Informal
1 Are you talking about the date?	You _____ the date?
2 Please, continue.	Go _____.
3 Wait a minute, please.	Hold _____ a sec.
4 I'm very surprised.	_____ way!
5 And what happened after that?	What happens _____?
6 "Leaves?" Could you explain, please?	What do you _____ "leaves"?
7 Is this true?	Are you _____?
8 I'm really sorry to hear that.	Oh, _____!

D ▶1.16 **Listen and practice the informal expressions in C, copying the intonation.**

E **Make it personal** Tell an anecdote.
1. In pairs, imagine what happened before, during, and after in cartoons 1–3.
2. In anecdotes, people often use the present tense so people and objects seem closer to the listener. In pairs, try telling the anecdotes from the pictures.

> So, I finish work and I'm walking to my car. I'm tired and really looking forward to getting home. I open ...

> Uh-huh. Yeah. And then ...?

3. **A:** Think of an anecdote of your own – a funny / embarrassing / scary situation like those in cartoons 1–3 – and tell your partner. Use informal language from **C**.
   B: Listen actively. Then change roles.

Common mistakes

~~saw~~ see
I get into the car, and I ~~saw~~ this huge mouse!

~~crash~~ crashed
I was running for the bus and ~~crash~~ into a street light.

 What do you mean? When you nod your head yes, But you wanna say no. What do you mean?

Writing 1   A personal profile

Where have you been
All my life, all my life?
Where have you been all my life?

A Read the profile. Which kind of social media network is it for?

☐ professional   ☐ dating   ☐ social

GetConnected

Pete Brill

1 _____

Hi, I'm Pete! I'm an adventure-seeking, outgoing, 22-year-old digital media studies graduate. Currently working in TV production and love it! Originally from Copenhagen and now living in London. I love the outdoors and socializing. Looking to meet like-minded, outgoing people for social and work-related connections. [a] PM me!

2 _____

OneStop Productions, London – Production Assistant
White Swan Clothing Co, London – Sales Assistant
Metropolitan University, London – 2015–2018
Copenhagen International School – 2007–2014

3 _____

Anything outdoors! I love skiing, surfing, running, and climbing. Anything adventurous! [b]
Taken part in four international triathlon events.
Eating out—Thai food is my absolute favorite. Know any good restaurants?

4 _____

Took a gap year and travelled through South America.
Highlights were teaching in a kindergarten in Bolivia, seeing Machu Picchu and being in Rio de Janeiro for Mardi Gras.
[c] Planning a tour in Norway next summer.

5 _____

Become a skydiving instructor!

6 _____

I mostly read non-fiction. [d]
Favorite book – *Sapiens* by Yuval Noah Harari.
[e]

7 _____

Anything by Spielberg—I love his imagination!
[f]

8 _____

Danish, German, English
[g]

9 _____

Friendship, running buddies, dinners out, movie trips, deep conversations, party partners, networking, [h]

B Complete 1–9 in the profile with these headings.

All about me	Ambitions	Books and music
Favorite movies	Interests	Languages
Looking for	Travel	Work and education

C Match the information about Pete to blanks a–h.

☐ Unfortunately, I broke my wrist on an Amazon canoeing trip.

☐ I enjoy live gigs and open mic nights.

☐ travel companions, travel tips, colleagues.

☐ I love science-fiction, too.

☐ Got any biography recommendations???

☐ I'd love to hear from you.

☐ Tried Mandarin!

☐ Just got my motorbike license!

D Read *Write it right!* and find examples of the features in Pete's profile.

✓ Write it right!

Social media profiles are usually divided into different sections with headings for you to fill in, e.g. *Favorite movies, All about me.*

To make them quick and easy to read, we often:

1 omit non-essential words such as pronouns and auxiliary verbs, e.g. *I'm looking forward to meeting you.*

2 use abbreviations, e.g. *PM (private message), Find me on FB (Facebook).*

3 use repeated punctuation marks, e.g. *Any good restaurant recommendations???*

4 ask questions to encourage reader interest, e.g. *Know any good local bands?*

E Rewrite 1–4 in social media profile style.

1 I am now living in California and looking for a job.

2 I can't stand romantic comedy movies.

3 At the moment, I'm working in public relations and I'm really enjoying it.

4 My dream is to visit New York City.

F *Your turn!* Write your own social media profile.

Before	Decide which headings you want to include. You don't have to complete all of them.
While	Make each entry short, friendly, and easy to read. Follow the tips in *Write it right!*
After	Show your profile to a classmate. Can they improve it in any way? Write a 'PM' back to each other in response, then email your profile to your teacher.

1 He said, she said

 Café

1 Before watching

A Match 1–6 to their definitions a–h.

1 close (friends)
2 to be over (somebody)
3 considerate
4 caller ID
5 gossip
6 chemistry
7 to figure
8 to gossip

a ☐ a phone feature that allows phone number recognition
b ☐ think, consider, or expect to be the case
c ☐ a romantic attraction between two people
d ☐ behaving in a caring way about another person's feelings
e ☐ talk about other people
f ☐ talking about other people or passing on untrue information
g ☐ no longer have romantic feelings for that person
h ☐ on affectionate terms

B In pairs, describe Rory and Genevieve. Who do you think calls who? Why? What are they saying?

Rory is about 25 and he's wearing ...

Maybe Genevieve calls Rory to gossip about a friend ...

2 While watching

A Watch to see if you were right, and check all you hear.

1 Genevieve's a musician. ☐
2 Genevieve hates the band Curious Fools. ☐
3 They're meeting at the Lexington Theater. ☐
4 August told Andrea that Rory likes Genevieve. ☐
5 Genevieve told Andrea that Rory was crazy about her. ☐
6 Genevieve said she found Rory attractive. ☐
7 Genevieve thought Rory would be over her by now. ☐
8 Genevieve and Rory don't have anything in common. ☐
9 Genevieve breaks up with boyfriends after one month. ☐
10 Andrea thinks Genevieve and Rory might have chemistry. ☐

B Watch again and order the events, 1–7. Did you notice any interesting phrases?

☐ Rory and Genevieve go to the concert.
☐ Andrea and Genevieve talk on the phone.
☐ Rory asks Genevieve out.
☐ Genevieve bumps into Rory.
☐ Rory is waiting for Genevieve at the theater.
☐ Rory gets tickets from his friend who's in a band.
☐ They agree to go to the after-show party.

C Complete 1–10 with *about*, *on*, *out*, *over* or *up*.

1 Rory finally asked you _____!
2 August said that Rory was thinking _____ it.
3 Why would your brother know _____ me and Rory?
4 They hang _____ all the time.
5 Rory told Auggie you'd probably never go _____ with him.
6 Rory likes you. He's crazy _____ you.
7 Really? I figured he'd be _____ me by now.
8 Do you and Auggie gossip _____ us?
9 When you date a musician, you end _____ breaking _____ with him.
10 All right. Let me sleep _____ it.

D Match seven phrasal verbs from **C** to their definitions.

☐ to wait a little before making a decision
☐ to spend time together
☐ to stop loving a person
☐ to date
☐ to end a romantic relationship
☐ to invite on a date
☐ to finally do or be something

3 After watching

A Complete 1–6 with the correct form of *have / have to*.

1 I was wondering if you _____ any plans.
2 I don't _____ anything in common with him.
3 You might _____ chemistry!
4 Rory _____ become close friends with August.
5 You _____ tell me how you met him.
6 And if you're interested, they _____ a party after their show.

B 🔴 **Make it personal** Do you think their date will be a success? Will they get along well? In groups of three, role-play their party conversation with Rory's friend, Max, from the band Curious Fools.

Hi Max. That was awesome! Thanks so much for the tickets!

17

2.1 How green are you?

1 Vocabulary Going green

A How are photos 1–10 each connected with being "green"?

> Well, 1 is plastic bottles. I think it takes a lot of energy to produce them.

> Yes, and the oceans are full of plastic waste …

B Match the highlighted words in the quiz to photos 1–10.

The "going green" Quiz

We all know what we should be doing.

But how green have you really gone?

1 Leaving appliances on stand-by mode isn't environment-friendly because it wastes energy. Do you always unplug your computer or cell charger when not in use?
Y / S / N

2 Disposable plastic bags can take up to 1,000 years to decompose.
Do you reuse plastic bags or take a reusable cloth bag when you go shopping?
Y / S / N

3 Leaving the faucet running when you brush your teeth twice a day can waste almost 8 gallons of water.
Do you turn the faucet off while brushing your teeth?
Y / S / N

4 Energy-efficient light bulbs last from 6,000 to 15,000 hours.
Do you use energy-efficient light bulbs in your house or office?
Y / S / N

5 Solar heating is a renewable energy source, and it can help you save as much as one-third off your monthly power bill. Does your house or apartment building have a solar heating system?
Y / S / N

6 It takes more than 30 million barrels of oil a year to make the plastic for the world's bottled water. Do you use refillable bottles for water at home?
Y / S / N

7 A Styrofoam cup takes 500 years to decompose. Do you use Styrofoam cups at work or home?
Y / S / N

8 A typical American family produces 30% more household waste than a typical Mexican family. Do you separate organic and non-organic household waste?
Y / S / N

9 More than 1.5 million Americans over the age of 17 are now vegan. "Flexitarianism"* is now on the increase, with a 60% global rise in new vegetarian branded products between 2011 and 2015.
Do you ever eat vegetarian meals?
Y / S / N

10 A carbon footprint calculates all the greenhouse gases we produce in our activities as individuals and measures them in units of carbon dioxide. The world average is about 4½ tons of carbon dioxide per person.
Do you ever feel concerned about your carbon footprint?
Y / S / N

*flexitarianism *n* following a vegetarian diet with the occasional inclusion of meat

Y = Yes   **S** = Sometimes   **N** = No

C 2.1 Listen, read, and answer the quiz. In pairs, compare answers. Who's greener?

> We're both similar, but …

Common mistakes

~~left~~
I ~~let~~ the lights on.

~~wastes~~
This fridge ~~spends~~ a lot of energy.

♪ *Heal the world. Make it a better place for you and for me and the entire human race.*

2.1

2 Pronunciation /ɑ/ and /oʊ/

▶ 2.2 Put these words in the correct column according to the underlined sounds. Listen to check.

b<u>o</u>ttle   cl<u>o</u>th   cl<u>o</u>thes   disp<u>o</u>sable   <u>e</u>co
pr<u>o</u>duct   pr<u>o</u>gram   s<u>o</u>lar   Styrof<u>oa</u>m

ɑ	oʊ
bottle	*clothes*

3 Vocabulary Adjectives from verbs and nouns

A We often form "green" adjectives by adding *-able*, *-efficient*, and *-friendly* to verbs and nouns. Match the endings to their meanings.

1 re<mark>us**able**</mark> cloth bag
2 energy-<mark>**efficient**</mark> light bulb
3 environment-<mark>**friendly**</mark> appliances

☐ that are safe for
☐ that use less
☐ that you can + verb

B ▶ 2.3 Make seven "green" phrases using the suffixes in **A**. Listen to check. Then ask about a partner's home.

1 water / faucets
2 environment / detergents
3 fuel / vehicles
4 recharge / batteries
5 energy / appliances
6 reuse / plastic containers
7 pet / insecticides

Do you have water-efficient faucets in your home?   *I have no idea!*

→ **Grammar 2A** p. 140

C 🎧 **Make it personal**   What could you do to be greener?

1 Look back at the quiz on p. 18. How could you be greener for each question? Make notes.
2 Compare your notes with a partner. Do you agree with each other?

I suppose I could try flexitarianism. I could be a vegetarian half the week.

That's a good idea. Vegetarianism is more animal-friendly and environment-friendly, too!

3 Then discuss how your school / class could be greener. Report back. Choose the top five ideas.

19

2.2 How long have you been studying here?

1 Listening

A ▶2.4 In pairs, interpret the poster. Is it for a comedy or a documentary? What do you think "No Impact Man" is about? Listen to / Watch the video to check your guesses.

Do you think he's some kind of superhero?

B ▶2.4 Remember what Colin said about these items. Then listen / watch again to check.

waste   travel and transportation
food and drink   shopping   money
health   relationships   happiness

I think he said he didn't buy tomatoes in January. Did you hear that?

C Make it personal In pairs, answer 1–3. Any big differences?
1 Why do you think he made these changes? What impact will they have on the environment?
2 What three things could you change to have less impact on the environment?
3 Would you consider going "no impact" for a year? A month? A week? Why (not)?

2 Reading

A ▶2.5 Quickly read Al's blog. How green is his lifestyle these days? Circle 1, 2, or 3.

This morning I ran into an old friend on my way to work. He could hardly recognize me. "You look so … different," he said. "Have you been working out or something?" Well, yes, I've been working out like crazy every day, but I guess it's the "something" that has made the difference.

You see, I've been trying to copy the idea I saw in a documentary called *No Impact Man*. It's about a guy called Colin Beaven, who tries to have zero impact on the environment for a year. So instead of simply switching to energy-efficient light bulbs, buying eco-friendly cleaning products, avoiding disposable cups, and stuff like that, he takes the whole thing to the next level: no TV, no elevators, no public transportation, no household waste … The list goes on and on.

No Impact Man has had such an impact (!) on me that my family and I are trying to green up our lifestyles, too. For example, I've been walking to work at least twice a week, taking the stairs, using recycled paper, and so on. At home, we're beginning to recycle, trying to unplug all appliances, installing water-efficient faucets—you name it. And you know what? We've all been feeling great lately. But I think that's really as far as I can go. I'd never be able to give up TV, sell my precious car (which I've only been driving since Monday!), or buy used clothes.

So my question is: Can I make a difference, or am I wasting my time?

B Reread and find key points to justify your answer in **A**. Compare in pairs. Do you disagree at all? Is he wasting his time?

C What do the highlighted expressions mean?
1 ☐ eventually   2 ☐ more and more   3 ☐ etc.

D Make it personal In pairs, share your own answers to Al's final question. Any conclusions?

I do what I can, but it doesn't feel like it's changing anything.

Yeah, but we have to start somewhere. The real problem is education.

3 Grammar Present perfect continuous

♪ Lately I've been, I've been losing sleep, Dreaming about the things that we could be.

2.2

A Sentences 1–3 are true. Find evidence in Al's blog in **2A**.
1 Al probably has a gym membership.   2 Al probably lives near his work.   3 Al has a new car.

B Follow the instructions in the grammar box.

> 1 Match examples a–c to the rules.
>   a **Have you been working out** or something?
>   b **I've been walking** to work at least twice a week.
>   c **He's been driving** a brand new car since Monday.
>
>   Sentences _____ and _____ emphasize the duration of an action or state.
>   Sentence _____ has a general meaning of *lately*.
>
> 2 Cross out the group of words that CANNOT complete this sentence.
>   I've been working out _____.
>
>   a How often?   regularly, every day, on and off, twice a week
>   b How much?   a little, a lot, like crazy, more and more
>   c Since when?   since April, for (five) years, lately, recently
>   d When?   three weeks ago, in 2015, yesterday, last year
>
> 3 Use *since* + a point in time (moment) and *for* + a period of time (duration). Complete with *for* or *since*.
>
>   _____ 90 minutes   _____ yesterday   _____ four years   _____ 6:30 p.m.
>   _____ my whole life   _____ the rest of the day _____ 2012   _____ June 4th
>
> ➜ **Grammar 2B** p. 140

⚠ **Common mistakes**

have been
I ~~am~~ walking to work once a week.

have been studying
I ~~study~~ English all weekend.

C Suzana has also watched *No Impact Man*. Use her notes to make sentences in the present perfect continuous. Which ones have you been doing recently?

		PAST	NEW HABITS	SINCE WHEN?
1	TV	watch a lot	watch far less	she saw the documentary
2	appliances	buy conventional	buy energy-efficient	lately
3	disposable products	use lots	try to avoid	past few months
4	car	use every day	walk to work	April
5	household waste	throw away	kids recycle	last two weeks
6	eco-friendly products	buy a few	husband buy lots	some time now

1 *She used to watch a lot of TV, but she's been watching far less TV since she saw the documentary.*

4 Pronunciation

A ▶2.6 Listen and copy the reduced form of *have / has*, the weak form of *been*, the stress, and the intonation.

       /əv/   /bɪn/   ↘   /əz/   /bɪn/   ↘
1 How **long** have you been **liv**ing in this **ci**ty?   2 How **long** has she been **try**ing to go **green**?

B ▶2.7 Listen to a friend giving you news. Pause after the "beep" and ask a *how long* question using the reduced form of *have* and *has*. Then listen to check.

> Guess what! I go to the gym twice a week now.

C 🗣 **Make it personal** In pairs, use these verbs to interview each other. Ask at least two questions for each verb. Any surprising answers?

> Really? How long have you been going there?

collect   drive   go   live   play   read   study   swim   watch   work

> Are you reading anything now?   Yeah, I'm reading a graded reader.   How long have you been reading it?

2.3 How has the climate been changing?

1 Vocabulary The environment

A ▶2.8 Match photos 1–9 to the headlines. Listen to check. Which ones are good news?

ENVIRONMENTAL NEWS FROM AROUND THE WORLD

- [ ] Droughts Seem to Be Getting More and More Severe
- [ ] Floods in All Parts of the World Have Been Getting Worse Year After Year
- [ ] Dumping of E-waste is on the Rise in Developing Countries
- [ ] Countries Like India Are Becoming Less Dependent on Fossil Fuels
- [ ] Officials Say Amazon Deforestation Is Not As Bad As It Once Was
- [ ] The UN Has Labeled the World's Rising Sea Levels "Alarming"
- [ ] Poaching in Latin America has Declined
- [ ] Experts Disagree on the Causes of Climate Change
- [ ] Threatened Species List Is Getting Smaller

B 🔊 Do some research and compare your views.

1 Choose a topic in **A** to research online. Find out five facts about the topic. Report back to the class.
2 Which facts did you all find interesting? Which topics do you now feel optimistic / pessimistic about?

> I feel a bit more optimistic about threatened species because there are lots of conservation groups trying to stop extinction.

2 Listening

A ▶2.9 You are going to listen to five scientists talking about points a–e. In pairs, guess what they will say. Then listen and match speakers 1–5 to a–e. How close were you?

a	[ ] Climate change is not just a problem for our future.
b	[ ] Climate change affects threatened animals.
c	[ ] The Earth is getting hotter, not the sun.
d	[ ] Climate change has happened before, but this time it's our fault.
e	[ ] Are we cooling down or heating up?

> I think the scientist who makes the first point will say climate change is also a problem right now.

B ▶2.9 Can you remember any of the missing words in extracts 1–8? Listen again and check. Who was the most convincing?

1 A number of independent measures of solar activity indicate that the sun _____ by a few degrees since 1960.
2 Over the last 35 years of climate change, sun and climate _____ in opposite directions.
3 Some people say, "Well, we _____ ice ages and warmer periods, so climate change is natural!"
4 This is like saying that forest fires _____ naturally in the past.
5 Climate researchers _____ papers for years.
6 Climate change deniers say the planet _____ since a peak in 1998.
7 However, experts _____ that in a climate being warmed by man-made carbon emissions …
8 A large number of ancient mass extinction events _____ to global climate change.

22

♪ *Everything is changing, And I've been here for too long. Going through the same things, I've been hurting too long.*

2.3

3 Grammar Present perfect simple vs. Present perfect continuous

A Read sentence pairs a–c and match them to uses 1–3 in the grammar box.
  a The earth has gotten warmer before.
     The earth has been getting warmer since 1998.
  b Tigers have lived in India for two million years.
     Tigers have been living in India for two million years.
  c In the last century, sea levels have risen by 10–20 cm.
     Sea levels have been rising over the last century.

> You can often use the *present perfect simple* or *present perfect continuous* interchangeably.
> Generally use the *present perfect continuous* to emphasize duration.
> Don't use the *present perfect continuous* with stative verbs.
> The *present perfect simple* emphasizes completion.
>
> | | Present perfect | Present perfect continuous |
> |---|---|---|
> | 1 ☐ | No difference | No difference |
> | 2 ☐ | Completed action | Process happening now |
> | 3 ☐ | How much / many? | Emphasis on how long |
>
> ➤ **Grammar 2C** p. 140

⏱ **Common mistakes**

　　　　has been
The problem ~~is~~ getting worse since 2010.

　　　　known
We've been ~~knowing~~ about climate change for ages.

B Read the environmental news below and circle the correct verb tenses. Sometimes both options are possible.

> New York's ¹**announced / been announcing** a plan to use human waste for renewable energy.

> Scientists from Ohio University have ²**found / been finding** a way to produce hydrogen from urine.

> In the past few years, the auto industry has ³**looked / been looking** into several different ways to produce vehicles that are less dependent on fossil fuels.

> The European Union has ⁴**tried / been trying** hard to meet the goal of at least a 27% improvement in energy efficiency by 2030.

> Despite poaching and a recent drought, Kenya's elephant population has ⁵**increased / been increasing** year after year. It has ⁶**increased / been increasing** by nearly 10% in the past three years.

> Although the world has ⁷**lost / been losing** 18% of the Amazon Rainforest, the rate of deforestation seems to be slowing.

C 👥 **Make it personal** In pairs, look back at **1A**. For each photo, answer 1–3. Compare your ideas with other pairs. Do they agree / disagree with you?
  1 Is this a major problem in your country / city?
  2 Has this problem recently gotten better or worse? How?
  3 Who's to blame for this, and why? What have they (not) done or (not) been doing?

> *Floods are a real problem in São Paulo.*

> *And it's gotten worse recently.*

D ▶ 2.10 👥 **Make it personal** **Dictation**. Write the five questions you hear. In pairs, answer them. Any similarities?

> *I've known my best friend for 15 years. We met in kindergarten!*

2.4 What's the best ad you've seen recently?

1 Reading

A Do you believe most ads you see? Why (not)? Read the pop-ups quickly. Which promise(s) do you find hard to believe?

1

Thinking of upgrading your phone? _____? With the new, gorgeous green Sun 360, you get all the features you love: an ultrafast processor, powerful 12 MP camera, and an internal solar panel that allows up to eight hours of heavy, uninterrupted usage. Sun 360 produces the greenest cell phone on the market by using recycled materials. All of this, and it will still fit into your pocket! Introductory price—$259. _____

2

_____? Try Moringa Miracle Powder—the Moringa plant is a superfood believed to be one of the most nutritious foods on our planet. The leaves are packed with at least 92 different nutrients, vitamins, and minerals for good health. Just add our Miracle Powder to tea, soups, and smoothies, and start experiencing the benefits immediately.

3

Feeling stressed out? _____? Then *Mindful Me* is the place to be. Our meditation retreat located in the beautiful countryside will help you deal with life's ups and downs with more peace and serenity. We welcome people of all ages and cultures. Every day, you will have the opportunity to participate in yoga classes, meditation groups, and enjoy vegan meals prepared by our chefs. N.B. _____, so no modern interruptions.

B ▶2.11 Reread and complete the ads with 1–5. Listen to check. Practice the pink-stressed words.
1. Need some time out
2. Tired of batteries that won't last
3. Not looking your best
4. No cell phones or tablets allowed
5. Offer limited to one unit per customer

Common mistake
least like
The one I'd ~~like least~~ to try is X.

C Read the information in the box and find eight examples of grammatical omission in the completed ads in **A**.

> To be shorter, friendlier, and sound more exciting, ads often omit articles, auxiliary verbs, or subjects.
> • (The) offer (is) only available in (the) U.S.
> • (Our Hybrid car is) greener than you thought.

I'd never try the Moringa stuff. I don't believe in all these "superfoods"!

Hmm ... I'd most like to try the retreat. I need a rest.

D Order ads 1–3 from *I'd most* to *I'd least* like to try.

2 Listening

A ▶2.12 Listen to the beginning of three conversations at a party. Which product in **1A** did each person buy?

B ▶2.13 Listen to the rest of the conversations. How many are satisfied customers?

I went to a retreat in India where you couldn't speak for 10 days!

C ▶2.14 True (T) or false (F)? Listen to check. Know any similar stories?
1. Beth has been on vacation.
2. Lorna doesn't believe in "superfoods".
3. Pedro's new cell phone battery dies after 90 minutes.
4. Pedro liked his old phone better.
5. Bruce left his old job because of the pay.
6. Bruce spent about a month away from New York City.

24

3 Grammar Simple past vs. Present perfect simple / continuous

🎵 *How long has this been going on? You've been acting so shady, I've been feeling it lately.*

2.4

A ▶ 2.15 Complete 1–6, and then listen to check. In pairs, remember all you can about each story.

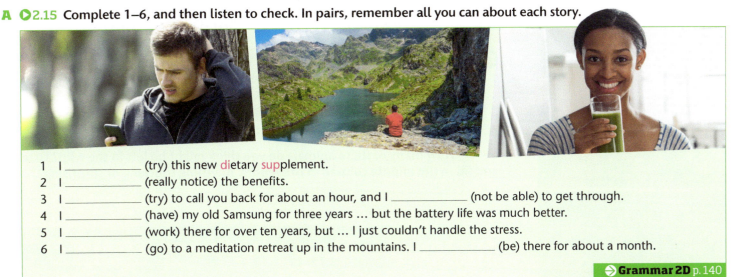

1 I _____ (try) this new dietary supplement.
2 I _____ (really notice) the benefits.
3 I _____ (try) to call you back for about an hour, and I _____ (not be able) to get through.
4 I _____ (have) my old Samsung for three years … but the battery life was much better.
5 I _____ (work) there for over ten years, but … I just couldn't handle the stress.
6 I _____ (go) to a meditation retreat up in the mountains. I _____ (be) there for about a month.

➔ **Grammar 2D** p. 140

She's been trying a new superfood. It's made her feel much better.

B ▶ 2.16 Form questions to ask the people in **A**. Listen to check. How do you think they would reply?
1 you / got / a new phone / yet?
2 you / look for / a new job?
3 try / yoga / at the retreat?
4 how long / you / take / this supplement?
5 how / it / affect / your health?

⚠ **Common mistakes**

James Dean's career ~~has lasted~~ *lasted* less than a decade.
I've ~~been having~~ *had* this new tablet since March. I love it!
~~For how~~ *How* long ~~do you have~~ *have you had* that smart watch?

C Read the pop-ups. Imagine you were tempted. In pairs, role-play a conversation about each one. Record the best one.

LEARN CHINESE IN 6 MONTHS!
Two hours a week, very little homework. Learn in your sleep! First month free of charge.

Tired of dogs, cats, birds, and goldfish? Maybe what you need is a **pet alligator!**
3000 happy owners can't be wrong. Come and choose yours today! 24-hour helpline: (555) 013-2689.

How much Chinese have you learned? When did you start?

Have you bought a baby alligator?

D 🎤 **Make it personal** In pairs, choose a topic and interview each other. Report back with anything interesting you found out.

a collection   an artist, band, or TV show you love
follow your favorite sport   a get-rich-quick plan
something you're trying to learn   a recent change in your life

I collect old vinyl pop records.

No way! How long have you been collecting them?

Well, it all started when …

25

2.5 Do you support any charities?

Skills Expressing numerical information

A **Make it personal** In groups, answer 1–3. Share your answers with the class.
1. Find the animals' names in the chart. Which of them have you seen, either in the wild, in a zoo, or stuffed in a museum? What do you know about them?
2. Give three reasons why some species are more vulnerable to extinction than others.
3. Suggest two ways to help people care more about threatened species.

B ▶ 2.17 How many of these animals do you think might be left in the wild? Listen and fill in the middle column in the report. Anything shocking or surprising?

> I can't believe there are only about 800 gorillas left!

Species we may never see again

	Origin / Habitat	Number left in the wild	Other info
Giant panda		fewer than ____	
Monk seal	Islands of Hawaii	fewer than ____	
Golden lion tamarin		around ____	
Mountain gorilla		about 800	discovered 120 years ago
North Atlantic right whale		fewer than ____	
Javanese rhino		approximately ____	
Ivory-billed woodpecker		maybe ____	

C ▶ 2.17 Can you remember any other information to complete the report? Listen again and fill in the other columns where possible.

D You are going to watch a video about threatened species. Before you watch, in pairs, circle the alternatives you think are correct.

> We are living in the age of the [1] **fifth / sixth** mass global extinction. Experts warn that within the next [2] **30 / 50** years, we'll lose [3] **20% / 10%** of the entire species on the planet. And if trends continue, we'll lose [4] **a third / half** of our species in the next [5] **100 / 200** years. [6] **15% / 25%** of our mammal species are at risk of dying out in the wild.

E ▶ 2.18 Listen / Watch to check. How does this extract make you feel? Why?

> It makes me want to do something.

> Me, too. I think it's actually worse. I heard recently we've lost more than half the world's wildlife since 1970!

Have you made any lifestyle changes recently?

2.5

ⓘⅅ in Action Encouraging and discouraging

⚠ Common mistakes

There are almost no / There are hardly any
~~Almost no have~~ pandas.

I love ~~the~~ nature, ~~the~~ animals, and all ~~the~~ wildlife.

A Before watching the rest of the video, in pairs, brainstorm five ways to raise awareness of threatened species and change people's behavior.

> *We should all be taught more about it at school.*

B ▶2.19 ▶ Read five extracts from the video. Then listen / watch and number them 1–5 in the order you hear them.

- ☐ Showing the loss of animals in faraway places may pull a few heartstrings ...
- ☐ ...: the single most important factor behind taking action is our childhood experience.
- ☐ It's not the depressing accounts of the wildlife we are losing that moves us. It's awe and wonder ...
- ☐ Have we forgotten what first inspired our love of nature?
- ☐ In all parts of the world, we're beginning to see that public awareness does lead to change.

> *I disagree. Remembering what we've lost make us more determined to ...*

C Choose the best summary of the video, 1–3. Do you agree with them all? Why (not)?

1 Developing a love of nature is more important than thinking about what we have already lost.
2 Children need to be encouraged to spend more time in nature.
3 Showing images of species we have lost increases donations to animal charities.

D ▶2.20 Listen to five people explaining how they're going to help threatened species. Match each speaker 1–5 to these actions. There's one extra.

- ☐ Collect for charity
- ☐ Raise awareness online
- ☐ Reduce waste
- ☐ Sponsor an animal
- ☐ Use an environment-friendly product
- ☐ Volunteer at an animal shelter

E ▶2.20 Listen again. Are the speakers' friends encouraging 😊 or discouraging 😞?

1 _____   2 _____   3 _____   4 _____   5 _____

F ▶2.20 Listen again and complete the expressions for expressing encouragement and discouragement. Write three words in each blank.

😞	Why ¹_____ to (adopt a whale)?
😞	What is ²_____ (spending money on) ...?
😊	Keep up ³_____.

😊	Wow, you are determined! ⁴_____.
😞	What's ⁵_____ (buying that)?
😊	Every time? ⁶_____!

I haven't been studying much outside class recently.

> *Don't give up. What's the point of paying for classes if you don't do homework?*

G 🔴 **Make it personal** Are you improving your lifestyle?

1 List three things (real or imaginary) that you have or haven't been doing, to improve your lifestyle.
2 In groups, take turns telling each other what you have or haven't been doing. Ask extra questions and use the expressions in **F** to encourage or discourage.
3 Share the most imaginative changes from your groups with the class. Which group is / has been making the most changes?

🎵 *I got the eye of the tiger, a fighter*
Dancing through the fire, 'Cause I am a champion

Writing 2 A report

♫ *Why do I find it hard to write the next line?*
Oh, I want the truth to be said,
I know this much is true.

A Read Nina's report and mark ➕ for the most popular and ➖ for the least popular practices.

- ☐ using solar energy
- ☐ reusing plastic bags
- ☐ separating waste
- ☐ recycling containers

To:	Ms. Lang, Geography Teacher	Going Green
From:	Nina Diaz	
Subject:	Going Green in the Neighborhood	

1 Introduction: The aim of this report is to describe the most and the least popular practices in this neighborhood to help save the environment. It also makes recommendations about what we can do to become greener. The findings are reported below.

2 The survey: This survey involved interviewing 30 people from the ages of 18 to 35 by asking them ten questions about popular practices to save the planet. Respondents had to say how often they did these things: always, sometimes, rarely, or never.

3 Most popular practices: The survey showed that the two most popular practices to protect the environment in our neighborhood are to recycle bottles, cans, and plastic containers, in addition to separating organic and non-organic household waste.

4 Least popular practices: The two least popular practices, according to the questionnaire, were reusing plastic bags, or using cloth bags for shopping, and installing solar heating systems in houses.

5 Conclusion: As we can see from this report, people in this neighborhood try to adopt some environmentally friendly practices. However, some simple things could also be done to make a difference to the planet. Therefore, I recommend we organize a campaign to stimulate the use of cloth bags and cardboard boxes for shopping.

B The report is divided into five headings. Which heading, 1–5:

- ☐ describes the survey?
- ☐ summarizes and makes suggestions?
- ☐ says why the report is being written?
- ☐ discusses the first point?
- ☐ discusses the second point?

C Read *Write it right!* Then mark 1–6 appropriate (A) or inappropriate (I) to include in a report.

1 I think this is a very important topic.
2 This report will present the results of a survey about protecting the environment.
3 In my opinion, respondents enjoyed the survey.
4 That's just great for the environment!
5 To summarize, the main ideas are easy to implement.
6 I also have some bad news!

✅ **Write it right!**

- Begin reports with the names of the recipient and the author, and then the subject.
- Keep to the facts. Use personal opinions only in the conclusion.
- Use paragraphs with headings for each subtopic.
- Use formal language and **fixed phrases** to organize ideas and add clarity.
- Don't contract and be careful with punctuation.

D Mark 1–8 introduction (I), reporting an observation (R), generalizing (G), making a recommendation (M), or summarizing (S).

1 The objective of this report is to present / review ...
2 The most / least common answer was ...
3 It was found that ...
4 In general ...
5 This report describes ...
6 In conclusion ...

E Identify and correct four spelling, one punctuation, and two style mistakes in this draft.

This report's based on recent interviews about tourists' expectations in our city. According to the people interviewed, our main problem is adequate accomodation. Tourists complained they can't find enough family rooms or rooms with air-conditioning! They also reccomended establishing more tourist information points to provide better information and sugestions for tourists.

F 🎤 **Make it personal** In pairs, choose one of the topics and prepare a five-question survey. Conduct it in class and record the results.

Use of technology for learning English.
Most popular free time activities.

G *Your turn!* Write a report in 100–180 words.

Before	Look at the results from **F**. What are your conclusions?
While	Follow the five tips in *Write it right!*
After	Ask a classmate to read it and check formality, spelling, and punctuation, then email it to your teacher.

28

2 Down to earth

 Café

1 Before watching

A Match the words to the photos. Which have you seen in real life?

- ☐ jaguar
- ☐ tamarin monkey
- ☐ logging
- ☐ toucan
- ☐ forest canopy

None of them except logging, sadly!

B 🔘 **Make it personal** In pairs, think of three ways we can help endangered species.

I guess we could build more zoos.

C In pairs, describe Daniel. What do you think he might be doing / saying?

He might be doing an interview about endangered species.

2 While watching

A Watch up to 1:30 to check your guesses, and then circle the correct alternative.

1 Daniel's in a **zoo** / **studio**.
2 He's been researching **wildlife** / **global warming**.
3 Daniel **has** / **hasn't** had a lot of pets.
4 He's been taking classes in **environmental science** / **climate change**.
5 He plans to be a **weatherman** / **reporter**.
6 Polar bears have been **dying of hunger** / **drowning in the sea**.
7 Lucy knows little about **endangered species** / **Antarctica**.
8 Daniel's talking about very **contemporary** / **controversial** issues.

B Watch from 1:30 to 2:40 and number these items as you hear them, 1–10. What else can you remember him saying?

- ☐ cover
- ☐ difference
- ☐ impact
- ☐ lights
- ☐ logging
- ☐ mankind
- ☐ recycling
- ☐ species
- ☐ walk
- ☐ victims

C Watch the second part again to check. Then, in pairs, answer 1–4.

1 Where has logging been going on?
2 Who have been victims of logging?
3 Which actions / things impact negatively on the earth?
4 Which actions make a difference?

D Watch from 2:40 to the end. Who said these words: Daniel, Lucy, or August? Can you remember the complete phrase?

1 coming
2 impressive
3 knowledgeable
4 heartbreaking
5 lunch place
6 dying to try
7 on me

3 After watching

A Complete 1–6 with the *present perfect* or *present perfect continuous* of the verbs.

1 He _____ always _____ a fanatic about weather and the environment. (be)
2 I _____ never _____ such an animal lover. (know)
3 _____ he _____ to be a weatherman? (study)
4 Daniel ___ ___ environmental science classes. (take)
5 The effects of global warming _____ serious harm to wildlife. (cause)
6 This _____ for the past several years and the results _____ devastating. (go on / be)

C 🔘 **Make it personal** Which items that Daniel talks about concern you most? In your opinion, what changes do we need to make to have the biggest positive impact on planet Earth?

I think using hybrid cars will make a big difference.

R1 Grammar and Vocabulary

A *Picture dictionary.* Cover the words and definitions on the pages below and remember.

pages	
8–9	6 stages of a relationship
13	10 personality adjectives
15	8 active listening expressions
18–19	10 "green" words
22	9 environmental problems
26	7 endangered animals
160	2 words for each vowel sound (not the picture words); say and spell them

B ▶R1.1 **Order the words to make questions. Listen to check, then ask and answer in pairs.**

1 like / people / do / new / you / meeting / ?
2 of / who / your time / spend / most / with / you / do / ?
3 follow / social media / who / do / on / you / ?
4 are / what / friend / qualities / in a / most important / ?
5 can / which / of / always / on / your friends / you / depend / ?
6 you / who / you / up / feel / when / cheers / down / ?

C 🔘 Make it personal **Match the sentence halves, then modify the underlined phrases to make them true. Compare in pairs.**

1 I sometimes fall
2 I often go <u>to the mall</u> to hang
3 I'm usually attracted
4 I don't get
5 When you want to get
6 If someone wants to get
7 The <u>family member</u> I can count

a ☐ to know someone better, you should <u>go camping with them</u>.
b ☐ to people who <u>have a good sense of humor</u>.
c ☐ out with my <u>friends after work</u>.
d ☐ back together with an ex-partner, they'd have to <u>be really romantic</u>.
e ☐ along well with people who <u>are too arrogant</u>.
f ☐ out with <u>my parents</u> over <u>using the car</u>.
g ☐ on the most is <u>my older sister</u>.

D **Choose three phrases from 1E on p. 9. Write a short story, leaving gaps for the phrases for your partner to guess.**

E **Circle the correct alternative.**

1 My family always _____ all our plastic bottles and food packaging.
   a recycles   b is recycling   c has recycled

2 Many scientists believe that the earth _____ warmer because of us.
   a gets   b is getting   c have gotten
3 My school _____ solar panels next month.
   a installs   b is installing   c has installed
4 I _____ a plastic shopping bag for three months.
   a don't use   b 'm not using   c haven't used
5 An aluminum can _____ between 200 and 500 years to decompose.
   a takes   b is taking   c has taken
6 Many people _____ that pandas will become extinct.
   a think   b is thinking   c have thought

F ▶R1.2 *The animal in you* **Follow instructions 1–3, then listen to find out what the combinations mean.**

1 Think of and write three names of animals.
2 Think of and write three personality adjectives.
3 Combine them.

G **Complete 1–5 with the verbs in the *present perfect simple* or *continuous*.**

1 The population of the earth _____ by over one billion this century. (grow)
2 Greenpeace is an international environmental organization. It _____ since 1971. (campaign)
3 It _____ for hours now! When is it going to stop? (rain)
4 I _____ a wild monkey before. (never see)
5 The mammoth _____ extinct for over 10,000 years. (be)
6 André _____ 5000m today. (run)
7 Sorry about the mess. We _____ all afternoon and _____ yet. (cook, not tidy up)
8 How many times _____ you _____ exercises like this? (do)

H **Correct the mistakes in each sentence. Check your answers in units 1 and 2.**

🔘 **Common mistakes**

1 *When you went in New York? (2 mistakes)*
2 *When did you feel in love to her? (2 mistakes)*
3 *Jed was engaged with Clara during six years. (2 mistakes)*
4 *With who are you usually hang out? (3 mistakes)*
5 *Sofía is thinking BlacKkKlansman is a sad movie, but Paulo isn't agree. (2 mistakes)*
6 *She don't often eats meat, but she did liked my barbecue. (3 mistakes)*
7 *Don't let your laptop in stand-by mode for too long. (1 mistake)*
8 *Leo is living in Boston since two years. (2 mistakes)*
9 *We has been knowing each other from 2008. (2 mistakes)*
10 *The tree in my garden been grown two meters I've planted it. (2 mistakes)*

Skills practice

 I've been running through the jungle,
I've been running with the wolves, To get to you, to get to you,
I've been down the darkest alleys, Saw the dark side of the moon to get to you

R1

A Listen to Al's blog ▶2.3 on p. 20 and pause after each paragraph. In pairs, summarize, then continue. Finally, read to check. Did you miss anything because:
  a it was too fast to understand?
  b you didn't think it was important?
  c you didn't remember the words?
  d of another reason?

B ▶R1.3 **Dictation.** Listen and write the numbers. In pairs, try to retell each fact. Listen again to check.

C ▶R1.4 Use the prompts to make questions 1–4. Listen to check and add the emphatic words.

1 nicknames?   *Do you have any nicknames?*

> Not really, no. Although my brother calls me "big ears." Oh, it _____ annoy me!

>> Aw! That's mean! They used to call me "potato" at school, but I've _____ no idea why.

2 first / notice / meeting / new?

> Oh, I'm _____ a shoe person. I always notice if people have dirty shoes.

>> Me, I don't notice clothes, but I _____ notice teeth. If they have something in their teeth … yuk!

3 more often optimistic / pessimistic?

> Oh, I don't know. I guess I'm about fifty-fifty.

>> No, you always seem _____ laid-back and happy. I think you're a _____ positive person.

4 only three electrical appliances?

> Hmm, difficult. Only three? Well, the first is my laptop. I _____ use it almost every day.

>> Lights? Do they count as an appliance? They _____ are important.

D ▶R1.4 In pairs, imitate dialogues 1–4 in **C**. Listen again to compare with the audio.

E Read the title of the magazine article and first paragraph only. Guess what *Boston500* involves.

> Maybe it's a plan to make 500 companies do more to be greener.

F Read the rest of the article and find:
1 two economic benefits of the scheme.
2 a reason for thicker walls.
3 a problem with current solar panels.
4 a use for windows.
5 a problem with using biodegradable waste.

Save the world, save your money!

The city of Boston, capital of Massachusetts, and the most populous city in New England, is already one of the greenest cities in the U.S. Public transportation is eco-friendly, all the taxis are hybrids, and, with Grow Boston Greener, the city is trying to plant 100,000 trees by 2020. Now, with *Boston 500*, it has set its citizens a challenge: to go even greener. City officials claim that if just 500 families join the *Boston500* scheme they can each save $100 a year on their energy bills, cut 25% of dangerous gases, and create lots of new "green" jobs for the community.

So what is the *Boston500* scheme?
The idea is to encourage people to live in more efficient homes. Construction workers have already started building houses with thicker walls to protect against both high and low temperatures. Many homeowners have installed more energy-efficient appliances and use solar panels to power them, but they still need to buy some electricity, as solar panels don't usually generate enough. The ultimate goal, say developers, is to create houses that generate enough electricity to provide power for others as well.

Scientists and engineers have been working hard on this problem and there are some very innovative ideas out there. One plan is to turn windows into solar panels to increase the total area of panels—and they already have a prototype that works. Another is to use biodegradable waste—a smelly but efficient solution.

If the *Boston500* scheme is a success, we could all be paying less for electricity in the near future!

G In pairs, brainstorm ways to save energy at home. How many can you think of in two minutes?

> Some people put aluminum foil on the roof to reflect the sun.

H ▶R1.5 **Make it personal** **Question time!**
1 Listen to and answer the 12 lesson titles in units 1 and 2.
2 In pairs, practice asking and answering. Use the map on p. 2–3. Ask at least two follow-up questions, too. Which was the most interesting conversation?

> So, do you know all your classmates?

>> No, there are a few new students I don't know.

3

3.1 Which city would you most like to visit?

1 Vocabulary Cities

A Look at photos a–g. Do you recognize any of the cities? Find the **highlighted** words in texts 1–4 in the photos. What else can you see?

These two look like fashionable neighborhoods …   *There's a bridge in this one.*

B Read the texts. Can you guess which cities the people are describing?

1
OK, my turn now. "You're at the heart of the city, in the middle of the world's largest city **square** and the country's most important **landmark**. This square separates the country's capital from the "Forbidden City". Which Asian city is it?"

Hmm, I don't know. Is it _____ ?

Yeah, well done. At last you got one right!

2
Marta: Hey! I thought you'd be busy sightseeing. What are you doing online?
Ed: It's raining. Just having coffee and waiting for the rain to stop.
Marta: So … how do you like _____ ?
Ed: Well, if you like avenues full of **skyscrapers**, **chaotic** traffic, dangerous neighborhoods, and the ugliest **harbor** I've ever seen, it's the place to go.
Marta: Well, OK … Anything you do like, Mr. **Grum**py?
Ed: Hmm … Well, streets and avenues are numbered, so it's easy to find my way around … I guess. And the city is mostly flat, so it's very easy to walk. It's very **li**vely, I suppose. Lots going on, some good shopping. Oh, and then there's the huge park. And the statue. Yep, I think that's about it.

3
Second day in _____ , this **mar**velous city. I'm at a beautiful beach right now, people exercising and sunbathing everywhere. Some of them even sunbathe standing up so they can be seen! Looking up to my right, I can see a magnificent statue, but to my left, up on the hill, is one of the most **rundown areas** of the city. It's really strange that only a few blocks away there's an **upscale, fa**shionable **neighborhood**. You gotta love this place—so many great tourist spots, such a lot to do.

4
" … such fabulous co**lo**nial **arc**hitecture. If you have time, be sure to go all the way up to the 44th floor. There's an observation deck where you'll get an ex**cep**tional view of _____ 's **sky**line. On a clear day, you can see the soccer stadium, lots of beautiful old churches, volcanoes, and even the **py**ramids. Problem is, this city is sometimes **smoggy** so we don't get too many really clear days, I'm afraid. "

*Concrete jungle where dreams are made of,
There's nothing you can't do,
Now you're in New York.*

3.1

f

g

C ▶ **3.1 Match each text to its type. There is one extra type. Listen to check.**
- ☐ Friends talking on WhatsApp.
- ☐ A guide talking to tourists.
- ☐ A vacation blog post.
- ☐ Friends playing a guessing game.
- ☐ Introduction to a guidebook.

D Write the underlined words and phrases in the texts next to their definitions. Describe examples of these features in your area.

1	_____ noun [C]	a well-known building or site
2	_____ noun [C]	places / attractions popular with visitors
3	_____ phrase	know where you're going
4	_____ phrase	I recommend it
5	_____ phrase	in the most important place

> *We have a beautiful square in the heart of our town. It's a real tourist spot because it has such great cafés and restaurants.*

E Match the **bold** adjectives in the texts to their synonyms. Which adjectives would you use to describe your town, city, or another place you know? Why?

con**fused** and dis**org**anized   ener**get**ic and active   expensive and chic
neg**lec**ted and poor   poll**ut**ed   popular

> *I'd say our city is chaotic. There's lots of traffic and millions of people.*

⚠️ **Common mistakes**

such
It has ~~a so~~ beautiful architecture.

are so
The people ~~is such~~ friendly.

2 Pronunciation /eɪ/

A ▶ **3.2 Cross out the words that do *not* have /eɪ/. Listen to check. Make a tongue twister with three or four of the words.**

 eɪ

ancient	Asian	chaotic	dangerous	~~fashionable~~
flat	skyscraper	stadium	statue	sunbathe
traffic	upscale	volcanoes		

> *A dangerous, ancient, Asian skyscraper!*

B 🗣️ **Make it personal** Think of a city you'd love to visit.
1. Spend a few minutes thinking about why you'd like to visit it and make some notes.
2. Describe the city, without naming it, for your partner to guess.

> *The city I'd like to visit has beautiful beaches, great music, and some of the best colonial architecture in South America. It's well-known for its mix of European, African, and indigenous cultures. Famous landmarks include …*

3. Share your ideas with the class. Is there one place everybody would like to visit?

3.2 Was your last vacation as much fun as you'd hoped?

1 Reading

A ▶ 3.3 Match the underlined words to photos a–h, and then circle the correct alternative in 1–9. Listen to / watch the video to check.

VISITING HONG KONG FOR THE FIRST TIME?

Here's what you need to know:

1. It's **usual** / **rare** for people to shake hands and bow slightly.
2. When you greet people, you **should** / **shouldn't** hug them and kiss them on the cheek.
3. When you're walking through a crowd, you should gently push your way through and **say nothing** / **apologize**.
4. When you receive a gift, it's good manners to open it **later** / **immediately**.
5. Clocks make **good** / **bad** gifts.
6. When drinking tea, you should pour your **own** / **friends'** cup first.
7. In Hong Kong, it's OK to blow on your soup / chew loudly.
8. Leaving your chopsticks straight up means **good** / **bad** luck.
9. After eating, you **should** / **shouldn't** leave a tip on the table.

B If you were going to Hong Kong, which social conventions would be hard to adapt to?

It would be difficult not to open a gift right away.

C 🔲 **Make it personal** What are the rules where you live? In small groups, write six tips for a foreign visitor and share them with the class.

You shouldn't really talk on your phone on the train. People get annoyed and don't like it.

2 Grammar Past perfect

A ▶ 3.4 Rita is in Hong Kong for the first time to meet her in-laws. Match these phrases with 1–5 in her travel blog. There's one extra. Listen to check.

☐ she'd made ☐ He hadn't told me ☐ I'd never seen anyone do that
☐ I'd left on the table ☐ I hadn't had it before. ☐ I'd said sorry

First few days in HK! I got mad at Hue. ¹_____ about the shaking hands thing here! Guess how surprised his dad was when I kissed him! Slightly embarrassing! Hue's mom gave me a gift ²_____. Fortunately, I remembered not to open it in front of her. Went out for lunch, and I saw a man blowing on his soup. ³_____ before. Then I forgot to tip the waitress directly. Luckily, Hue went back and took the money ⁴_____ and gave it to her. I was walking through crowded streets this afternoon when this man suddenly looked at me strangely. I realized ⁵_____ to him. Typical tourist! To be honest, it's so unnatural for me not to apologize! But loving being here.

3.2

*For some reason I can't explain,
Once you'd gone there was never,
Never an honest word,
And that was when I ruled the world.*

B Reread the blog in **A** and complete the grammar box.

1 What happened first?
Hue's mom <u>gave</u> me a gift that <u>she'd made</u>.
☐ She gave the gift. ☐ She made the gift.

The past perfect has only one form for all persons: had / hadn't + past participle. The past perfect shows a relationship with another past event. Use the past perfect for the earlier event and the simple past for the later event.

2 Match pictures a and b to the phrases below.
☐ When I arrived, everybody started leaving.
☐ When I arrived, everybody had left.

→ **Grammar 3A** p.142

a
b

C Complete Rita's tweets with the *past perfect* of these verbs. There's one extra verb.

be   com**mit**   finish   make   read   not told   visit

In HK to meet the in-laws! I ¹_____ (never) on a long-haul flight before, so I was exhausted when we landed! #jetlag #experiencechina #exploreHK
← Reply   ⟳ Retweet   ★ Favourite

When Hue's parents began their meal, I ⁴_____ (nearly) mine! I didn't know I was supposed to wait for the hosts! #HongKong #dinnerout
← Reply   ⟳ Retweet   ★ Favourite

I ²_____ once that some of Hong Kong's skyscrapers had no 13th floor. Guess what? It's true! #superstitions
← Reply   ⟳ Retweet   ★ Favourite

Blew my nose in public yesterday, and everybody looked at me as if I ⁵_____ a crime. What did I do? #cultureshock #HongKongculture
← Reply   ⟳ Retweet   ★ Favourite

Made the mistake of wearing white yesterday. @Hue2008 ³_____ me that it's the color of death. #embarrassing
← Reply   ⟳ Retweet   ★ Favourite

On way to HK airport. Hue said I ⁶_____ a good first impression. His parents actually liked me. #relieved
← Reply   ⟳ Retweet   ★ Favourite

D Bruno was an exchange student in London last year. Choose the correct alternative.
1 I loved most of the landmarks. I **thought** / **'d thought** Big Ben was amazing.
2 At first I hated the food, but by the time I left, I **got** / **'d gotten** used to it.
3 I was shocked to find out how fast Londoners **spoke** / **'d spoken**.
4 It was nice to hear all the words I **learned** / **'d learned** in class over the years.
5 By the time my stay was over, I **visited** / **'d visited** most of the tourist spots.
6 My first car ride wasn't too bad. I **never drove** / **'d never driven** on the left side of the road.

⚠ **Common mistakes**

been
I'd never ~~gone~~ to L.A. before.

gone
He'd already ~~went~~ when I arrived.

E 🎤 **Make it personal** *Mystery Monologue!* A: Use questions 1–7 to plan a one-minute monologue about a place you've been to. Don't name the place.
B: Wait until A finishes, and then guess the place or ask more questions. Then change roles. How many of you have been to the same place?
1 When did you go? How long did you stay?
2 Had you been there before? If so, how many times?
3 Had you heard a lot about this place / seen it on TV?
4 What were you surprised to discover?
5 Did you do / see / eat anything you'd never done / seen / eaten before?
6 What were the people like? Any different from what you'd imagined?
7 Was anything else special? Would you recommend it?

Last year I went to this amazing place. I'd never been there before, and to my surprise, it was completely empty. I'd expected it to be full!

35

3.3 Do you ever want to get away from it all?

1 Vocabulary Urban problems

A Read the magazine and match the highlighted words to the photos.

The stresses of CITY LIVING

"The traffic is a nightmare. There's construction everywhere, and you get stuck in traffic jams every day. Drivers sometimes go through red lights and it's impossible to find a parking spot."

"There is so much pollution! The air is smoggy, there's trash everywhere, and there's noise pollution from the cars. People are always honking!"

"The crime rate is high. There is a lot of vandalism, car theft, and pickpocketing. I don't feel safe in my neighborhood."

"It's difficult to find a work-life balance, and there just isn't enough "me-time," We are all in debt and constantly connected to the Internet, but not to each other, so a lot of people suffer from loneliness and anxiety."

B ▶3.5 Reread and listen to check the pronunciation of the highlighted words. Do you agree with all four opinions of city living?

That sounds just like where I live!

C 🔸 **Make it personal** In pairs, from the photos, choose the five most serious problems in your city. Can you agree on the order?

I think the worst problem by far is the traffic.

No way! I'd say vandalism is a much more serious issue.

🔸 **Common mistake**

In my neighborhood, there is trash ~~in every place~~.
everywhere

2 Reading

A In pairs, list five ways you could escape the problems mentioned in **1B**.

B ▶3.6 Read the article on p. 37. Are any of your ideas mentioned? Complete the article with a–f. Then listen to check echoing the pink-stressed words.

  a Overcome this by volunteering at an animal shelter.
  b Finding a quiet place to switch off and enjoy peace is so important.
  c Use lavender for relaxation and peppermint to invigorate.
  d Try by your window or on your balcony.
  e Try going to events to inspire your creative self.
  f It's not easy to find these things in the city, though.

It's like a jungle, sometimes it makes me wonder how I keep from going under. A-huh-huh huh-huh.

3.3

How to *get away* from it all

Living in a lively city is amazing, but the stresses and strains of urban life can affect our mental and physical health. Read the following tips to help you find a more balanced, peaceful city life.

Nature
Natural light and fresh air will instantly make you feel better. ¹_____ Try to find a park and go for a walk there, or just sit and read a book. You'll be amazed how these simple activities can improve your mood.

Indulge your sense of smell
Clearly, the city does not smell pleasant. You can really transform your home environment and mental health with smell. ²_____

Get some pet therapy
If you've lived in the countryside, you'll notice how disconnected city dwellers are from nature and animals. ³_____ Bonding with an animal naturally reduces anxiety, and loneliness can never be a problem while walking a dog!

Grow something
Nowadays we're disconnected from where our food comes from. Even though you might not have a garden, you can grow food anywhere. ⁴_____ Producing your own vegetables makes you appreciate food more, waste less, and feel closer to nature.

Find some silence
We live among permanent noise—roadworks, traffic jams, phone calls, advertising, even our own minds are noisy. ⁵_____ Just a few minutes every day will make you feel more positive.

Do what you love
Everyone has a talent: painting, playing an instrument, or gardening, but we rarely spend time nurturing these gifts. When we take the time to do what we love, we feel more grounded. ⁶_____ Life isn't all about work, money, and success!

C 🔊 **Make it personal** **In groups, discuss these questions.**
1. Which of the activities in the article have you tried to "get away from it all"? Which would you like to do?
2. What other things do you / people you know do to reduce the stress of modern life?

My brother turns off his phone for an hour every day. He says he enjoys the peace and quiet.

I do the opposite. I listen to music or play video games.

③ Listening

A ▶3.7 **Listen to three city dwellers describe changes they made in their lives. Complete the chart.**

	Problem	Change
Raul		
Tomiko		
André		

B ▶3.8 **Complete 1–6 with these words. There is one extra. Then listen to check.**

| bother | driving | find | 'm | mind | stand | takes |

1. ... and my nonstop lifestyle was _____ me crazy.
2. I'm still just as busy, but it doesn't really _____ me as much.
3. Now, I _____ it annoying if I don't have time to eat properly.
4. It takes more time, but I don't _____ that.
5. I couldn't _____ coming home to an empty apartment every day.
6. I still find the city a bit lonely sometimes, but I _____ OK with it.

C **Read** *Common mistakes*. **Then circle the correct alternatives in 1–4.**
1. The noise **drive / drives** me crazy! Absolutely insane!
2. I love my city, but the huge lines really **annoy / annoys** me.
3. I can't stand people who **go / goes** through red lights.
4. There are massive traffic jams in my city, but that **don't / doesn't** bother me at all. I'm a cyclist!

D 🔊 **Make it personal** *City Stress Survey*. **Choose a topic from the article. Write three questions and interview your classmates. Report your findings.**

How often do you go for a walk in a park or the countryside?

> ⚠ **Common mistakes**
>
> drive
> All the traffic jams ~~drives~~ me crazy.
> (traffic jams = they)
>
> bothers
> Littering ~~bother~~ me a lot.
> (littering = it)
>
> doesn't
> The traffic ~~don't~~ bother me.
> (traffic = it)

37

3.4 Have you ever missed any important dates?

1 Listening

A ▶3.9 From the pictures, imagine Juan and Sandra's stories. Listen to check. Were you close?

OK, so it looks like Juan's going to work.

Juan Alvarez from Bogotá

Sandra Machado from São Paulo

B ▶3.9 Listen again. True (T) or false (F)? How much more did you understand the second time? Who do you feel most sorry for? Why?
1. Juan had high hopes for the job interview.
2. Juan gave himself one hour to get there.
3. Sandra bought the tickets two weeks before the show.
4. Sandra and her friend managed to watch 30 minutes of the show.

I feel most sorry for … because …

C Read ▶3.9 on p. 165 and write the underlined expressions in the chart.

 Common mistake

missed
I ~~lost~~ my flight.
You lose objects, but you miss transportation, events, and opportunities.
I missed the chance to see U2 because I was sick.

Listening actively	
1	I'm not sure I understand.	*What do you mean?*
2	I'm sorry this happened to you.	
3	I'm not surprised to hear that.	
4	What happened in the end?	
5	I'm very surprised.	

38

You only get one shot, do not miss your chance to blow. This opportunity comes once in a lifetime, yo.

3.4

D 🔵 **Make it personal** Have you ever been stuck in traffic for a long time? In pairs, take turns sharing your stories. Remember to listen actively. Who has the funniest story?

I was going to visit my grandparents once, and we got stuck on the highway for four hours.

Oh, no. You poor thing. What happened?

2 Grammar Past perfect continuous

A Read the example sentence and answer 1–3 in the grammar box.

> When we finally **got** to the stadium, **she had been singing** for well over an hour.
> 1 When they arrived:
>   a) was Taylor Swift already singing?   b) did the music stop?
> 2 Do we use the past perfect continuous for an action that:
>   a) had finished?   b) was in progress before another past action?
> 3 Is the form had(n't) +   a) being?   b) been + verb + -ing?
>
> ➡ **Grammar 3B** p. 142

B Complete 1–8 with the *past perfect* or *past perfect continuous* of these verbs. Use contractions.

> arrange   dream of   drive   get up   go through   try   rain   wait for

1 Juan _____ to find a job as an architect for months.
2 He wasn't worried about the traffic as he _____ at 6.
3 He heard on the radio that a bus _____ a red light.
4 He didn't get the job he _____ since he graduated.
5 Sandra bought tickets for the show she _____ since she was 16.
6 Sandra's friend _____ to pick her up in her car.
7 They _____ for a little while when the car broke down.
8 They were stuck in traffic because it _____ nonstop.

C Complete the grammar box with the tenses below. Then, in pairs, role-play Juan and Sandra telling their stories. Retell the stories in your own words.

> Past perfect   Past perfect continuous   Past continuous

> **Narrative tenses**
> The simple past is the most common past tense. In general, use the others like this:
> ¹_____: an action in progress at a point in the past.
> *I was chatting* online when you called. Sorry!
>
> ²_____: one action that happened before another in the past.
> By 8 p.m. Jo **had done** all her work, so she went home.
>
> ³_____: action in progress or repeated before a point in the past.
> But she'**d been working** so hard she fell asleep in the car.
>
> ➡ **Grammar 3C** p. 142

🔴 **Common mistakes**

So, I was going for a job interview. I'd been looking for a job as an architect for ages, so I was really nervous.

D 🔵 **Make it personal** Have you ever missed or forgotten anything important? In groups, share stories and choose the saddest and funniest ones. Use these questions to plan what to say first.
1 What was the important date or event?
2 Had you been looking forward to it?
3 Why did you miss or forget it?
4 What happened?
5 How do you feel about it now?

Well, it was my cousin's birthday, and I'd been planning ...

Had you spent many birthdays together in the past?

39

3.5 Do you always follow the rules?

ID Skills Understanding rules and regulations

A ▶ 3.10 Match the signs to photos a–i. Listen to check. In pairs, think of two places where you might find each one. Which four are intended to be funny?

> That one could be at a public beach

DOGS MUST BE ON LEASH.

TRESPASSERS WILL BE PROSECUTED (IF THE DOGS DON'T GET YOU FIRST.)

SPEED LIMIT 10 MPH

ATTENTION, DOG GUARDIANS! PLEASE PICK UP AFTER YOUR DOG. THANK YOU. **ATTENTION, DOGS!** GRRRR, WOOF. GOOD DOG.

DON'T EVEN THINK OF PARKING HERE! UNAUTHORIZED VEHICLES WILL BE TOWED AWAY AT OWNER'S EXPENSE.

PLEASE FASTEN SEAT BELT WHILE SEATED. LIFE VEST UNDER YOUR SEAT.

SMILE! This building is under **24 hr surveillance.**

SWIM AT YOUR OWN RISK – THE SHARKS WILL BE DELIGHTED! BY THE WAY, NO LIFEGUARDS ON DUTY HERE.

IN ORDER TO MAINTAIN A RELAXING ENVIRONMENT, PLEASE REFRAIN FROM CELL PHONE USE.

a

b

c

d

e

f

g

h

i

B ▶ 3.11 Match 1–10 to their meanings. Listen to a teacher to check.

	Verbs		Meanings
1	refrain from		remove someone's car using another vehicle
2	pick up after		avoid
3	tow away		close securely
4	fasten		clean up someone's mess
	People		
5	a lifeguard		someone who enters private property without permission
6	a trespasser		someone who helps swimmers in difficulty
	Expressions		
7	under surveillance		whoever owns it will pay all costs
8	on duty		although you know it's dangerous
9	at owner's expense		working
10	at your own risk		monitored

C In groups, create and share signs for places 1–6. Any funny ones?
1 an airport   3 your favorite beach   5 a theater
2 a hospital   4 your English school   6 a zoo

D 👤 **Make it personal** Have you, or people you know, ever broken any of these (or similar) rules? Would you ever break any of them?

> My parents never used to pick up after their dog, but now they always do.

When did you last break a rule? 3.5

ID in Action Explaining and questioning rules

A ▶ 3.12 Listen to three dialogues and circle the correct signs on p. 40. Which speakers 1–3 don't accept the regulations easily?

B ▶ 3.13 Complete 1–7. Listen, check, and copy the stress and intonation.

Stating a rule	1	I'm a_____ you c_____ park here.
Apologizing	2	I'm sorry. I didn't r_____ that.
Questioning a rule	3	What do you m_____ I can't park here? S_____ who?
	4	Oh, c_____ on! Be reasonable!
Reinforcing	5	I'm afraid s_____.
	6	I'm afraid n_____.

Common mistakes

~~I'm afraid yes.~~ → I'm afraid so.
~~I'm afraid no.~~ → I'm afraid not.
~~I think no.~~ → I don't think so.

C ▶ 3.14 Match these confessions to photos 1–4. What rule(s) had they broken?

☐ Well, a few years ago I was on a work trip to Poland. I was crossing the street when these police officers suddenly stopped me and tried to give me a fine for crossing in the wrong place! I had no idea it was illegal! I didn't speak any Polish and pretended not to understand. In the end, they let me go with just a warning. Weird!

☐ Once, my brother was taking photos in the countryside in Egypt. Suddenly, two soldiers appeared and confiscated his camera. Apparently, without knowing it, he'd taken photos of a military installation. And he'd thought it was just a nice bridge over a river!

☐ My wife and I were visiting Rome and the Vatican. I'd been wearing shorts all day, around the museums and stuff, no problem, but then they wouldn't let me in to St. Peter's. I had to wait outside while my wife got to see it all. Anyway, lucky for me, it's a beautiful square.

☐ My wife used to get into trouble all the time at school for not wearing the right uniform. The wrong shoes, the wrong shirt, she never wore a tie, dyed her hair purple … She was a real punk and it all seemed so stupid to her. Actually, she's still a bit of a rebel today. That's why I love her!

D In pairs, role-play a sign from p. 40. Act it out for the class to guess which sign you chose.

> Excuse me, ma'am. Haven't you read the sign?

> No, I'm sorry, I haven't. Is there a problem?

> Well …

E 🎤 **Make it personal** **Confessions!** Have you / your friends ever gotten in trouble for breaking a rule? Share stories in groups. Who has been the most disobedient?

> Hmm … well, the police stopped my uncle for using his phone in the car.

> Did he get a fine, or did they let him go with a warning?

🎵 *I don't want to go to school, I just wanna to break the rules.*

Writing 3 A narrative

♪ *Little did I know...*
That you were Romeo, you were throwing pebbles,
And my daddy said, "Stay away from Juliet",
And I was crying on the staircase
Begging you, please, don't go.

A *Innovation* magazine has held a "best vacation narrative" competition. Read the winning entry and circle the correct photo for the story.

A vacation to remember
By Stef Stiller

1 ☐ My best friend Karen hadn't had a vacation for a long, long time. ☐ She was desperate to go somewhere new and do something she had never done before. ☐ So, last winter, after looking into many options, she decided to go skiing in Courchevel, a resort in the French Alps.

2 When Karen arrived, she was so excited about the comfortable hotel, delicious food, and such incredible views. ☐ The following day, she joined a ski-school. The other skiers seemed like fun-loving, sociable people, so she knew she'd have a great time. Karen had never skied before, but the instructor Alain, was great and reassured her.

3 However, she found skiing so hard she almost gave up. She kept trying, but then a horrible thing happened. While she was going down a hill, she fell badly and broke her leg. Her special trip had turned into a nightmare. Unable to move, she was stuck in a hospital in Courchevel.

4 But she had a wonderful surprise. ☐ They visited every day and brought gifts. Karen began to fall in love with the French Alps and decided to stay and get a job. She worked in a ski-chalet, learned to ski, and guess what? Now she's an instructor herself!

B Which paragraph, 1–4, answers these questions?
☐ What was the hotel like?
☐ Why did she go there?
☐ Where did she decide to go?
☐ Who is the main character?
☐ What happened while she was there?
☐ What happened in the end?
☐ Who did she meet?
☐ When did she go?

C Reread and underline examples of *simple past* (SP), *past continuous* (PC) and *past perfect* (PP).

D Read *Write it right!* and notice the nine time expressions in the story. Can you think of any others?

> ✓ **Write it right!**
> - To enrich a narrative, use a variety of past tenses.
> - Sequence it with a mix of time expressions to start, end, and connect sentences.
> - Use plenty of adjectives and adverbs to add color to your story and *so* and *such* to emphasize them.

E Complete 1–5 with a time expression and the correct form of the verbs in parentheses.

| after | ago | finally | occasionally | while |

1 _____ leaving all her bags in the hotel, she _____ for a walk. (go)
2 _____ Karen _____ on her own. (travel)
3 This story _____ a few months _____. (happen)
4 _____, she _____ to go skiing. (decide)
5 Her new ski-friends and Alain _____ her the whole time _____ she _____ in bed. (help / recover)

F Match 1–5 from **E** to the boxes in Stef's story.

G Circle the correct word in each pair.
1 Courchevel was **so** / **such** **beautiful** / **beautifully** that she didn't want to leave.
2 The days passed **so** / **such** **slow** / **slowly**.
3 It was **so** / **such** a **special** / **specially** trip that she'll always remember it.
4 That trip **complete** / **completely** changed her life.
5 Alain was **so** / **such** a **friend** / **friendly** guy.

H *Your turn!* Choose one of this year's topics for *Innovation* magazine's competition and write an entry in 100–180 words.

> *That was really embarrassing!*

> **What a frightening experience!**

Before	Note down the main events in your story. Use the questions in **B** to help. Number the events in the order you want to tell them.
While	Write four paragraphs. Follow the tips in *Write it right!*
After	Ask your partner to check spelling and punctuation and give suggestions before emailing it to your teacher.

3 Global swarming

ID Café

1 Before watching

A Are the photos city (C), coast (Co), landmark (L), or scenery (S)? In pairs, describe them in detail and include these adjectives.

| amazing | awesome | beautiful | buzzing |
| chaotic | congested | crowded | historic |

Photo 4 looks like somewhere in Asia.

B 🔵 **Make it personal** In pairs, describe your favorite place or historical landmark.

I saw the pyramids in Egypt five years ago. I'd never seen anything so old before!

2 While watching

A Do you think 1–9 will be true or false? Watch and check (✓) your guesses. How many right?

1. ☐ August and Andrea had lived in many places before they moved back to the U.S.
2. ☐ Rory wants to go somewhere he has been before.
3. ☐ Silicon Valley is home of the computer nerds.
4. ☐ Rory has never been to Quebec City before.
5. ☐ August doesn't think New York is so chaotic.
6. ☐ Andrea and August lived in Buenos Aires.
7. ☐ Mexico City and New York are very crowded.
8. ☐ Rush hour in Mexico City is similar to New York.
9. ☐ Quebec City has lots of little cafés.

B Watch again and check the features of each place.

	Buenos Aires	Mexico City	New York	Quebec City
architecture				
cafés				
chaotic				
good public transportation				
historic landmarks				
scenery				
traffic				
unpredictable weather				

3 After watching

A Circle the correct alternative(s).

1. The siblings had a lot of passport stamps because their **father / mother** was a photojournalist.
2. Rory goes to Dublin every year to **play soccer / visit his grandparents**.
3. August said they'd lived in **more than ten cities / more cities than he could name**.
4. Andrea and August mention "swarming like bees" to describe cities buzzing with **people / the noise of the traffic**.
5. Genevieve's gigs at the café draw **big / small** crowds.

B Complete 1–5 with the *simple past* or *past perfect*.

1. Rory _____ about visiting the West Coast. (think)
2. Rory didn't know they _____ in Argentina. (live)
3. Before Genevieve arrived for her gig, she _____ the others several times. (text)
4. August and Andrea _____ Rory pictures of Buenos Aires. (show)
5. Rory _____ in Dublin before he moved to the U.S. (live)

C 🔵 **Make it personal** Compare cities you know with those mentioned in the video. What would be your dream vacation destination?

I've never been abroad, so I don't know any of these places.

Me neither. My home town, Trujillo, is a much smaller city, but it has some great colonial architecture.

43

4

4.1 Does your school system work well?

1 Reading

A In groups, compare your thoughts when looking at photos 1–8.

All the books remind me of my school bag. It was really heavy!

B Say the subjects on the school schedule together. Pay attention to the pink-stressed syllables. In pairs, compare how you feel / felt about each one. Any good stories?

	Monday	Tuesday	Wednesday	Thursday	Friday
7:10	Literature	Geography	Biology	Math	Chemistry
8:05	Math	Art	Information and Communication Technology	Math	Physics
9:00	Biology	Chemistry	History	Languages	Math
9:50	Break	–	–	–	–
10:05	Music	Math	Geography	Chemistry	Art
11:00	Physical education	Math	Languages	Physical education	Music
11:55	Lunch	–	–	–	–
12:30	History	Physics	Art	Literature	Literature
1:25	Languages	Philosophy	Music	Economics	Geography
2:20	Physics	Literature	Politics	Biology	Physical education

I used to hate math because the teacher couldn't explain it to us.

C ▶ 4.1 Guess which countries have the world's best education systems, and why. Listen, read, and complete the first part of an article to check.

Common mistake

subject
My worst ~~material~~ was math.

HEY, TEACHER, THOSE KIDS ARE DOING GREAT!

A certain education minister once joked that his country's education goal was a modest one: to be one of the best in the world. Well, looks like he's been successful. His country—which also has one of the largest per capita cell phone use on the planet—has the world's best school system, and 66% of its five and a half million population are university graduates. Here are some reasons why _____'s school system works so incredibly well and is considered the best in the world.

4.1

D Why might this country's system be so good? Make a prediction about 1–8.

1 class size   4 number of tests   7 popularity of arts subjects
2 discipline   5 public vs. private education   8 uniforms
3 homework   6 teachers' qualifications

♫ *Hey, Teacher, leave them kids alone! All in all you're just another brick in the wall.*

Maybe they have lots of expensive private schools.

Yes, I guess the teachers are well qualified, too.

E ▶ **4.2** Read the rest of the article to check your predictions. How many were correct? Match the highlighted phrases to photos 1–8.

▶ Tuition fees? Forget it. Education is free and there are very few private schools.

▶ Classes are small, with rarely more than twenty students. The atmosphere is relaxed (lots of students don't wear uniforms or even shoes, only socks!), but students rarely behave badly. They hardly ever get kicked out of class or cheat on exams.

▶ Students in grades one through nine spend a lot of time each week taking classes in subjects such as art, music, and cooking. This helps to generate interest and motivate students.

▶ In Finland, kids have a lighter schedule than American students and do less homework, too— half an hour per day, tops. Having too much homework, they believe, can interfere with a child's passion for learning.

▶ During the first few years of school, students don't take tests. Instead, they get continuous feedback and a report card twice a year so their parents know if they're doing well. Students are actively encouraged to make mistakes and learn by doing.

▶ If students get low grades and fail* a test, they have extra support and one-on-one tutoring, if necessary. And it works really well. Every classroom has a teaching assistant to help students who are experiencing difficulties and everyone makes progress.

▶ What really makes the difference, though, is the status teaching enjoys in Finland. Education is the most competitive professional field in Finland— more so than medicine and law—and you must have a master's degree if you want to become a teacher.

* the opposite of *pass*

② **Vocabulary** School life

A Check the correct *verb + noun* collocations. Then scan the article in **1E** and *Common mistakes* to check.

do	get	make	take	
1				a class / tests
2				a low / high grade
3				homework
4				kicked out of class
5				mistakes
6				well (in school)

🕐 **Common mistakes**

doing
My wife is ~~making~~ an MBA.

take
She'll have to ~~make~~ an exam at the end.

passes
If she ~~gets~~ the exam, she'll get a promotion at work.

make
She hopes she doesn't ~~do~~ too many mistakes.

B ⬤ **Make it personal** Follow the instructions.

1 In pairs, use the highlighted phrases and collocations in the article to compare the Finnish system with yours. How many differences can you find? Which would you introduce in your country?

They have one-on-one tutoring sometimes. We don't get that if we fail a test.

2 Describe your ideal school, its policies, and schedule. Who came up with the best ideas? Any disagreements?

It'd be a nice modern building. We would only do a little homework every day and not take a lot of tests. And I think uniforms are a good idea.

No way! I love wearing my own clothes.

45

4.2 What's the ideal age to go to college?

1 Listening

A ▶ 4.3 Listen to / Watch the trailer of a documentary about the education system in the U.S. Is it mostly positive or negative?

B ▶ 4.3 Listen / Watch again and check the three problems mentioned. Ignore the second column for now. Does it make you want to study there?

	The U.S.	My school
Too much homework.		
Too much pressure to get into a good university.		
Overcrowded classrooms.		
Badly paid and demotivated teachers.		
Too much emphasis on tests and grades.		
Poor use of technology.		
Discipline problems.		
Not enough career counseling.		

2 Grammar *too / enough*

A Read the phrases in **1B** and the rules in the grammar box. Then correct the mistakes in the typical student errors 1–9 below.

1	*too* = more than necessary	Our classes start too early. The classrooms get much too hot.
2	*enough* = the necessary amount	There was enough time to check my work. Do you work hard enough?
3	*not enough* = less than necessary	There aren't enough chairs for everyone. I wasn't sitting close enough to see.

too goes before an adjective or adverb
(not) enough goes after an adjective but before a noun

→ Grammar 4A p.144

1 My school was ~~too~~ *a lot of* fun. I really enjoyed it.
2 Are there windows enough in your classroom?
3 It was a too hard class. I didn't understand anything.
4 There was not money enough to buy new projectors.
5 I have too many friends at school. I feel lucky!
6 My teacher is too helpful. She's really friendly as well.
7 This is too difficult homework. I can't do it.
8 This exercise was very easy. It wasn't enough challenging for me.
9 I gave up Chinese because it was a too difficult language.

B **Make it personal** Complete the *My school* column in **1B**. In pairs, share your experiences. Overall, are your feelings positive or negative? Any big differences?

At my school, students have too much homework. It takes me four or five hours a day.

Well, when I was in high school, I had a lot of homework, too.

C **Make it personal** Read the Education Debate statements.
1 How much do you agree with them? (1 = strongly agree, 5 = completely disagree)
2 Research online to support your ideas.
3 In pairs, share your opinions and evidence. Do you have similar ideas?
4 Share your thoughts with the class. Any disagreements?

🎵 Baby, we don't stand a chance,
It's sad but it's true,
I'm way too good at goodbyes.

4.2

Education Debate

1. Pressure and competitiveness are positive for students.
2. Technology helps students learn better.
3. Training good teachers is the best investment a country can make.
4. There are too many problems with my country's education system.

I think too much pressure can be very stressful for students.

You're absolutely right, but without enough competition, students can get lazy.

3 Vocabulary College life

A Match the highlighted words in the website article below to their definitions.

1	_____	to specialize in a subject in college	4	_____	to enter
2	_____	to begin again	5	_____	your main subject of study
3	_____	money to pay for your education	6	_____	to stop going to

B ▶ 4.4 Reread and match classic mistakes 1–6 to the typical examples. Listen to check. Have you, or anyone you know, made these mistakes?

WAYS TO PICK THE **WRONG CAREER**

Are you going to be a graduate soon? Choosing a career is one of the most important decisions you'll ever make, so you'd better do it right. Here are six mistakes to avoid.

BY GABI WATSON

A backup plan might be a good idea, in case 'being a celebrity' doesn't work out....

CAREERS ADVISOR

Classic mistakes
1. Living someone else's dream.
2. Doing what everybody else is doing.
3. Following your head, not your heart.
4. Being afraid to make big changes.
5. Being afraid of failing.
6. Not planning for the future.

Typical examples

☐ "I can't throw away $40,000, drop out of college, forget about my business major, and start over."

☐ "I'd love to get a scholarship to go to Harvard, but it's so hard I won't even try."

☐ "All my friends will major in business, so that's what I'll do."

☐ "My parents have always wanted me to get into medical school. I can't disappoint them, and they are desperate for me to succeed."

☐ "I'd love to get a degree in music. I've already got my intermediate piano certificate, but what will I do when I graduate? How will I get a decent job?"

☐ "I have all the education I need. I'm not illiterate! It's time for fun, fun, fun!"

C **Make it personal** Complete 1–5 with words from **A**. In pairs, ask and answer. Any disagreements?
1 If you could get a _scholarship_ to study anywhere in the world, where would you go?
2 How difficult is it to _____ a good college in your country?
3 What did you / would you like to _____ at college? Why?
4 Do you know anyone who _____ college? How did things go for him / her?
5 If you could _____ at high school, what would you change?

I'd study gastronomy at the Sorbonne in Paris!

⚠ **Common mistake**

I *am* graduated from law school. =
I majored in law. /
I have a law degree.

4.3 What do you regret not having done?

1 Listening

A In pairs, discuss the questions.
1. What kinds of regrets do people sometimes have about school?
2. Guess what these three people studied / are studying? What might they regret now?

B ▶ 4.5 Listen to three interviews about career choices and complete 1–3.

1. Justin says he should have studied _____ instead of _____.
2. Zoe studies _____, but she says she _____ writing.
3. George dropped out of _____ and became a _____.

C In pairs, do you know anybody who had trouble choosing a career? Are they happy now?

> Yes, me! I tried three completely different jobs until I found the right one for me.

> Really? What did you do?

2 Grammar *should have*

A ▶ 4.6 Match the sentence halves. Listen to check. Any resonate with you?

1 Dad wanted me to follow in his footsteps, but	☐ I should have <u>chosen</u> another major.
2 I'm way too old now.	☐ I should have <u>gone</u> to music school years ago.
3 Basically, journalism's not my thing.	☐ I shouldn't have <u>listened</u> to him.
4 I know it was a stupid decision, and	☐ Should I have <u>persevered</u> a little more?
5 Every day I wake up and ask myself:	☐ I should have <u>thought</u> about it more carefully.

Common mistakes

~~I should studied~~ *have* English when I was a kid.

I regret ~~to not learn~~ *learning* English before.

B Reread 1–5 in **A** and the grammar box. Then answer 1–2.
1. What form are the underlined verbs in? Complete the form below.
   subject + *should (not)* + *have* + _____
2. How do you form questions?

> Use **should have** to express regret about something in the past.
>
> *I should have thought about it more carefully.* (= I didn't think about it carefully, and I'm sorry.)
> *I shouldn't have listened to him.* (= I did listen to him, and I regret that.)
>
> Also use **should have** to ask for or give advice about a past event.
>
> *What should I have studied instead?*
> *You should have been more open.*
> *You shouldn't have kept it secret.*

➤ Grammar 4B p. 144

♪ *Too young, too dumb to realize that I should have bought you flowers and held your hand.*

4.3

C ▶ 4.7 *Should've* is common in informal speech and writing. Listen and write down regrets 1–5. Notice the weak sound in the contractions /ʃʊdəv/ and /ʃʊdntəv/. In pairs, practice saying the sentences dramatically!

1 *We should've gone by train.*

D Think of four regrets about your school days. Share them with your partner and then the class. What is the most common / unusual regret?

I shouldn't have missed so many classes.   *Me, too. I should have participated more.*

E In pairs, write two *should have / shouldn't have* captions for each photo. Compare with other pairs. Choose the best caption for each photo.

I should have stayed home with Mom!

F 🟢 **Make it personal** *Oops, I did it again!* We've all done things we regretted later. What's your story?

1 Choose a topic below and prepare your story. Include a lie.
2 In groups, share your stories. Can you spot the lie?

| Your hair / looks | Dis**as**trous vacations | Eating / drinking | Things you bought |
| Things you said | Relationships | Missed opportunities | Studies | Career |

I shouldn't have told my sister I didn't like her new dress.

Why would you say such a thing? I think you're lying about that!

4.4 What would you do if you won a million dollars?

1 Listening

A Match the two halves of the quotes. Which ones do you like the most? Why?

1. If I had my life to live over,
2. If you never try,
3. If you don't know where you're going,
4. If you realized how powerful your thoughts were,
5. Dream as if you will live forever;
6. If you always do what you've always done,

- [ ] you'll probably end up somewhere else.
- [ ] live as if you'll die today.
- [ ] you'd never think a negative thought.
- [ ] you'll always get what you've always got.
- [ ] I'd dare to make more mistakes next time.
- [ ] you'll never learn.

I like number 4. Positive thinking is very powerful.

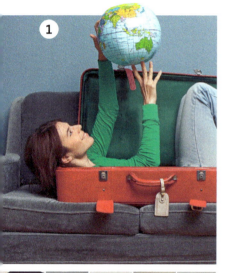

B Look at photos 1–6. What are the people's aspirations? Match them to these categories.

| Career | Education / skills | Family life | Health and fitness | Travel |

C How can these people achieve their goals? Do you have any similar goals?

This couple want to own their own property.

They'll have to save a lot. Buying an apartment is so expensive. I'll never be able to get my own place.

D ▶ 4.8 Listen to three people talking about their goals and aspirations. Match them to the photos in **B** and complete what they say.

Speaker 1: My big dream is …
Speaker 2: My main wish is …
Speaker 3: My ultimate aim is …

E ▶ 4.8 Listen again and complete 1–6 with the verb forms. There's one extra. Who do you think will achieve their goal?

| 'll go backpacking | 'll prove | didn't train | were |
| work hard | wouldn't be able | 'll have | |

1. If I didn't live at home, I _____ to save anything.
2. If I _____ and save my money, I'll see the benefits later.
3. If there _____ nine or ten continents, I would still want to visit each one!
4. If I save enough this year, I _____ around Southeast Asia.
5. If I pass this level, I _____ to myself that I can do anything I want.
6. If I _____ in martial arts, I wouldn't be the person I am now.

F 🟠 **Make it personal** In groups. Do you know anyone who has achieved their dream? What are your current aspirations? Share your best stories.

My ultimate aim is to be a DJ.

If I could turn back time, If I could find the way, I'd take back all those words that hurt you, And you'd stay.

4.4

2 Grammar First and second conditional

A Study the examples in the grammar box and complete the rules with these words.

"unreal" or impossible   real and possible   past   present (x2)   future

---

First conditional
if + simple present, *will* + infinitive
If I have time, I'll come and visit you.

Use the first conditional to talk about something that is ^{1}_____ .
The *if* clause uses a ^{2}_____ tense and talks about a ^{3}_____ situation.

Second conditional
if + simple past, *would* + infinitive
If you had to spend a year with just one person, who would it be?

Use the second conditional to talk about something that is ^{4}_____ .
The *if* clause uses a ^{5}_____ tense and talks about a ^{6}_____ situation.

*Remember: use the zero conditional (*if* + present simple, present simple) for facts or things that are generally true.
If you heat ice, it melts.
Don't tell me you need me if you don't believe it. (Ed Sheeran)

➔ **Grammar 4C** p.144

B Look back at the quotations in **1A**. Is each one in the first or second conditional?

C ▶ 4.9 Circle the correct alternative to make either first or second conditional sentences. Listen to check, and then repeat.
1 If I **have / did have / had** more time, I **'d practice / did practice / practice** the piano more.
2 If you **'ll save / would save / save** money now, you **'d have / 'll have / had** a good pension when you retire.
3 If we **knew / 'd known / know** the answer, we **told / 'd tell / tell** you.
4 You **are / 'll be / were** late if you **didn't take / won't take / don't take** the bus.
5 I **bought / 'd buy / 'll buy** an apartment if I **have / 'll have / 'd have** enough money.

⚠ Common mistakes

If you ~~will~~ study hard, you will pass your test.

            had
If I ~~would have~~ more space, I'd get a dog.

I'll be at school tomorrow unless I~~'d~~ still feel ill.
                                    I

D In teams of two, race around the game. Write an ending for each segment before you go again. Which team can get to the end first?

E 🟢 **Make it personal** Think of a goal you have. Use the categories in **1B** to help you.
1 What is your goal and why? Prepare your answers to these questions.

What is your goal?   What are you going to do to get there?
Why do you want to achieve this?   What will the challenges / difficulties be?
How will you feel if you achieve your dream? And if you don't?

If I get my driver's license soon, I'll be able to get a better job.

What kind of job would you get if you passed your test?

2 In pairs, share your goals. Ask and answer follow-up questions. Any similar ones? Who has the most unusual goals?

51

4.5 What makes someone a genius?

Skills Predicting and checking predictions

A Look at the photo and headline. Guess what the items below refer to.

| 5,000 | IQ (intelligence quotient) | autism | trouble sleeping |
| learning disability | researcher | Stephen Hawking | huge equations |

Maybe he earns $5,0 a day?

B Read in pairs to check. A: Read paragraph 1, B: Paragraph 2. Share what you remember. Then repeat. A: Read paragraph 3, B: Paragraphs 4 and 5.

SMARTER THAN EINSTEIN?
Meet the 19-year-old who might change the way we see the world

1 Jacob Barnett is what we might call a genius. He has an IQ of 170 and, in his free time, is developing an expanded version of the theory of relativity. Not bad for a 19-year-old, especially one who was diagnosed with Asperger's syndrome (a mild form of autism) and has trouble sleeping because he constantly sees numbers in his head! Not bad at all!

2 At the age of two, Jacob—or Jake, as most people call him—still hadn't learned how to talk, so his parents suspected he might have a learning disability. As he grew up, however, they realized their son was actually incredibly gifted. By the age of three, Jacob could easily solve 5,000-piece jigsaw puzzles, calculate the volume of the cereal box while having breakfast, and learn by heart every single highway on the Indiana state road map. Just a few years later, while other kids were playing soccer or watching TV, Jake was having fun drawing complex geometrical shapes and writing huge equations on the living room windows.

3 By the time he had reached fifth grade, aged eight, it was clear that his mathematical ability was unusually high (at the level of a doctorate degree, actually!), so he dropped out of elementary school, taught himself all the math he needed to know in only one week, skipped high school, and enrolled at Purdue University, where he was allowed to attend advanced astrophysics classes. Five years later, Jake moved beyond the level of what his professors could teach him, so he eventually became a paid researcher—at only 13!

4 After college, Jake moved to Perimeter Institute, a place where the world's top thinkers, including Stephen Hawking, have taught. Jake was Perimeter's youngest ever student and submitted his master's thesis at 15. Today, he's still at Perimeter and the University of Waterloo.

5 For now, though, Jake's long-term plans are probably similar to the average teenager: to be happy doing something he finds challenging and rewarding. I wonder if he blames his autism for his early difficulties. If he wasn't autistic, however, he wouldn't be at the place he is right now. Autism is his way of viewing the world and it's because of that that he's able to do what he does so well.

C ▶ 4.10 True (T), false (F), or not mentioned (NM)? Listen and reread to check.
1 Jacob's speech developed when he was two.
2 Jacob enjoys playing soccer.
3 Jacob didn't attend high school.
4 Jacob has a "normal" social life.
5 Jake's very happy with his life.

D ▶ 4.11 In pairs, try to pronounce these words. Then listen to check. Any difficult ones?

3 syllables	theory	actually	constantly	easily
4 syllables	ability	incredibly	unusually	eventually
5 syllables	relativity	elementary	disability	

Guess the word!
1 point = the right word
2 points = the right word and stress

E ▶ 4.12 Play **Guess the word!** Listen to the first part of the sentence, then say the missing word from **D** after the beep.

F Make it personal   In pairs, answer 1–3. Any similar views?
1 Do you know anybody with a very high IQ?
2 Would you like to be like Jacob or have kids like him?

Apparently, anyone with over 160 on an IQ test is 'profoundly gifted'. My dad scored 161!

52

How do you deal with criticism?

4.5

ID in Action Sympathizing and criticizing

A ▶4.13 Listen to four dialogues and match them to the situations in the photos.

B ▶4.14 Listen again. After each beep, predict the next line from those in the chart. How many correct guesses?

Dialogue	Sympathy	Criticism
1	It could have been worse.	Will you ever learn?
2	Don't let it get you down.	You should have known better.
3	What's done is done.	How could you do such a thing?
4	It's not the end of the world.	What were you thinking?

C ▶4.15 Listen and repeat the expressions in **B**. Copy the intonation for each. In pairs, practice the expressions.

Common mistake

have
He shouldn't ~~had~~ bought that car.

D In pairs, answer questions 1–3 for each situation.
1 What should / shouldn't each person have done?   *The first person should have ...*
2 Who do you feel most sorry for?
3 Have you or people you know ever had any problems like these?

E **Make it personal** In pairs, tell a new story. Then change roles. Who was the most sympathetic listener? Whose story was funniest?
A: Choose a context (a–f) and plan what to say.
B: Ask follow-up questions and react to A's story using sentences from **B**.

a an accident that could have been a lot worse
b an image or message you sent by mistake
c something you bought on impulse
d something important you forgot / missed
e an unpleasant meeting
f a disastrous meal / vacation

♪ *I should've known better than to cheat a friend, And waste a chance that I've been given. So I'm never gonna dance again, The way I danced with you.*

Writing 4 A blog

♪ *We could have had it all,
Rolling in the deep,
You had my heart inside of your hand,
And you played it, to the beat.*

A Use the title and photo to guess what the blog post will be about.

> It might be about contractions or funny expressions.

B Read the post. Did you guess correctly? Do you think it is too late for the writer?

"Shoulda, Coulda, Woulda"

"I shouldn't have done this." "I should've done that." (a) _____ Regret is something we all experience in life. I know, I have tons, but what's my biggest regret? My biggest regret is my choice of career. Yep, my career! Pretty big thing to get wrong, huh? Well, I did. (b) _____ Let's go back …

When I was eight years old, I started to learn to play the piano. I did it because my big bro was having lessons, too. Turns out I was way better at it than he was! (c) _____ Really, good, in fact. By the time I was 14, I had passed my grade 8 test. I loved it and played whenever and wherever I could. I started to compose my own stuff, and even had a gig playing in a local restaurant when I was 16. The tips were great! (d) _____

At 18, I had to make tough decisions. What did I want to do with the rest of my life? At that age, I was pretty focused on money. I wanted to do something I knew would give me a good income and stable future. (e) _____ playing piano in a restaurant wasn't that. So, I took a finance degree and I became a financial advisor, but I really regret that now. I had the dough, the stable future, but ten years down the line, what's missing?

I miss the music! I work long, hard hours and my piano is gathering dust. I hardly have time to play. (f) _____ I shouldn't have looked for the money. I should've stuck with something that gave me joy and fulfillment, but I guess it's too late now.

What do you think? Have you any shoulda, coulda, wouldas of your own? (g) _____

C Match 1–7 to a–g in the blog.
1 You guessed it,
2 Please share your regrets, and if you've managed to moved on from them!
3 Ever find yourself using these words?
4 How could I have let go of something so important to me?
5 Thank you to the generous patrons of Mama's Italian.
6 So, where did I take a wrong turn?
7 (Sorry, Mitch!)

D Read *Write it right!* Then match 1–7 in **C** to the different features commonly found in blogs.

> ✓ **Write it right!**
>
> Common features of blogs are:
> - rhetorical questions (a question asked to make a point rather than elicit an answer)
> - humor
> - informal / "chatty" language
> - direct communication with the reader
> - asking the reader for their ideas / opinions / experiences

E Find informal words and phrases in the blog to match the more formal ones below. Why are blogs written using this kind of informal language?

1 should have, could have, would have
2 many
3 That's correct
4 Isn't it?
5 brother
6 considerably
7 job
8 money

F Study the highlighted phrases in the blog. Then complete these sentences with the correct form of the verbs.

| take | go out | not listen | send |

1 I regret _____ to my heart.
2 I shouldn't have _____ last night.
3 I would've _____ my dad's advice if I'd known.
4 I regret _____ that email.

G *Your turn!* Write a blog post in 120–180 words.

Before	Choose a regret to write about.
While	Use informal language and the *Write it right!* tips.
After	Ask a partner to read your blog post, check spelling and punctuation, and leave a comment. Then send it to your teacher.

4 AIQ: Artificial Intelligence Quotient!

 Café

1 Before watching

A Match 1–6 to their definitions a–f.

1 disciplinary action
2 calculated
3 input
4 outcome
5 procrastination
6 sophomore

a ☐ the result of something
b ☐ delaying things, not managing time
c ☐ punishment for breaking a rule
d ☐ planned
e ☐ a second year college student (U.S.)
f ☐ enter data into a computer

B ⊙ **Make it personal** Check the bills you pay monthly. Any paper bills or is it all online?

☐ cell phone   ☐ insurance   ☐ water
☐ electricity   ☐ Internet   ☐ other
☐ gas   ☐ mortgage

The only mail I still get are fliers advertising services!

C Guess which four bills August gets, and what's in the large envelope.

2 While watching

A Watch to 3:19 and check your ideas, and then check the three synonyms you hear for *intelligent / intelligence*.

☐ brilliant   ☐ crazy   ☐ Einstein
☐ genius   ☐ IQ   ☐ insane
☐ socially gifted

B Watch again and complete 1–5.

1 If you hadn't _____ the phone, I would've totally _____ insane.
2 Whatever happens, you _____ have done things any differently.
3 If only I hadn't been _____ of class ... for _____.
4 Look, if I'd _____ more confidence, I would have _____ it immediately.
5 He _____ 've made me get up.

C How does his AIQ machine work? Order these steps, 1–5, then watch from 3:19 to the end to check. Do you think the letter will contain good news or bad?

☐ He inputs the presence or absence of people.
☐ The robot / machine calculates the outcome.
☐ It sends him a message.
☐ August types in his situation.
☐ He enters data about the scholarship.

3 After watching

A True (T) or false (F)? Correct the false statements.

1 August tried to contact several people.
2 Rory gives August good advice.
3 August was punished for a disciplinary action.
4 Daniel woke August up early.
5 August's program doesn't have a name yet.
6 August was in a higher physics class than Rory.
7 August lacks self-confidence.
8 His project results were great.
9 August won a scholarship for $25,000.

B Check all the correct answers. Do you ever procrastinate like this?

Yes, quite often. It took me a long time to decide to ...

1 Why doesn't August want to open the letter?
   a ☐ He's not confident.
   b ☐ He's worried about the outcome.
   c ☐ He already knows the result.

2 Why is August the "king of procrastination"?
   a ☐ He keeps changing the subject.
   b ☐ His project is incomplete.
   c ☐ He won't open the letter.

C Why do we say it? Write C (change a subject), E (express regret), G (get a subject back on track), R (reassure) or S (speculate about the past).

1 ☐ If you hadn't ..., I would've ...
2 ☐ If only I hadn't ...
3 ☐ You couldn't have done things any differently ...
4 ☐ Hey, remember that time ...
5 ☐ Stop changing the subject and get on with it.
6 ☐ If I'd had more confidence, I would've ...

D ⊙ **Make it personal** In pairs, use the expressions in C to share past regrets or experiences. Any coincidences?

If I'd had more confidence, I would have sung at the karaoke competition.

Do you think you'd have won?

You never know. The winner wasn't that good.

55

R2 Grammar and Vocabulary

A *Picture dictionary.* Cover the words on the pages below and remember.

pages	
30–31	6 features of a city
34	8 social rules in Hong Kong
36	10 urban problems
38	5 more active listening phrases
40	10 verbs from regulations
44	8 school words & 16 school subjects
55	5 types of shopper
160	2 words for each diphthong (not the picture words); say and spell them

B ▶R2.1 Complete 1–6 with the correct form of the verbs in parentheses. Listen to check.

1 If you _____ as I tell you, you _____ into trouble. (do / get)
2 I can't understand what he's saying. If he _____ more slowly, I _____ more. (speak, understand)
3 When we _____ out of the restaurant, my car _____ there. Someone _____ it. (come / not be / take)
4 The authorities _____ that the athlete _____ drugs for months so they _____ him. (discover / use / disqualify)
5 I _____ to visit you if I _____ enough money, but I'm broke. (come / have)
6 I was really excited when I _____ in Barcelona. I _____ to it for ages. (arrive / look forward)

C ▶R2.2 In groups, imagine the rest of the story in pictures 1–3. Use a variety of tenses. Listen to compare stories and write the six past verb forms you hear. Have you had an experience like this?

> The three of them had spent the day packing all their camping stuff, and then they took the bus to the festival.

D 🔴 Make it personal In pairs, circle *a*, *b* or *c* for 1–5 and explain your reasons.

1 Homework from this class:
 a too much b the right amount c not enough
2 Tuition fees in your country:
 a too low b a fair price c not low enough
3 Green spaces in your city:
 a too small b perfect size c not big enough
4 Buses or trains in your town / city:
 a too many b a good number c not enough
5 Tourists in your capital city:
 a too many b the amount c not enough

> I'm happy with the homework. And you?

> Hmm. I don't think we do enough.

E ▶R2.3 Match 1–5 to a–e to make short exchanges. Imagine who is speaking in each one. Listen to check.

1 Are we lost?
2 That was a dirty game.
3 I'm sorry. I shouldn't have said that.
4 I can't believe I crashed my car.
5 What! Vic's going out with Jill?

a ☐ You didn't know? Forget I said anything. I shouldn't have mentioned it.
b ☐ You really should have known better than to drive that fast.
c ☐ Yes! There should have been three red cards.
d ☐ Maybe. I think we should have turned left.
e ☐ I agree. But we all say stupid things sometimes.

F Correct the mistakes in each sentence. Check your answers in units 3 and 4.

🔴 Common mistakes

1 I'm graduated of math. (2 mistakes)
2 If you would got up earlier, you wouldn't lose the bus every morning! (2 mistakes)
3 "Did you do many mistakes?" "I think no." (2 mistakes)
4 He loves traveling. He's gone in every place in Europe. (2 mistakes)
5 L.A. is so big city and the people are such nice! (3 mistakes)
6 Studying hard don't mean you will get the test, but it helps. (2 mistakes)
7 I feel bad. I shouldn't to have ate all that pizza. (2 mistakes)
8 You should went at the party last night. (2 mistakes)
9 He was angry because he was waiting during 40 minutes before the police arrived. (2 mistakes)
10 People who goes to Miami are often surprised because they haven't expected Spanish speakers. (2 mistakes)

56

Skills practice

♪ *I should have changed that stupid lock,
I should have made you leave your key.*

R2

A Read and listen to the four stories ▶3.14 on p. 41 and underline any words that are difficult to hear / understand. Listen again. Are they difficult because:
a   these words link to the following word?
b   they're unstressed and virtually disappear?
c   their pronunciation changes in context?

B ▶R2.4 Listen and complete extracts 1–6 from videos in units 3 and 4.
1   Kissing _____ cheek _____ hugging _____ not practiced.
2   Gifts _____ never opened _____ person _____ gave them.
3   Fill _____ tea cups _____ others before pouring _____ own cup, _____ their cups _____ not empty.
4   In America, _____ you don't earn _____ money, something _____ wrong.
5   Everyone expects _____ superheroes.
6   You have _____ smart and you have _____ involved _____ arts.

C ▶R2.5 Listen to and imitate each phrase.

D Look at the photo and title. Guess what these words refer to. Read the text to check your predictions.

| Netflix | 12 years old | Spain | Calvin Klein |
| Drake and Maroon 5 | youngest person ever | | |

Maybe she's the daughter of the owner of Netflix?

E Reread. True (T) or false (F)?
1   Millie Bobbie Brown had won nine awards before *Stranger Things*.
2   She's half English, half Spanish.
3   She has lived in at least three different countries.
4   Her family moved to L.A. a week after she was spotted by a talent agent.
5   She's also also worked as a pop singer and a model.
6   She had appeared in two movies when this article was written.

F ▶R2.6 Cross out the word with the different underlined sound. Listen to check, then in pairs create a funny sentence with the remaining words. Say them slowly, then quickly.
1   afr<u>ai</u>d ~~<u>a</u>pples~~ <u>A</u>sia th<u>ey</u> volc<u>a</u>no
    In Asia they are afraid of an eruption from the volcano.
2   cr<u>a</u>zy f<u>a</u>shionable st<u>a</u>tue t<u>a</u>xi tr<u>a</u>ffic
3   aw<u>ay</u> <u>eigh</u>t p<u>ai</u>r st<u>ay</u> str<u>aigh</u>t

G *Role-play.* Social rules
1   In pairs, list three more "social etiquette" rules. Then exchange with another pair.
2   **A**: You're a tourist. Mime breaking each rule.
    B: Explain the rules to **A**.

H ▶R2.7 🟠 **Make it personal**   *Question time!*
1   Listen to and answer the 12 lesson titles in units 3 and 4.
2   In pairs, practice asking and answering. Use the map on p. 2–3 and choose the two most interesting questions from units 3 and 4. Which one produces the most interesting conversation?

Which city would you most like to visit?   *There are lots of cities I'd love to see, but number one has to be …*

Millie Bobby Brown

Name: Millie Bobby Brown
Born: 19 February 2004
Occupation: actor and model

Next big thing?

Many people say that Millie Bobby Brown is the next big thing in Hollywood. What do they mean? She is already there!

Brown caught the attention of the world in 2016 with her role in the hit Netflix series *Stranger Things*, which she won approximately nine awards for! She achieved that when she was only twelve years old, but she had already acted in five different TV series. Pretty incredible, huh? Well, it's even more amazing when you realize that she was actually born in Spain to English parents, moved to England when she was four, and then to the U.S. when she was eight. In 2011, she was spotted by a talent agent at a drama class. Her family later moved to L.A. and after only a week, Millie was meeting talent agencies. After only three months in Hollywood, she was given her first TV role.

What a career so far! Millie is extremely hardworking. The adults she works with praise her for her maturity and talent. Although she is so young, she has already played some very challenging roles. Apart from film and TV, she has also starred in music videos with Maroon 5 and Drake and modeled for Calvin Klein. In 2018, she was the youngest person ever included on *Time* magazine's list of the "World's most influential people". In 2019, she'll be in her first movie, *Godzilla: King of the Monsters*.

Watch out for this girl in the future!

57

5

5.1 Are you a shopaholic?

1 Reading

A In pairs, list five things you expect from a store when shopping. Are your shopping habits and expectations similar to your parents'?

I expect good customer service.

Yes, and I like it to be well organized, so I can find things easily.

B Look at the cartoons. Who or what do you think Generation Z is? Read the introduction to the article to check.

Gen Z TRANSFORMING THE SHOPPING EXPERIENCE

Generation Z, born between 1996 and 2012, came into a digital world with technology at the center of everything. This generation is expected to have a huge impact on the future of shopping. Let's examine how.

TECHNOLOGY. Members of Gen Z have a device they interact with constantly so, while shopping, they compare prices, read reviews, and even buy online. They still want to do in-store shopping, but they want an experience, and technology has to be at the center of this experience. Stores need smart phone self-checkouts, interactive screens, and virtual try-ons. A discount code and loyalty programs are an incentive and should be accessible online. Gen Z expects free Wi-Fi in stores. In fact, it is wise for stores to provide charging stations, so shoppers can keep their batteries full.

HIGH EXPECTATIONS. Gen Z is demanding. If the in-store experience doesn't meet their expectations, they move on. They want a store that embraces technology and makes products easy to test, but they still want human interaction. They have less patience and will instantly share a poor experience on social media. Attractive prices are still essential, or they'll just have Amazon deliver it to their door, again!

INFLUENCERS. Gen Z is influencing the decisions of the whole family. Apparently 70 percent of parents ask their kids for advice before they shop. Gen Z trusts friends rather than advertising and has a strong social media presence. Gen Zers post their thoughts and images of products on Snapchat, Instagram, and YouTube and want to connect directly with the brand. There is even a rising trend in videos, which are posted online, of shoppers displaying items they have recently bought and talking about them. Brands should use this user-generated content if they want to encourage brand loyalty with Generation Z.

C In groups, brainstorm how you think Generation Z is changing shopping. Then each read a different paragraph and report back. Were your ideas mentioned?

Well, they probably all shop online and don't go to real stores anymore.

D ▶5.1 Listen, reread, and give the author's answers to 1–5. Do you agree with them all?
1 What should stores provide Gen Z shoppers with for in-store shopping?
2 What does Gen Z expect from a store in addition to technology?
3 What happens when Gen Z has a negative shopping experience?
4 How does Gen Z influence their parents?
5 How can stores encourage brand loyalty?

E 🗣 **Make it personal** How might shopping evolve in the next 30 years? Will there still be any small stores?

Maybe we'll have chip implants so we won't need cash or credit cards.

Common mistakes

expect everything to be
My parents ~~wait that all is~~ really cheap.

most successful brand
Apple is the ~~mark of most success~~.

♪ Baby, I don't need dollar bills to have fun tonight.

5.1

② Vocabulary Shopping

A Match the highlighted words in the article to the photos.

B Complete 1–8 with the words in **A**. Which ones do you hear / say often?
1. There's no need to stand in that long line. They have _____ here.
2. My battery is running out. Are there _____ in here?
3. Smart brands use customers' _____, such as YouTube videos and blog posts, to advertise their products.
4. I would rather do _____ than shop online. At least you can try things on.
5. I've got a _____ for that store—you get 10% off everything today.
6. I can't get online to check the reviews. They don't even have _____ in here!
7. These glasses looked good on me with _____, but they don't look good in real life.
8. I don't have much _____ except for my cell phone—I'd never consider getting any other make.

C 🧑 **Make it personal** In pairs, answer 1–3.
1. Are you a member of Generation Z?
2. Which points in the article do you agree / disagree with, and why?
3. How many of the people in the class shop like a Gen Z?

> I agree with a lot of it, but I still prefer to buy things online. It's so much easier!

③ Listening

A Do you ever post images or videos of things you buy on social media? Why (not)? Have you seen (YouTube) vloggers describe things they have bought?

> No way, what for? Who would care about my shopping?

B ▶ 5.2 You're going to listen to a radio program about "shopping haul" and "anti-shopping haul" videos on YouTube. Guess what these videos are.

C Listen again and complete 1–5.
1. A "shopping haul" video shows a vlogger _____ they've bought.
2. People watch these videos because it's satisfying to see how _____.
3. In an "anti-haul" video, vloggers talk about products they don't plan to buy because they think they are _____.
4. Kimberly Clark's first "anti-haul" video has had _____ views. Now there are over _____ "anti-haul" videos online.
5. Research shows that Millennials would much rather _____.

D 🧑 **Make it personal** In pairs, make a "shopping haul" or "anti-shopping haul" video. Follow these instructions.
1. 📶 Decide which type of video to make. Search online for examples of these videos to give you ideas.
   - **Shopping haul:** Make notes about products you have bought recently (where, how much, why, how happy you are with them, etc.)
   - **Anti-shopping haul:** Make notes about products you don't think people should buy, explaining your reasons why.
2. Practice what you want to say. Then record yourselves using a cell phone or act out your video for the class. Who made the best one? Any future YouTube stars?

> **Common mistake**
> Buying
> ~~Buy~~ things online is much ~~more easy~~.
> easier

> Today, we're gonna be showing you things that we're not actually gonna buy, then explain why.

59

5.2 What shouldn't you have spent money on?

She was 18 when she started getting into debt.

1 Listening

A How do people get into debt? List five things they can do to get out of debt.

B ▶5.3 Listen to a college graduate giving a talk to some freshmen about debt. Answer the question in **A** for her. Did she mention any of your ideas?

C ▶5.3 Listen again. What is the significance of the following numbers?

| 18 | 25 | 30 | 50 | 2,000 | 12,000 | 20,000 |

D Match the verb and noun collocations. Check your answers in ▶5.3 on p. 167.

Money collocations		
1	take out / pay back / pay off	☐ debt
2	go on	☐ money
3	run out	☐ of money
4	waste	☐ a shopping spree
5	be in / get into / get out of	☐ a loan / a credit card / an overdraft

E 👤 **Make it personal** Is there a lot of debt in your country?

Absolutely, and not only students. Most of us spend our lives owing money to someone.

2 Pronunciation Silent consonants

A ▶5.4 Pronounce these words. Listen to check. Know any others?

| debt | listen | castle | thumb | subtle | high | bought |

> **Common mistake**
> had
> If the word hadn't ˇ silent letters, I would have pronounced it correctly.

B ▶5.5 Listen and cross out the two silent consonants in 1–5. In pairs, say the sentences simultaneously, as fast as you can.
1. I have no doubt you'll be able to pay off your debt.
2. The traffic cop whistled and told me to fasten my seatbelt.
3. It's difficult to understand signs in a foreign language.
4. My neighbors' daughter has moved out.
5. The police will climb the mountain to look for the bomb.

3 Grammar Third conditional

A Look at the example and answer 1–5 in the grammar box.

> *If I'd **listened** to some advice, I wouldn't have **gotten** into financial mess.*
> 1. Is she imagining changing the past or the present? Is that possible?
> 2. Did she take advice? Did she get into a financial mess? Can she change what happened?
> 3. What form are the bold verbs: simple past or past participle?
> 4. What is the full form of *I'd listened*: *I had listened* or *I would listened*?
> 5. Complete the form:
>   If + subject + *had (not)* + _____, subject + _____ + past participle + phrase
>   If you are not sure about the result, you can use *might / could have*:
>   *If I'd listened to advice, I might not have gotten into financial mess / could have avoided it.*
>
> ➔ **Grammar 5A** p.146

60

5.2

♪ It's a bittersweet symphony, this life.
Trying to make ends meet.
You're a slave to the money, then you die.

B ▶5.6 Complete the third conditionals 1–5 with the verbs. Use contractions. Listen, check, and repeat.
1. If you _____ (tell) me you were in debt, I _____ (lend) you some money.
2. If he _____ (be) more sensible, he _____ (save) more money.
3. I _____ (not buy) a new car even if I _____ (earn) enough money last year.
4. If we _____ (pay) the bill on time, they _____ (not cut off) the electricity.
5. The bank _____ (might give) you a credit card if you _____ (ask) for one.

> **Common mistake**
> had
> If I ~~would have~~ paid to park my car, I wouldn't ~~get~~ a parking fine.   have gotten

C Make sentences about the speaker in ▶5.3 using the third conditional.

> *If she hadn't gone to college, she might not have gotten into debt.*

D 🟢 **Make it personal** Think about a mistake you made or something you wish you'd done differently. In pairs, share your stories. Ask follow-up questions. Whose was the biggest mistake?

> *If I hadn't played so many video games, I'd have been better at sport!*
>
> *Which sports would you have played?*

4 Reading

A Look at the photos and read the first three lines of the website. What do you think Volunteer2Zero is?

B Read on to check. A: Read the main text, B: Read *How it works*. Then share. Were you right?

C ▶5.7 Cover the text and remember the five benefits of Volunteer2Zero. Listen and reread to check. Any surprises?

Volunteer2Zero

Do you have a student loan?
Wondering how you're going to pay it back?
That's where Volunteer2Zero comes in …

Volunteer2Zero is a crowdfunding idea with a difference. We all know that crowdfunding is getting lots of people to give small amounts of money in order to fund a project. But, with **Volunteer2Zero**, instead of just fund-raising to pay back your debts, you can give a little more in return and help make the world a better place.

With **Volunteer2Zero**, you can reduce your student debt by volunteering. In exchange for your time and skills, you will:
→ receive donations from your community
→ improve your professional skills
→ develop professional contacts
→ improve your community
→ increase your chance of graduating debt-free

HOW IT WORKS
→ You register with us as a volunteer or donor
→ You say where and how much time you can volunteer
→ Our donors decide what help they need and how much to sponsor you
→ You do work in your community and receive donations for every hour you volunteer
→ You pay off your debt and pay back your community. It's simple!
Volunteer2Zero

D 🟢 **Make it personal** Discuss.
1. Would Volunteer2Zero work in your country? Is crowdfunding common? Would you register with an organization like this?
2. List three things you could volunteer to do in your community.
3. In pairs, role-play a conversation with someone who got out of debt by joining Volunteer2Zero.

> *I'd volunteer to help with reading at my local elementary school. I think some parents would donate to V2Z.*
>
> *If I hadn't joined V2Z, I wouldn't have escaped from debt.*

61

5.3 Have you ever borrowed money from a relative?

1 Listening

the website Kickstarter

the Statue of Liberty

Mozart

British rock group Marillion

the Pebble smart watch

A In pairs, share what the photos make you think of. Then guess what they have in common.

Could Kickstarter be something to do with old motorbikes?

B ▶ 5.8 Listen to a lecture and check your ideas for **A**. Have you ever donated to a crowdfunding project?

My cousin ran a marathon last year to raise money for cancer research. I donated to that.

Common mistake
~~The~~ crowdfunding is a great idea.

C ▶ 5.8 True (T) or false (F)? Listen again to check.
1 Crowdfunding has existed much longer than the Internet.
2 Only wealthy people funded the Statue of Liberty.
3 Crowdfunding has changed a lot over the years.
4 Marillion fans paid for the band's tour and albums.
5 Pebble Technology holds the record for the most money ever raised through crowdfunding.

Let's raise money to clean our polluted river.

D **Make it personal** In groups, think of a project you could start with crowdfunding and why.
1 Make notes on your ideas. Use these questions to help you.

> How will you organize it?   Why should people donate to it?
> How much do you want to raise?   What will donors get in return?

2 Present your project to the class. How many people want to "donate" to it? Which one gets the most "donations" from the class?

2 Grammar Modals of possibility / probability

Common mistakes
We really must ~~to~~ go home.
 be able to
I'd love to ~~can~~ help in some way.

A ▶ 5.9 Try to complete excerpts 1–4. Listen to check.

1 Their fans _____ really love their music.
2 It _____ be bad for young entre**pren**eurs.
3 You _____ be surprised to learn.
4 It _____ work for you!

♪ *I might be young, but I ain't stupid,*
Talking around in circles with your tongue.

5.3

B Study 1–4 in **A** and check the correct definitions in the grammar box. Then read the information. Do you find any of these difficult?

	must	can't	might	could
I'm 100% sure this is true.				
I'm 100% sure this isn't true.				
Maybe this is true.				

The opposite of *must* is *can't*. (NOT ~~mustn't~~)
You must be ready for the exam. You've studied a lot.
You can't be ready for the exam. You haven't studied at all.

You can use *may* instead of *might* or *could* in affirmative sentences.
The business may / might / could close because it isn't doing very well.
But *couldn't* does not mean the same as *may not* or *might not*.
The business is doing better so it may not / might not close. (NOT ~~couldn't close~~)

→ **Grammar 5B** p.146

Common mistake

was able to
I ran and ~~could~~ catch the last bus.

Use *was / were* able to to express success in the past.

C Complete these comments about crowdfunding projects with *must* or *can't*.

1 Surely you _____ be serious. You want me to donate $1,000?! You're joking.
2 You _____ be so excited about the project. It's almost fully funded!
3 That _____ be right. It's not possible to fund a business for that little money.
4 You _____ seriously expect people to buy this product! It's a pile of junk.
5 You _____ be really determined. This is the third time you've tried crowdfunding.

D ▶ 5.10 Listen to five different extracts. In pairs, guess and note your answers.
1 Who's Alberto talking to?
2 Where's Laura?
3 What's Ernie talking about?
4 Why's Tony breathing in and out like that?
5 What kind of problem does Susie have?

I think he must be talking to his son.

Hmm ... Not sure. I think he might be talking to a friend.

E ▶ 5.11 Listen to the complete conversations and check your guesses. Who's in the most difficult situation?

F *Fact or fiction?* In pairs, say whether 1–5 may be true.

1 Chewing gum is good for your teeth.
2 An ant can lift fifty times its own weight.
3 The brain is approximately 80% water.
4 Humans are the only living beings that can cry as the result of emotions.
5 You're more likely to have a heart attack on a Monday than on any other day.

I think the first one might be true, but I'm not really sure.

Really? I actually think it could be bad for your teeth.

G **Make it personal** In groups, speculate about each other's lives. Who's the best guesser?

Favorite free time activities?
Favorite shops / restaurants?
Musical taste?
Reasons for learning English?
Soccer fan? If so, what team?
Use of cell phone / the Internet?
How green they are?

You must be quite green. You always bring a reusable bottle of water.

Yeah, and you never use plastic bags.

Yep—you're both right. I'm actually a member of Greenpeace!

5.4 Have you ever bought a useless product?

1 Reading

A Listen and read the introduction of an article about infomercials (= information + commercial). The writer:

☐ wants a refund on items she / he bought. ☐ is often entertained by infomercials.
☐ is often disappointed with the products. ☐ is angry about infomercials.

TWO USELESS PRODUCTS I'VE BOUGHT

As far as I'm concerned, infomercials are an unappreciated art form. I mean, they are pure comedy, and who doesn't love to laugh? The truth is, though, that staying up and watching them can seriously interfere with my common sense. You see, I bought apparently useful products that promised to give me the physique of a good-looking fashion model, make me a math genius, and help me pass my exams. Yet, shockingly, guess what: I'm actually heavier now, I still have trouble understanding my credit card statement, and I'm currently taking all my exams again. Now, I don't want to generalize, but here, for your enjoyment, are two of the most useless gadgets I've ever bought.

1 "READY TO SNUGGLE UP ON THE SOFA?"
But, you can't reach the remote or hold your cup of cocoa! Hug Rug, the blanket with sleeves, is the solution! Hug Rug is a blanket with sleeves, which means you can change channels, have a drink, or check your phone without getting cold. Hug Rug is super-soft to the touch and comes in eight gorgeous bright colors. Enjoy the convenience of free movement while also experiencing the comfort of a warm blanket. Read, watch TV, text your friends, even get takeout with Hug Rug, the blanket with sleeves."
OK, it is really cosy, but it looks ridiculous. And "free movement"?! Once I got into it, I couldn't figure out how to get out. Stick to a blanket.

2 "FEELING THE EFFECTS OF SITTING AT YOUR DESK ALL DAY?"
It's time to tighten that tummy and get the flexibility you've been dreaming of with the Wonder Chair! Wonder Chair helps you flatten your abdominal muscles, massage your lower back, and improve your fitness. By doing our recommended exercises, you can fully train your upper, lower, and side abs. Help tone your lazy, aching muscles and get rid of your stiff appearance! This remarkable device also offers comfortable support for your spine, thighs, and arms. Don't waste another second! Sit at your desk with the Wonder Chair and wave good-bye to aches, pains and lethargy."
You'd better hope your office mates have a sense of humor. Sadly, mine didn't, so the chair stayed at home, and I got a gym membership.

B ▶5.12 In pairs, each read about one product and match it to a picture. Then tell your partner about it. Listen to check each other's answers.

C Match the underlined words to their definitions.

1	_____ adj.	very beautiful or pleasant	6	_____ adv.	now
2	_____ adj.	very special, amazing	7	_____ noun	cooked food from a restaurant that you buy to eat somewhere else
3	_____ adv.	in fact			
4	_____ verb	make flat / level	8	_____ noun [U]	pleasure
5	_____ verb	tone / make tighter	9	_____ adj.	good for nothing

D ▶5.13 Listen to two friends talking about the product that isn't mentioned in the article. Why wasn't she happy with it? Which was the worst purchase?

I bought a hairdryer. It didn't work and I wasn't able to send it back.

E 👤 Make it personal Think of an item you bought because of an infomercial / ad. Describe the product and ad to your partner. Why did you buy it? Did it work? Would you recommend it? Why (not)?

2 Vocabulary Word formation

♪ *I'm advertising love for free, so you can place your ad with me.*   **5.4**

A Complete the chart with the highlighted words from the article. Underline the suffixes.

Nouns	Verbs	Adjectives	Adverbs
enjoyment			

> ⚠ **Common mistakes**
> My phone is full of useful~~l~~ features.
> Please listen care~~fuly~~. → carefully

B ▶ 5.14 Complete 1–8 with forms of the words in parentheses. Listen to check.
1. I bought it on impulse. It was pure __madness__! (mad)
2. It can't work the way they _____ it would. (advert)
3. I felt really _____ afterward. (guilt)
4. It seemed like a _____ product ... (wonder)
5. ... but it was such a _____. (disappoint)
6. This stuff is _____ quite _____. (actual / danger)
7. They go on and on in the infomercial about how _____ it is. (nature)
8. I guess it's just so _____ these days. (fashion)

C 👤 **Make it personal** Think about 1–8 in **B**. When was the last time you felt like that? In pairs, each choose and share an experience. Whose was worse?

> 💬 *I bought some very expensive sunglasses and left them in a taxi. I felt really guilty afterward—and stupid, too.*

3 Grammar Adjective order

A Study the examples and circle the correct alternative in the grammar box. Then read the information below and underline the fact adjectives in **1A**.

> You'll get the physique of a [handsome] [fashion] model.
> They can buy them in [gorgeous] [bright] colors.
> Help tone your [lazy], [aching] muscles.
> Tom's a [nice] [little] kid.
>
> If we use two or more adjectives before a noun, [opinions] usually come **before** / **after** facts.
>
> I'm wearing the most expensive, round, contemporary, black, Korean, titanium, multi-function smart watch.
>
> If you have more than one fact adjective in a sentence, they tend to go in a particular order:
> number – size – shape – age – color – nationality – material – purpose + noun
> But don't worry, it isn't usual to use more than three adjectives together!
>
> → **Grammar 5C** p. 146

B Read infomercials 1–7 and correct five adjective order mistakes.

1. A spray that promises more attractive dark hair—instantly!
2. Glamorize your look with these star-shaped fashionable earrings.
3. A Japanese camping miraculous knife that can cut through anything!
4. A bizarre green plastic blanket with sleeves to keep you warm while watching TV.
5. Jeans that look fashionable, but feel like cotton comfortable pajamas.
6. A SMALL METAL INCREDIBLE ACCESSORY THAT CREATES GORGEOUS HAIRSTYLES INSTANTLY!
7. Throw out your leather brown ugly shoes and buy our fantastic waterproof boots today!

C 👤 **Make it personal** 📶 In small groups, search online for a funny or interesting infomercial. Act it out or describe the product to the class. Can your classmates guess what the product is? Who found the best / worst / funniest products?

65

5.5 Do you often buy things on impulse?

ID Skills Reading for confirmation

A In pairs, match the areas to photos a–c. Then list six more items in the photos. Which aspects of grocery store shopping do / don't you enjoy?

the bakery   a checkout   fresh fruit and vegetables

B Guess what "supermarket psychology" refers to? Read the introduction to the article to check. Who are "they"?

> I'd say it's probably about consumer behavior.

C In pairs, brainstorm how grocery stores "assault our five senses." Give an example for sight, hearing, touch, taste, and smell. Then quickly read and match each sense to a paragraph. Were your ideas mentioned?

D ▶5.15 Listen and reread carefully. A: read 1–4, B: read 5–8. How else do grocery stores make us spend more and how can we avoid it? Share your information.

Supermarket PSYCHOLOGY

Ever noticed that whichever grocery store you go to, you'll inevitably find the same basic arrangement of products? It's a trick they play on us so we buy more and more things, even stuff we don't really need. Virtually all the products are carefully displayed to affect our shopping experience. Psychological tactics, you know. Clever devils! Read on to find out how grocery stores assault our five senses.

1 You can rarely leave the grocery store through the same door you walked in. This means you'll have to go around the whole place and maybe buy more stuff on your way out. They even let you try tasty food and drink items to tempt you further, so you feel like you're eating for free while you explore this "wonderful world."

2 Fresh fruits and vegetables are always right near the entrance. You think this is just by chance? No way. It's so you will feel fresh and happy at the start of your shopping adventure. They're nice to touch, too, and you feel you can choose the best ones for yourself. Plus, it's best to have these items near the entrance because of the sunlight. Smart, huh?

3 Everyday items like dairy, meat, or rice are always at the back of the store. They know you want to get to the checkout as fast as possible, so they make you go all the way to the back, past the clothes, watches, and gadgets—the most lucrative items. You know, just in case.

4 Ever feel hungry when you're doing your weekly shopping? Grocery stores know that food aromas make us hungry, so they have an in-store bakery and sometimes a restaurant, and the smell of food inspires us to buy more. They even use a manufactured bread-smell to catch customers on the street.

5 Want to buy shampoo? Well, don't look straight ahead: the products at eye level are always the more expensive ones. The cheaper ones are either placed at the very bottom or really high up, on the top shelves. Yeah, right there.

6 And why those long, endless aisles filled with unrelated products? Like cereals for breakfast next to a treat like candy. Well, parents usually buy boxes of cereal for their children, and when they make the mistake of taking them to the store, the magic happens: "I want to buy candy, Mommy. Pleeeaaaase."

7 Ever find yourself singing as you shop? There's a reason you're more likely to hear The Eagles or Celine Dion than Foo Fighters or Iron Maiden. Slower music creates slower traffic, which means people shop for longer. Genius, huh?

8 So, if this all sounds familiar, wise up! If you don't want to be a victim of these strategies, here's my advice: make a shopping list and stick to it!

E **Make it personal** In pairs, ask and answer 1–4. Do you regularly succumb to 'shopping psychology'? If so, what's your best example?

1. Which grocery stores do / don't you usually shop at? Why?
2. Do you visit every aisle? Do you stick to your list, or do you ever buy more?
3. Which tactics from the article have you noticed? Any others?
4. What psychology do you find in other stores? (travel agents, technology, clothes, cosmetics …)

> Supermarket psychology doesn't work on me. I only buy what I need.

When did you last complain in a store?

5.5

ID in Action   Shopping problems

A ▶5.16 Listen to three dialogues. What are the three problems? Which were successful shopping experiences? Which one is most familiar to you?

B ▶5.16 Match the phrases and mark them C (customer) or SC (store clerk). Listen again to check. Have you ever worked in a store?

> **Common mistakes**
> My credit card was
> ~~rejected / refused~~.
>   declined
> What size (of shoe) do you ~~use~~?
>   take

	Choosing		
1	I like these shoes. Can I	☐	charge?
2	What size do you	☐	refund.
3	Do you have a size 10	☐	take?
4	I'm sorry ma'am,	☐	card, please.
	Paying	☐	declined.
5	Cash or	☐	we're sold out.
6	Insert / Tap / Swipe your	☐	in stock?
7	I'm afraid your card has been	☐	receipt.
	Complaining	☐	try them on?
8	Unfortunately, we can't give you a	☐	exchange it for another one.
9	But we'd be happy to		
10	I just need to see your		

C In pairs, cover the endings in **B** and test each other.

D ▶5.17 Can you remember the missing words? Listen to check.
1 It _____ impossible to _____ larger sizes. Can you _____ me when you _____ some in stock?
2 _____! I don't _____. It's a new card, and I _____ I'm not over my limit. There _____ be a problem with your card machine.
3 I'd _____ to _____ this phone. I _____ it here the other day, and it's _____.

E In pairs, choose a situation from **B** and read ▶5.16 on p. 168 for one minute. Then role-play the situation. Who complained successfully?

F 🔘 **Make it personal** In pairs, role-play a situation, 1–3, below. Use sentences from **B** and **D**. Who complained successfully?

> Hi. Are those shoes in the sale?
>
> I'm afraid I'm unhappy with this phone.

1 You bought a smart phone last week, but you don't like it anymore. You want to get a refund or exchange it for a new one. There's a slight scratch on the screen, though.

2 You bought two pairs of jeans last month, but couldn't try them on because the store was too crowded. They don't fit. You want to exchange them or get a refund.

3 You bought some strawberries at the grocery store, but when you got home, you noticed that some of the fruit was rotten. You want a refund.

🎵 There's a lady who's sure all that glitters is gold,
And she's buying a stairway to heaven.

Writing 5 An advert

*Come on, vogue,
Let your body move to the music,
Hey, hey, hey
Come on, vogue,
Let your body go with the flow.*

A Read the ad and circle the correct alternative.
1. Shape U Shoe is mainly for people who **do / don't** go to the gym.
2. Shape U Shoe shoes come in **"one size fits all" / various sizes and colors**.
3. They are good for **your arms and legs / your legs and body position**.
4. To get the benefits you need to walk with Shape U Shoes 20 **times per week / minutes a day**.

Are you ¹constantly trying to get ²fitter?

³Always needing to tone up those muscles?

⁴Joined a gym several times but kept giving up ⁵'cos you ⁶can't find the time—or willpower—to go?

YES

If your answer is to any or all of these, then we have ⁷the perfect solution for you:

Shape U Shoes

Shape U Shoes are a revolutionary, 100% effective product that help you get fit and tone up fast, in a safe, almost effortless way. They're ⁸the most modern and intelligent answer for those who, like you, are concerned about their health but are too busy to go to the gym. Walk in our shoes instead!

Shape U Shoes come in various gorgeous, stylish designs and colors. They strengthen legs and thighs, by boosting your muscle activity by up to 35% simply by walking. Imagine that! Shape U Shoes can also improve your posture. You will soon look and feel fitter, ⁹less tired, and get that shape you've been dreaming of. ¹⁰All these benefits without any risks!

Shape U Shoes are ¹¹the scientific solution that was missing in your life. Walking for just 20 minutes a day is ¹²the secret to ¹³a better and happier life! Remember, ¹⁴it's no miracle. It's Shape U Shoes!

Available online for next-day delivery. Satisfaction guaranteed!

B Read *Write it right!*, then match **highlighted** items 1–14 to rules a–d.

✓ Write it right!

To write a good ad,
a use comparatives and superlatives. ☐☐☐☐
b use emotive, exaggerated language to make opinions sound like facts. ☐☐☐☐☐
c remove articles, auxiliaries, or subjects to make it short and exciting. ☐☐
   *(Our new car is) faster than you thought.
   (The) offer (is) limited to the United States.*
d use informal language, such as contractions and abbreviations. ☐☐☐
   *Don't wait any longer!
   You're gonna love this!*

C Complete 1–6 with the adjective or adverb forms of the words in parentheses.
1. You'll be _____ _____ by the fast results. (total / surprise)
2. This product is 100% _____. (safety)
3. The most _____ solution to your problems. (efficiency)
4. Use it _____ to see _____ results. (regularity / wonder)
5. Achieve _____ results. (success)
6. Feel _____ _____ all the time. (complete / energy)

D Circle the correct alternative in 1–7.
1. Get **long beautiful / beautiful long** hair.
2. Looking for a **perfect new / new perfect** solution?
3. Feel like **an attractive young / a young attractive** model!
4. Take only one **gentle short / short gentle** walk a day.
5. A **strong new / new strong** body!
6. It's the **better / best** and **modernest / most modern** solution.
7. Learn English using the **faster / faster** method with the **less / least** effort.

E *Your turn!* Write an ad in 130–150 words.

Before	Choose a product (e.g. from **3C** in Lesson 5.4 on p. 65) and note down five adjectives to describe it. Think who it's for and how you can "sell" it.
While	1 Begin your ad with a question or a catchy sentence. 2 Use tips a–d in *Write it right!* 3 End with a powerful statement.
After	Show your ad to three different classmates. Would they buy your product? Then email it to your teacher.

5 Shop around

 Café

1 Before watching

A Match 1–7 to five of the definitions a–e.

1 A clothes hoarder
2 A discount shopper
3 A loyal shopper
4 An online shopper
5 A reluctant shopper
6 An upcycler
7 A shopaholic

a ☐ loves shopping sprees
b ☐ reuses materials (e.g. clothes, furniture) to create something new
c ☐ shops around to buy things when they're cheaper
d ☐ always buys clothes at the same store
e ☐ keeps all their clothes, never throwing any out

B ◉ Make it personal Which of 1–7 in **A** best describes you and your friends?

> I guess I'm 4 for most things except clothes. I like to try things on before buying.

2 While watching

A Watch the first two minutes and check: Andrea (A), Genevieve (G), or Lucy (L)?

		A	G	L
1	Has beautiful, sophisticated clothes.			
2	Needs beautiful, new clothes.			
3	Likes to wear dark clothes.			
4	Works with demanding actors.			
5	Used to be a mad shopper.			

B Watch again and check all you hear.

1 What is Lucy doing?
☐ Demanding things. ☐ Working with actors.
☐ Starring in a film. ☐ Shooting a film.

2 How does Andrea describe her past behavior?
☐ Anxious. ☐ Creative genius.
☐ Kidding. ☐ Tired.

3 What does Andrea want to do?
☐ Make her own clothes. ☐ Have better taste.
☐ Stop shopping. ☐ Sew curtains.

C Study Andrea's clothing rental website. In pairs, explain how it will work. Who might use it? What are the benefits? Would you use it?

> It could be good for clothes hoarders.

> Yeah, they could sell clothes they haven't worn.

D Watch the rest and number 1–9 the order these are mentioned.

a performance ☐   Genevieve ☐
all the girls on   Lucy's actors ☐
campus [1]   make curtains ☐
dark clothing ☐   make money ☐
design clothing ☐   save money ☐

3 After watching

A Match the noun and adjective used to describe it.

1 best   a ☐ clothes
2 crazy   b ☐ friend
3 creative   c ☐ genius
4 mad   d ☐ sizes
5 different   e ☐ shopper
6 shopping   f ☐ shopping
7 sophisticated   g ☐ spree

B Complete 1–4 with the correct adverb.

| actually | definitely | probably | seriously |

1 I _____ went a little crazy on spending.
2 No, _____ I believe it.
3 _____, I have an idea.
4 You are _____ the best friend anyone could ask for!

C ◉ Make it personal In pairs, compare your usual taste in clothes and colors. Any surprises?

> I like to wear dark colors, especially at night.

> Not me. I'm into bright shirts or T-shirts.

69

Mid-term review

Game: 55 seconds

There are four games in each Unit square. ■ You have 55 seconds for each game. ■ The winner is the first team to get to 40 points.

RULES
- 4 players: divide into Teams 1 and 2.
- Flip a coin to decide which team starts.
- Team 1 starts at Unit 1, Team 2 starts at Unit 5.
- Each team plays TOPIC TALK. Monitor the time (55 seconds) while the other team plays.
- Then take turns playing the other games in this order:
  DESCRIBE ▶ DISCOVER   COUNT THE QUESTIONS
- Then move to the next unit. Read the instructions and scoring for each game before you start.

UNIT 1
Relationships
Friendship
Personality

UNIT 2
Going green
The environment
Endangered species

UNIT 3
Cities
Stress and relaxation
Rules

70

INSTRUCTIONS

TOPIC TALK

The opposing team chooses a topic and counts the mistakes.
Talk about the topic together. Give opinions on the ➕ and ➖ points.
Score: Start with 10 points. Lose:
- 1 point for each mistake the opposing team notices.
- 1 point each time you pause for five seconds or more.

Calculate the points at the end. Use each topic only once.

DESCRIBE ▶ DISCOVER

The opposing team chooses one noun, one adjective, and one verb from that unit, writes them on a piece of paper, and gives it to player A.
A: Define and describe three words without using the word itself.
B: Discover the word.
Score: 5 points for a correct discovery.

COUNT THE QUESTIONS

The opposing team chooses a photo and counts the correct questions.
A: Ask your partner questions to find "the story behind the photo." The more questions you ask, the more points you score!
B: Answer A's questions however you like. Use your imagination!
Score: 1 point per correct question. Use each photo only once.

ROLE-PLAY

Act out the situation in the cartoon. Be creative! You have 30 seconds to prepare.
Score: Start with 10 points. Lose:
- 1 point for each mistake the opposing team notices.
- 1 point each time you pause for five seconds or more.

Calculate the points at the end.

UNIT 4

TOPIC TALK
- Education
- Career choices
- Regrets

DESCRIBE ▶ DISCOVER

UNIT 5

TOPIC TALK
- Shopping
- Spending habits
- Useless products

DESCRIBE ▶ DISCOVER

6

6.1 What are you watching these days?

1 Vocabulary TV genres and expressions

A ▶6.2 Match photos a–h to eight of the TV genres in question 1 of the survey. Listen to question 1 and repeat the genres. In your opinion, which are the best / worst shows on TV these days?

> ... isn't the worst show on TV, but it's not as good as it was.

TV OR NOT TV?
CHECK YOUR VIEWING HABITS!

1 Which kinds of TV shows are you into?
- cartoons
- stand-up comedy
- game shows
- medical dramas
- news programs
- sitcoms
- cooking programs
- sports events
- documentaries
- music programs
- *a* talk shows
- reality TV
- soap operas
- wildlife programs

2 Are / Were you addicted to any show or genre?
- yes
- no   If so, which? _____

3 Is there any TV genre you can't stand?
- yes
- no   If so, which? _____

4 How do you prefer TV shows in other languages?
- dubbed
- with subtitles

5 Do you subscribe to any TV streaming services?
- yes
- no

6 When did you last watch an entire season of a show?
- never
- ages ago
- recently (specify _____)

7 What has the most influence on what you watch?
- favorable reviews
- friends' comments
- trailers
- other (specify _____)

8 How many of each of these devices do you have at home?
- computer
- tablet
- smart phone
- TV

Which do you use most to watch TV?

Common mistake

watch
I like to see TV at night.

♪ *There's nothing on the TV, nothing on the radio that means that much to me.*

6.1

B ▶6.1 Match the highlighted words in **A** to their meanings. Listen to a talking dictionary to check.

1	_____ noun [C]	ads for a movie, showing extracts of it
2	_____ noun [C]	critics' opinions
3	_____ verb	pay regularly to receive something
4	*be into* verb	really like something
5	_____ noun [C]	all the episodes in one year of a series
6	_____ noun [C]	on-screen translation of speech
7	_____ verb	spoken in the viewer's native language
8	_____ adj.	unable to stop doing something

C Complete the comments with the items from **B**.
1 More than 100 million people worldwide *subscribe to* Netflix.
2 The latest *Star Wars* movie received great _____ from all the critics.
3 Sometimes, I can't read the _____ fast enough, and I miss some of the dialogue.
4 I used to love *Downton Abbey*, but I got bored after the third _____ and stopped watching.
5 I saw a _____ for the new series of *Stranger Things* yesterday. Exciting!
6 I don't like _____ TV shows. It's better to hear the original language.
7 I used to be _____ *The Simpsons* when I was younger. I could watch episode after episode.
8 Everyone _____ *Game of Thrones* these days, but I don't like it.

D ▶6.2 🎤 **Make it personal** Listen and do the survey in **A**. In pairs, compare answers. Any big differences? Who's the class TV addict?

I was totally addicted to How I Met Your Mother *a few years ago.*

2 Listening

A ▶6.3 List five ways TV and viewing habits have changed since your parents' generation. Listen to a father and daughter and check any of your points that you hear. Are any other ideas mentioned?

People can watch TV anywhere and everywhere now.

Yes, and my parents didn't use to have a remote control.

B 🎤 **Make it personal** In groups, ask and answer 1–3. Any big differences?
1 Where do you watch TV? Who with? How much TV do you watch at home / somewhere else every week?
2 Would you prefer to watch TV the way the father did or the way the daughter does now? Why?
3 What's positive / negative about recent changes to TV programs and viewing habits? Is it similar for radio?
4 Does public TV have a future or will it all be private soon?

Well, these days you can subscribe to lots of different services, so we have a lot more options.

True, but there are too many options sometimes.

I sometimes watch English language programs with subtitles to practice my English.

73

6.2 What's your favorite TV show ever?

1 Reading

A What do you know about *Stranger Things*? What genre is it?

It looks like a sci-fi show.

B ▶6.4 *Stranger Things* is a TV show that almost didn't make it past the pilot episode. Listen to two friends talking about it and answer 1–3.
1 How many times was *Stranger Things* rejected by TV companies?
2 Why was it rejected?
3 How many seasons have there been so far?

C List five reasons why a show might get canceled.

Maybe it's had really bad reviews.

D In groups of four, each read about a different show. Report back all you remember. Were any of your reasons in **C** there?

E ▶6.5 Listen, reread, and answer 1–6. Which show do you think sounds the best / worst? Why?
1 did the critics hate?
2 was a sci-fi program?
3 failed because the relationship between the actors wasn't realistic?
4 was a reality TV show?
5 involved three big Hollywood names?
6 managed to get one episode on TV?

The Secret Talents show sounds awful! Who wants to know about celebrities' other talents?

Heat Vision and Jack

This pilot starred Jack Black and Owen Wilson and was directed by Ben Stiller. The plot centered around an astronaut who developed super powers. Black played the lead role and Owen Wilson was the voice of his talking motorbike! It sounds far-fetched and was not picked up by a TV station, but with such huge Hollywood actors, surely it deserved one series! Perhaps the superhero theme was ahead of its time.

Mr. & Mrs. Smith

After the success of the movie with Brad Pitt and Angelina Jolie, ABC planned a spin-off television series. The story was set six months later and followed assassins John and Jane Smith's "normal" life in the suburbs with some spy action thrown in. Martin Henderson, who starred in *Grey's Anatomy*, and Jordana Brewster from *The Fast and The Furious* were chosen for the lead roles. However, critics said there was no chemistry between the two actors, and the series was never made. It's too bad, as it seems like a show that would appeal to fans of the movie!

THE SHOWS THAT NEVER MADE IT PAST THE PILOT

Secret Talents of the Stars

In this show, celebrities displayed talents we didn't know they had, and viewers would vote on the most talented celebrity. It sounds like a good idea, doesn't it? Unfortunately, in the pilot episode, the stars displayed talents that were similar to the ones they were already famous for. For example, ice skater Sasha Cohen showed off her acrobatic skills. Not entirely different from figure skating! The audience didn't see anything surprising or "secret," and the program was canceled after one episode because of low ratings.

The Osbournes: Reloaded

The Osbournes were huge on MTV. Ozzy Osbourne's career was reborn, and the family became famous. When the MTV series ended, the Osbournes tried making a variety show for Fox. The show consisted of comedy, celebrity interviews, and live music. The network spent a lot of money on making and promoting the series. However, it cut the first episode from one hour to thirty-five minutes, and it was very heavily criticized by critics and viewers. Five episodes were filmed, but the show was canceled after just one.

♫ Want you to make me feel
Like I'm the only girl in the world
Like I'm the only one that you'll ever love

6.2

F **Match the underlined words and phrases in the article to the definitions.**

1   based on something that already exists
2   difficult to believe because it is very unlikely
3   much more advanced / modern than most other things
4   to include something extra
5   the estimated audience size of a TV or radio show.

G 🔵 **Make it personal** **In pairs, can you remember the pilot (or first) episode of your favorite TV show or movie series? What happened?**

> *I loved the first episode of* Mad Men. *It was so stylish!*

> *I'm old enough to remember going to the first* Star Wars *movie! We were amazed by the special effects.*

② Grammar Restrictive relative clauses

A **Match the sentence halves, then do the grammar box. Circle the right answer in 1 and 2 (ignore rule 3 for the moment).**

1   *Heat Vision and Jack* is about <u>a man</u>
2   *Mr. & Mrs. Smith* was <u>a TV series</u>
3   *Secret Talents of the Stars* starred <u>celebrities</u>
4   *The Osbournes: Reloaded* was <u>a TV show</u>
5   Winona Ryder plays <u>a mother</u>

a ☐ **that** was based on a movie.
b ☐ **whose** talents the audience had not seen.
c ☐ **who** develops superpowers.
d ☐ **whose** son has gone missing.
e ☐ **that** got canceled after one episode.

⚠ **Common mistakes**

~~who~~
She's the actor ~~that~~ was in those awful comedies.

They sent us an app that we found ~~it~~ very useful.

	whose	that	who
people			
things			

1   Use restrictive relative clauses like those in a–e to give **essential / extra** information about someone or something.
2   The clause usually comes **before / after** the noun it describes.
3   When the pronoun is the object, you _____ a relative pronoun.

➡ **Grammar 6A** p.148

B **Which sentence doesn't need a relative pronoun (*that, whose, who*)? Check in the article on p. 74. Then complete rule 3 in the grammar box.**

1   It seems like a show that would appeal to fans of the movie!
2   In this show, celebrities displayed talents that we didn't know they had.

C **Complete 1–5 with relative pronouns. Which two sentences don't need a relative pronoun?**

1   *Glee* is a show _____ features high school students _____ can sing and dance.

2   Oprah Winfrey is a TV host _____ talent made her the most powerful woman on TV.

3   *Friends* is a sitcom _____ adults and kids still watch, even after 25 years.

4   Homer Simpson is a cartoon character _____ keeps saying "d'oh."

5   *The Tonight Show*, *The Late Show*, and *The Daily Show* are talk shows _____ millions of Americans watch.

D 🔵 **Make it personal** 🔊 **In small teams, write a 5-question quiz about TV, movies, or music. Search online to find and check information. Play against another team. Who can get more answers right? Try to use restrictive relative clauses.**

> *1* _____ *is the actor who starred in "24" and whose father is also a famous actor.*
> *2* _____ *is the TV show that was canceled by Fox and renewed by NBC the following day!*
> *3* _____ *is the musician who's married to Jay-Z and was in Destiny's Child.*

> *I know the first one. It's Kiefer Sutherland, so that's one point to us.*

> *And I have a feeling the answer to number two is "Brooklyn Nine-Nine."*

> *And number 3 is definitely Beyoncé!*

75

6.3 What was the last movie you saw?

1 Reading

A Which of the movies in the posters have you seen? Describe the plot for each in only four sentences, like this one for *Romeo and Juliet*.

"A boy and a girl fall in love and marry. They're forced to separate so she pretends to kill herself. Then he thinks she's dead so he kills himself. She finds him dead and really kills herself."

B ▶ 6.6 Insert phrases 1–4 in gaps a–d. Listen to check. Any pronunciation surprises? Do the gapped sentences in the article make sense without the phrases?

1 whose popularity was at its peak
2 who had been diagnosed with terminal cancer
3 who played Jake Sully
4 which became the fastest movie in history to reach a worldwide gross of $1 billion at the box office

FOUR *curious* MOVIE FACTS

Avatar's Na'vi is an actual language. Director James Cameron asked a renowned linguist to create a language that would integrate well with the story and also be relatively easy for the actors to learn. How easy was it? Well, actor Sam Worthington, [a _____], said in an interview that it was easier to master Na'vi than to fake an American accent, which he had to do for the movie.

James Cameron, who also directed *Titanic*, initially didn't want the movie to have a theme song, even during the closing credits. Composer James Horner, however, secretly asked Celine Dion, [b _____], to record a demo of "My Heart Will Go On." Horner then played the song to James Cameron, who immediately changed his mind. The song won an Oscar and became one of the best-selling singles in history.

Actors Mark Hamill, who played the legendary Luke Skywalker, and John Boyega persuaded *Star Wars* director J.J. Abrams to allow *Star Wars* super-fan Daniel Fleetwood to see the movie before it was officially released. Fleetwood, [c _____], got to see the movie in a special screening at his home before he passed away.

Avengers: Infinity War, [d _____], was one of the best kept movie secrets ever! In order to keep the plot of the movie secret and avoid spoilers, Disney decided to give the cast* fake scripts**. The directors wanted to protect the movie, which eventually came out in 2018, because it had taken ten years to make. They wanted the audience to have the best experience possible when they went to see the movie.

*the group of actors in a movie or show
**the written story and instructions

2 Grammar Non-restrictive relative clauses

A Reread the movie facts article with the additions from **1B** and circle the correct alternatives in the grammar box.

1 Non-restrictive clauses give **essential** / **extra** information.
2 Non-restrictive relative clauses **use** / **don't use** commas.
3 You **can** / **can't** use *that* in a non-restrictive clause.
4 Non-restrictive clauses **always** / **don't always** need a relative pronoun.

➜ Grammar 6C p.148

B Find and underline five more examples of clauses like this in the article.

Common mistake

My favorite Batman movie is The Dark Knight, *that* won four Oscars.   which

*When the sharpest words wanna cut me down,
I'm gonna send a flood, gonna drown them out,
I am brave, I am bruised, I am who I'm meant to be,
This is me.*

6.3

C Connect sentences 1–4 with relative pronouns. Have you seen this movie?

Did you know …?

1 *The Greatest Showman* was directed by Michael Gracey, who. ~~He~~ had never directed a movie before.
2 This musical movie had a very popular soundtrack. It included hits like "This is Me" and "A Million Dreams".
3 The plot is based on the life of circus owner PT Barnum. He was born in 1810.
4 The main character is played by Hugh Jackman. His family is from Australia.

D Rewrite 1–4 using non-restrictive clauses. Write one more of your own.

1 Robert Downey Jr. was voted the best Marvel actor of all time by fans. He plays Iron Man.
2 The first *Iron Man* movie helped relaunch Downey Jnr.'s career. It was made in 2008.
3 Scarlett Johansson plays one of Marvel's first female superheroes in *Black Widow*. Her other movies include *Lost in Translation* and *Sing*.
4 *Avengers: Infinity War* is one of the highest grossing movies in history. It's the third *Avengers* film.
5 Stan Lee created many of the Marvel characters. He played cameo roles in many of the movies.

Robert Downey Jr., who plays Iron Man, was voted the best Marvel actor of all time by fans.

3 Pronunciation Pauses in speech

A ▶6.7 Listen to part of a radio quiz about movie director Ryan Coogler. Circle the correct answer for each question in the quiz.

1 *Infinity Wars*   *Black Panther*   *Guardians of the Galaxy*
2 Soccer   Motor racing   Boxing
3 Barack Obama   Steven Spielberg   Morgan Freeman

B ▶6.7 Pausing when you speak gives you time to think and helps the listener to follow you. Insert speech pauses (//) in 1–5 where necessary. Listen again to check. In pairs, practice imitating the speaker.
1 This week we've been talking about moviemakers who have changed American cinema.
2 The first question is about Ryan Coogler, who many people consider to be one of the finest new moviemakers around.
3 *Creed*, which also starred Sylvester Stallone, was a spin-off from a classic series of movies, *Rocky*.
4 Well, it's a kind of sport that involves two people and a ring.
5 The movie, which won Stallone a Golden Globe, was highly acclaimed by critics.

C 🧑 **Make it personal** Write a short description of a movie you know. Then in groups, read it for the others to guess the movie. Use non-restrictive relative clauses.

> _____, which was written in 1990, inspired one of the most successful movie franchises of all time. The stories are based on the science-fiction novels by Michael Crichton, who is an American author, screenwriter, movie director, and producer.

That's easy. I've seen all four of those movies. I do love dinosaurs. It's Jurassic Park.

77

6.4 Where do you usually watch movies?

1 Vocabulary Movies

A ▶6.8 In pairs, take our quiz and find out who knows more. Listen and choose the answer from the options given. Then listen to the correct answer to check.

Think you're an expert on movies and media? Try this quiz and prove it!

1 Which fantasy **prequel** to *The Lord of the Rings* did director Peter Jackson **shoot** in New Zealand between 2011 and 2013?

2 The video for which song by Luis Fonsi and Daddy Yankee became the most watched video in YouTube history, with over five billion views?

3 *Avengers: Infinity War* is an action movie about superheroes. The cast is like a "Who's Who" of Hollywood and includes many big names. Can you name three of them?

4 One of the biggest YouTube memes of 2013 was "Harlem Shake." There were over 33 hours of "Harlem Shake" **clips** uploaded every day. What did people do in the videos?

5 British actor Tom Holland **stars** as which wall-climbing superhero?

6 Andy Serkis, who was the gorilla in *King Kong*, had to learn to move like a chimpanzee in which famous trilogy?

7 What **role** does Liam Hemsworth play in the blockbuster *The Hunger Games*?

8 Which romance movie **set** in Indianapolis portrays two teenagers who are suffering from cancer?

9 Who wrote the script and directed the first *Star Wars* films?

B Match the **highlighted** words in the quiz to the definitions.

1	_____ *noun [C]*	a movie that is released after another, but tells the story before it
2	_____ *verb*	to take photos for a movie / to film
3	_____ *verb*	to put a story in a certain time and place
4	_____ *noun [C]*	an extract from a video; a short video
5	_____ *noun [C]*	the part, or character, that an actor plays in a movie
6	_____ *verb*	to be the main character in a movie

C ▶6.9 Listen to dialogues 1–3. Which three movies from **A** were they discussing?

D ▶6.9 Listen again. In which dialogues do they disagree? Who do you agree with?

E **Make it personal** Have you seen 1–9 in **A**? What did you think of them? Compare opinions in groups. Any similarities? Who has seen the most?

> I've seen lots of "Harlem Shake" videos. My class made one and uploaded it.

> Really? I didn't like them to be honest. I thought they were weird.

⚠ Common mistakes

"*Despacito*" is a catchy ~~music~~.
　　　　　　　　song / tune

　music　　　　　*is*
The ~~musics~~ in that movie ~~are~~ great!

　　　like
Adele sings ~~as~~ a bird.

　　as
She stars ~~like~~ Jay's second wife.

2 Listening

🎵 *You still look like a movie.*
You still sound like a song.
My God, this reminds me
Of when we were young.

6.4

A In pairs, decide what is important to consider about the items below when making a video.

| filming | light | permission | sound | story |

> You need a quality camera with a good lens and plenty of memory space.

B ▶ 6.10 ▶ Listen to / Watch the instructions on how to make a short video and see if your guesses are mentioned.

C ▶ 6.10 ▶ Read the summary notes on the video and try to remember the missing words. Then listen / watch again and fill in each blank with two words.

Tips and tricks to making a SHORT VIDEO

PLAN YOUR SHOOT
Think about: the topic. ¹_____ people? What do you want the video to ²_____ in the end?

USE THE TECHNOLOGY AVAILABLE TO YOU
You could use:
A ³_____, a camcorder, a webcam, or a ⁴_____.

CAPTURE YOUR CLIPS
Press the ⁵_____ a few seconds before you start. Use a tripod to stop the camera from moving. Extra shoots and ⁶_____ might be useful. Don't ⁷_____ the top of the subject's head.

BE CAREFUL WITH LIGHTING
Shoot in a well-lit area.
⁸_____ there is no bright light behind the subject.

PLAN THE LENGTH OF SHOOT
Plan ⁹_____ in advance.
Don't talk about one thing for ¹⁰_____.

D Read ▶ 6.10 on p. 169 to check. Compare the underlined items with those in **C**.

E Make five pieces of moviemaking advice and decide what elements in **A** they refer to.

1	<u>Always</u>	☐ you are allowed to film in public places.
2	<u>Think about</u>	☐ have a beginning, a middle, and an end.
3	<u>Make sure</u>	☐ moving shots, try attaching the camera to a skateboard or office chair.
4	<u>Never</u>	☐ continuity. If you have a shot from the middle of the day, the next scene shouldn't be at night.
5	<u>If you want</u>	☐ underestimate the emotional power of silence.

F 📶 In groups, brainstorm and search online to find advice to include in a "how to" video on one of these topics. Use the underlined phrases from **E**.

| How to get more views on YouTube | How to learn English faster | How to become a better dancer |
| How to live longer | How to study effectively | How to meet new people |

G 🎙 **Make it personal** In groups of three, choose a title and decide your story. Tell the class and award an Oscar for the best idea. If you really like your idea, go out and film it—in English, of course!

One Wednesday evening

Rob and Rex

Thanks for everything

- *This retired couple fell in love a long time ago.*
- *But then they separated and married different people.*
- *Years later, they meet again and fall in love, and the movie is about how their children feel.*

6.5 Who are the wildest celebrities you know?

🆔 Skills Understanding details

A Complete the text about Sia with these words.

2014	Australia	broke	five
hits	musician	rising	single

¹_____ Sia Kate Isobelle Furler was born in ²_____ on December 18, 1975. Before ³_____, she'd made ⁴_____ unsuccessful solo albums, but written huge ⁵_____ for other artists, including "Titanium" with David Guetta, "Diamonds" with Rihanna, and "Wild Ones" with Flo Rida. Sia finally ⁶_____ through as a solo artist with her sixth studio album, "1000 Forms of Fear" and the hit ⁷_____ "Chandelier." Since then, Sia's star hasn't stopped ⁸_____.

B In pairs, share what you know about Ellen DeGeneres and her TV show. Imagine three questions Ellen asked Sia. What would you like to ask Sia?

> Ellen's an American TV host who interviews famous people.

> I think she asked Sia why she wears a wig like that.

> She must have done. It's the most obvious question.

C ▶ 6.11 Listen to Sue telling Joe about Ellen's interview with Sia. Where did Sue watch the show?
☐ on TV   ☐ live in the studio   ☐ on YouTube

D ▶ 6.12 Listen to the second part of the dialogue and check the picture that best represents what happened.

E ▶ 6.13 Listen to the full dialogue. True (T) or false (F)? Correct the false ones. Did you understand most of it this time? Read ▶ 6.12 and ▶ 6.13 to check. Compare in pairs. If you missed anything, try to figure out why.
1 Both Sue and Joe like Ellen.
2 Joe knows more about Sia than Sue.
3 Ellen asked a surprising question.
4 Sia doesn't like going to the grocery store.
5 Joe didn't know Sue was in the audience.
6 Sia did not reveal her face.

> I love James Corden's Carpool Karaoke, where he sings with musicians. Have you seen any of them? He actually did a great one with Sia!

F 🟠 **Make it personal** In pairs, answer 1–2. Any similarities?
1 Do you often watch / listen to / read celebrity interviews? If so, which shows / magazines / sites are you into?
2 Describe a funny / interesting / embarrassing celebrity interview you've seen.

⊘ Common mistake
It's not my thing.
~~It's doesn't go with me.~~ / ~~It's not the mine.~~

When were you last surprised? 6.5

ID in Action Expressing surprise

A ▶6.14 Use your intuition to complete 1–5. Listen to check. Say them as emphatically as you can.

1	What? Get _____ of here!	4	_____ you serious?
2	Really? You're _____, right?	5	_____ goodness!
3	_____ way!		

B ▶6.15 Listen to these extracts and underline the stressed syllables. Which are the most stressed?
1 She wrote those?
2 You were actually in the audience?
3 You mean they were just pretending?

Pronunciation Showing surprise

C ▶6.16 Read the information and listen to the mini-dialogue. In pairs, practice it, paying attention to stress and intonation. Who is the better mimic?

- To show surprise, echo information using a questioning intonation.
- Use word stress to highlight the really surprising information.
- Notice the use of *actually* to show something is really true.

A Did you know Lady Gaga's real name is actually Ste**fa**ni Jo**a**nne Ange**li**na Germa**not**ta?
B Huh? Her name's Stefani? No way! She doesn't look like a Stefani!
A Well, you didn't think it was really Lady Gaga, did you?!

D ▶6.17 Listen to the mini-dialogues. What is each speaker's question implying?

1 ☐ Not your sister?
☐ Not buying?
☐ Not pizza?

2 ☐ Not your wife?
☐ Not rent?
☐ Not bigger?

3 ☐ Not Paula?
☐ Not a cat?
☐ Not for Christmas?

4 ☐ Not five?
☐ Not months?
☐ Not vegetables?

E In pairs. A: read aloud questions from ▶6.17 on p. 169, stressing one of the underlined words. B: Listen and choose the correct option from **D**.

F 🟠 Make it personal In pairs, play *Surprise me!*
A: Tell **B** three surprising facts about yourself. One should be imaginary.
B: Express surprise. Say if you think they're true. Change roles.

> Did I ever tell you that my sister once shared a cab with Emma Stone?

> No way! You mean your sister actually met Emma Stone?

> Yes, she offered to share her cab from the airport.

> That can't be true. I don't believe you.

🎵 *I'm gonna swing from the chandelier, from the chandelier*
I'm gonna live like tomorrow doesn't exist, like it doesn't exist

Writing 6 A movie / book review

*I think your love would be too mu[ch]
Or you'll be left in the dust
Unless I stuck by ya
You're the sunflower.*

A Read the review and circle the correct alternative in 1–4.
1. The movie is based on a **book / true story** and the reviewer liked it **more / less** than she had expected.
2. The main characters are four **teenagers / robots** trying to **win / lose** a game.
3. **Some / All** of the characters are interesting and original and develop **well / badly**.
4. It's **boring / funny** and follows on **badly / well** from the original movie.
5. The reviewer **was / wasn't** impressed and would give it **two / four** stars out of five.

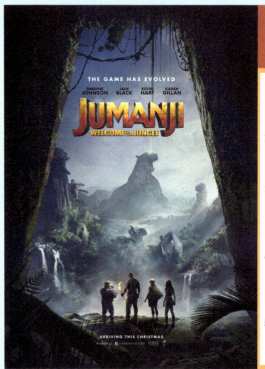

REVIEW SECTION Jumanji: Welcome to the Jungle

1. If you like action and adventure, try *Jumanji: Welcome to the Jungle*. Based on a children's novel, and sequel to the much-loved 1995 film of the same name, this te**rr**ific movie definitely ex**cee**ded my expectations.

2. The story is about four high school kids who discover an old video game console. They somehow end up in the game and become the avatars they chose. They have to beat the game or they will be stuck in Jumanji forever!

3. The movie **cap**tivates, not only because of the amazing special effects but also because of the int**ri**guing new characters we meet. Unfortunately, the male and female characters are a bit ste**re**otyped, but the story does focus on the way the characters change and think about themselves.

4. As well as the action-adventure element, this story has a lot of comedy and heart. Fans of the original movie will not be disappointed, as this version makes nos**tal**gic references to the first. Because of that, those who loved the hi**lar**ious Robin Williams will be deeply touched by the **tri**bute this film makes to the wonderful actor.

5. In my opinion, this is a great version as it will keep the original fans happy and combines action, special effects, comedy, and nostalgia. I'd say it's a must-see and I'd certainly suggest you watch it.

B In which paragraph, 1–5, does the reviewer:
- ☐ recommend it or not?
- ☐ mention the positive points?
- ☐ describe the plot?
- ☐ mention any negative points?
- ☐ describe what's being reviewed?

C Read *Write it right!* Then find extreme adjectives meaning:
1. very good (x3)
2. very interesting
3. very funny
4. very popular

✓ Write it right!

In reviews, use a variety of adjectives, including extreme adjectives with appropriate adverbs (*really, absolutely, completely, not very*).
- names as adjectives
  Star Wars fans / X-Men movies / Twilight lovers

To give extra information, use non-restrictive clauses between commas:
- *Spider-Man: Into the Spider-Verse*, which is the seventh Spider-Man movie, is the first computer-animated version of Stan Lee's story.
- Spielberg, who is famous for action movies, directs *Ready Player One*, a sci-fi fantasy where technology offers an escape from overpopulation and climate change.

D Reread *Write it Right!* and punctuate this short review with three commas, two periods, and one question mark. Capitalize where necessary.

wonder woman which was released in 2017 tells the story of Diana, Princess of the Amazons when a pilot crashes on her remote island and tells her about the war in the world outside Diana leaves her home and sets off on a mission to save the world. israeli actor Gal Gadot plays Wonder Woman while stopping the war can Diana find out her true destiny

E *Your turn!* Choose a book / movie to review in 140–180 words.

Before	Make notes for five paragraphs as in **B**.
While	Write your review. Follow the tips in *Write it right!* and use a friendly, informal style.
After	Ask a partner to read and check it. Then send it to your teacher.

82

6 Best in show

1 Before watching

A Match the photos to descriptions 1–6.

1. ☐ *The Brady Bunch* was a popular American TV show from the 1970s about a family.
2. ☐ A character from *X-Men* was called "Wolverine."
3. ☐ Starbuck was a fighter pilot on a popular science fiction TV show.
4. ☐ Lucille Ball was a famous redhead who had a show called *I Love Lucy*.
5. ☐ *The Addams Family* was a very creepy family that was on TV and on Broadway.
6. ☐ Lily Munster was a very nice "monster" who lived at 1313 Mockingbird Lane.

B 🗣 **Make it personal** Do you know any characters from **A**? Which are / were your favorite TV characters / sitcoms / series / theme tunes?

I think I've seen that Lucy show.

As a kid, I used to love the Addams Family *theme tune!*

2 While watching

A Watch to 3:12. Check all you hear.

1. ☐ Andrea looks like Lady Gaga and Morticia Addams.
2. ☐ Lucy doesn't know any 1960s TV shows.
3. ☐ The party will be full of nerds and geeks.
4. ☐ For the costume party, you dress as a character that you really like.
5. ☐ Andrea once won the "Best in Show" prize for her Superman costume.
6. ☐ Andrea thought dubbed TV shows were hilarious.
7. ☐ Diana Prince is Wonder Woman's alter ego.
8. ☐ Andrea says August is the family mutant.

B Order the story, 1–6. Then watch the rest to check.

☐ Andrea admires other costumes.
☐ Andrea confirms she isn't.
☐ August sees Paulo dressed as Superman.
☐ August thinks he'll win.
☐ Lucy says he did predict he'd lose to the perfect Superman.
☐ Lucy worries she's the only one from the 50s.

C Watch and check: August (A), Andrea (An), Lucy (L) or Paulo (P)?

		A	An	L	P
1	put on his wig first.				
2	tried on long and short wigs.				
3	repaired a costume.				
4	didn't really want to go.				
5	convinced her to go.				
6	forgot to check something.				
7	beat August last year.				
8	really expected to win.				
9	felt attracted to Paulo.				
10	felt defeated again.				

3 After watching

A Complete the extracts with *who* or *that*.

August She was the one ¹_____ kind of looked like a vampire.
August And the people ²_____ will be there are cool people, not just nerds.
Lucy   We watched so many American shows ³_____ were dubbed in Spanish.
Lucy   Am I the only one here ⁴_____'s dressed as a character from the 1950s?
Lucy   Well, didn't you say that the only person ⁵_____ was going to beat you this year …

B Play 20 questions! **A**: Think of a famous person. **B**: Ask **A** *Yes / No* questions. How many questions did you have to ask before you guessed correctly?

Is this an actor who was on TV?   *Yes, it is.*

83

R3 Grammar and Vocabulary

A *Picture dictionary.* Cover the words or definitions on the pages below and remember.

pages	
60	5 money collocations
64	9 "product" words
67	the endings of 10 shopping phrases
72–73	8 TV genres
78	10 words from the quiz
161	2 words for each sound in lines 1 and 2 of the consonants chart (not the picture words)

B Order the **bold** words in 1–4 to make adjective phrases and cross out the word that doesn't fit.

1. These **boots / hiking / comfortable / strange** are perfect for the mountains.

2. *Set in Love* is a **romantic / short / novel / well-written** of over 800 pages.

3. Lose yourself in this **new / video game / tasty / exciting**.

4. Make your own TV show with our **old / equipment / digital / easy-to-use**.

C In pairs, think of two endings for 1–8. Compare with another pair. Who has the funniest endings?
1. If you hadn't posted that photo, …
2. My parents wouldn't have got married if …
3. I'd have sent you a text if …
4. If I'd been born in the U.S., …
5. We'd have watched the show if …
6. If my father hadn't studied law, …
7. If I'd gone to bed earlier, …
8. We wouldn't have missed the bus if …

D ▶R3.1 Match 1–5 to the correct response a–e. Listen to check.
1. Have you seen my keys anywhere?
2. Uh … my … dog ate my homework.
3. So there was this documentary about the UFOs in Roswell and …
4. Allan isn't answering his phone.
5. Hey, what language are they speaking?

a ☐ Have you tried Skyping him? He might be online.
b ☐ Oh, come on! You can't believe that, surely.
c ☐ I don't know. It can't be English because I don't understand a word.
d ☐ Not again! They could be anywhere!
e ☐ Oh really? You must think I'm stupid.

E In pairs, write a mini-dialogue to extend one of a–e in **C** by at least four lines. Role-play it for the class.

Well, I had them this morning. Can you help me look for them?

F ▶R3.2 Add commas to these relative clause sentences if necessary. Listen, repeat, and copy the intonation.
1. I love my <u>MP3 player</u> which <u>has over 2,000 songs</u>.
2. I really like people <u>who laugh easily</u>.
3. <u>Javier Bardem</u> who starred in *No Country for Old Men* is one of my favorite actors.
4. <u>My son just graduated</u> which made me very proud.
5. It's difficult to find <u>people who you can count on</u>.
6. I'd like to get a phone that <u>takes better photos</u>.

G 🔵 **Make it personal** Change the underlined phrases in **F** to make 1–6 true for you.

H In pairs, add two more words with the same ending to each group. Mark the stress in the new words.
1. ac**tu**ally / **cur**rently
2. use**less** / care**less**
3. **ac**tion / **ques**tion
4. a**bi**lity / se**cu**rity
5. **com**fortable / re**cy**clable
6. **ce**lebrate / **gra**duate

I Correct the mistakes in each sentence. Check your answers in units 5 and 6.

🔵 **Common mistakes**
1. If I knew you were here, I had have called. (2 mistakes)
2. Rob borrowed his phone for me. (2 mistakes)
3. That shirt look good. You should buy her. (2 mistakes)
4. It must to be difficult to be on debt. (2 mistakes)
5. When you pay with credit card online, you have to be carefull. (2 mistakes)
6. People which talk in theaters they annoy me. (2 mistakes)
7. That's the house in that they live. (2 mistakes)
8. Bruce Banner is a scientist who turn to the Hulk. (1 mistake)
9. Panama, that is famous for the canal, is a city amazing. (2 mistakes)
10. If I had eat less lunch, I wouldn't been so sleepy in the afternoon. (2 mistakes)

Skills practice

♪ *Where did I go wrong?*
I lost a friend somewhere along in the bitterness.
And I would have stayed up with you all night,
Had I known how to save a life.

R3

A ▶R3.3 Listen to five sentences. What do they mean? Circle the correct alternative.
1. I'm **very sick** / **not joking**.
2. I think somebody **broke** / **will break** your machine.
3. He **likes** / **doesn't usually like** kids' movies.
4. They had **no money left** / **stolen money**.
5. They are **very popular** / **a waste of time**.

B Read the article and answer 1–6.
1. What do people receive from GoFundMe?
2. What does Peg want to do?
3. How did Peg learn about GoFundMe?
4. Who is Dan?
5. Do you pay to try GoFundMe?
6. Have you ever asked for sponsorship? If so, what happened?

> *I asked my friends and family. Only some of them gave me money though.*

Help on the Internet

Why is everyone talking about GoFundMe? Because GoFundMe has helped thousands of people raise many millions of dollars online for amazing personal causes like school tuition, rock bands, medical bills, volunteer trips, business ideas, parties, travel expenses, even for animals and pets.

Let's take Peg, for example. Peg has a terrific opportunity to volunteer overseas but needs enough money for the flight and food. Luckily for Peg, her friends told her to check out GoFundMe, the easiest way to raise money online. Convinced by thousands of success stories, Peg decides to create her very own fundraising page on GoFundMe. Choosing a color, selecting a photo, and writing your information only takes a minute.

Now Peg's ready to tell the world about her cause. Inviting contacts and sharing with Facebook friends couldn't be easier. Peg's friend Dan notices her GoFundMe page on Facebook. Dan is happy to support his friend and gives her some money. He even helps tell other people for Peg. Peg gets an email each time a new donation is made. In just a few short days, she's nearly reached her goal. Once Peg's ready to get her money, she simply provides her banking information and receives the cash days later.

GoFundMe has helped Peg, and hundreds like her, raise lots of money online and can do the same for you. Click the "try it free" button and get started in less than a minute.

C ▶R3.4 Listen and underline ten differences between the text and the audio. Listen again to check. How many different expressions mean the same as what you read?

D *Feel 'n' Guess!* Play in groups.
A: Secretly put an object in a bag.
B, C, D: Feel it and speculate what it might be.

> *It's soft so it can't be a DVD.*   *Yes, it might be a ...*

E *Keep, Kill, Ignore.* Talk about the options in 1–6 and choose one to keep, one to kill, and one to ignore.

1	a news programs b soap operas c sitcoms	4	a Horror b Romance c Fantasy
2	a cartoons b sports events c documentaries	5	a Dance music b Rock music c Rap
3	a YouTube b Facebook c Twitter	6	a cell phones b laptops c vacations

> *I guess we could kill news programs. I get most of my news online anyway.*

F *Shopping problems role-play.* In pairs, decide what kind of store you want to set your role-play in.
A: You're a customer. Buy something in the store, and then try to return it later.
B: You're the store assistant. Invent as many problems for the customer as you can.

> *Hi, do you have this in a bigger size?*   *I'm sorry, we're all on our break now.*
> *On your break? Are you serious?*

G ▶R3.5 **Make it personal** *Question time!*
Listen to the 12 lesson titles from units 5 and 6 in random order. Pause after each one to ask and answer in pairs. Ask follow-up questions, too. Any surprises?

> *Would you ever lend money to anyone?*   *Well, that would depend on who it was.*

85

7.1 Does technology rule your life?

1 Reading

A In pairs, what's the message in the cartoon? Did it make you smile? What complaints about technology have you heard (recently)?

> I heard something about a virus that made private social media information become public.

> Yes, I heard about that, too.

PROTESTING AGAINST NEW TECHNOLOGY – THE EARLY DAYS

B ▶7.1 In pairs, read only the introduction and first paragraph heading. Guess what the author will say. Then listen and read to check if you were right. Repeat with the other four paragraphs.

> I guess he or she will say we can check anything on our phones.

> And to be careful about fake news!

⊘ **Common mistake**

~~Technology means~~ *effortless* communication ~~without effort.~~

MODERN TECHNOLOGY –The Bright Side!

Every day, we hear so much negativity about modern technology and its impact on society: There are no jobs. We have no social skills. It's killing our creativity. Beware of Identity Theft! World destruction! The list goes on … But let's just calm down. We know technology has a down side, but, for a moment, can we focus on the many benefits it brings to us?

Access to Information
Our parents used to have to go to a library and take out a book to find out the information they needed. Now, we access whatever we need to know instantly and anywhere. With the vast amount of data on the Internet, we can read the news, check the stock market, and buy tickets to a concert, all while we're on the train!

Innovation and Creativity
The possibilities seem limitless. It was difficult to start a business years ago, but now with online selling platforms, anyone can set up a business at home. Creative people can easily sell their work online. Another example is crowdfunding. This leads to the creation of new businesses, further creativity, and more technology!

Communication
Apparently, we are all zombies with our faces glued to our screens. Yes, we know we need to cut down on screen time and have more face-to-face time, but modern technology has made communication effortless! Before, it took weeks to get a letter to a relative in Australia. Now, we have email, cell phones, video conferencing, text messaging, and social media. You can reach anyone, anywhere, at any time.

Entertainment
Where would the entertainment industry be without technology? We can store and enjoy endless music and movies with streaming apps. Like that new song you just heard on the radio? Download it instantly! We can play games with people on the other side of the planet. It also makes it easier for artists to break into the entertainment industry. Ed Sheeran and Justin Bieber were both discovered on YouTube.

Education
Students can access courses remotely with distance learning. Of course, we also use technology in the classroom. Tablets and smartboards are commonplace, and lessons are much more engaging with visual information. But don't forget the countless educational apps you can download to help you pick up everything from French to ballroom dancing!

86

They took the credit for your second symphony. Rewritten by machine on new technology.

7.1

C In pairs, reread and find …
1. two old-fashioned ways to access information.
2. three improvements to entertainment.
3. two ways technology increases innovation.
4. three improvements to education.
5. five ways dialogue has become easier.

D Complete 1–7 with the underlined items in the article. Which are true for you? Modify the others to make them true.

1. I know how to protect myself against _____.
2. Some people say that Millennials don't have good _____ because they spend too much time on their smart phones.
3. I find it really annoying when I'm _____ a movie and the Internet goes down!
4. Children should be limited to one or two hours of _____ a day.
5. I'd like to take a _____ course one day.
6. I think face-to-face meetings are much better than _____.
7. I like buying secondhand items from _____.

E 🟠 **Make it personal** *Technology – the dark side!* Imagine you're a member of an "I hate everything about technology" group. In threes, list all the negative aspects imaginable. Then share with the class. Which, if any, do you think are, or will be, serious problems?

> There are too many choices now. It was easier to focus before.

> Effortless? No way! It takes ages to learn to use technology well!

> Yes, and people had better memories. You don't have to remember anything anymore. Your phone knows everything!

② Vocabulary Phrasal verbs

A Match the **highlighted** phrasal verbs in the article to the definitions. Any you didn't know?

1	_____	learn a new skill
2	_____	continue or persevere
3	_____	begin to feel more relaxed and less emotional
4	_____	start doing less of something
5	_____	get something officially from somewhere
6	_____	discover a fact or piece of information
7	_____	start something such as a business
8	_____	start to have success in your career

🟠 **Common mistakes**

    cut down on
My five-year-old needs to ~~reduce the~~ sugar.
    pick up
I ~~take~~ a lot of English from subtitled movies.
    taken out   for
We've ~~asked~~ a loan to pay ‸ our wedding.

B ▶ 7.2 The phrasal verbs are in the wrong sentences. Put them into the correct places. Listen to check. In pairs, imagine the context 1–8 were said in.
1. I don't want to work for someone else. I'd rather cut down on my own company.
2. You'll break into Spanish quickly if you spend time in a Spanish-speaking country.
3. When did you go on these loans on your credit card? Now you've got a huge debt!
4. I don't know what time the train is, but I can easily calm down.
5. Please pick up with what you're doing, and don't let us interrupt you.
6. I'm trying to set up the amount of caffeine I drink.
7. She was angry at first, but we managed to take her out.
8. It must be difficult for artists to find out the U.S. music industry.

> This sounds like a person who is fed up with their job.

C 🟠 **Make it personal** *Three of each!* Write down …

- three things you should cut down on.
- three ways to pick up a new language.
- three things that help calm you down.
- three things you've found out so far during this course.

In groups, compare and ask questions. Any coincidences? Share one unusual response with the class.

> Do you know any good apps that can help you pick up a language?

> Yes, there are lots! Duolingo is a good one.

87

7.2 What was the last little lie you told?

1 Reading

A In your experience, do salespeople always tell the truth? What kinds of promises might they make or lies might they tell?

> They might say a color looks great on you when it really doesn't!

Common mistakes

I try to not ~~say~~ lies. → tell

They sometimes exaggerate the ~~true~~. → truth

B Read sales promises a–f and guess what device each one refers to.
a "Some of the keys are different, but it's basically the same thing."
b "Oh, yes, you can mount it on the wall yourself."
c "You'll be able to use it in any country, don't worry."
d "It works just as well as the famous brand, but at half the price."
e "There's lots of technical support online."
f "Look! It just arrived!"

> I think the first one could be a piano.

C Read the article and match promises a–f in B to tips 1–5. There's one extra promise.

But How Was I to Know?

Christmas is just around the corner and chances are you'll be buying someone you love a new digital device of some sort. Today we bring you five hot tips to guide your holiday shopping and avoid trouble down the road.

1 [f] Our first tip basically applies to any new gadget or household appliance. Companies race to launch new products before their competitors. This means the early versions of the new technology may contain all sorts of horrendous bugs and break down in a matter of weeks. Allow brand new products time on the market so the most serious defects can (hopefully!) be corrected.

2 [ ] Well, theoretically, yes, but if you miss a screw or two, the TV may come crashing down on you after a week. These things weigh more than 100 lbs, so either put it on a table or get a professional to do the job because the warranty doesn't cover stupidity.

3 [ ] The Rolex that your dad has been dreaming of is way too expensive, I know, but stay away from the cheap imitations you find on the streets. They might look good today, but what about next month? Not to mention that buying fake goods is illegal—Dad certainly won't thank you if the police catch him! Remember: If something looks too good to be true, it probably is.

4 [ ] Buying a cell phone abroad can save you a few bucks, but first you've got to check whether you can even use it back home. Make sure it's unlocked (that is, not tied to a particular carrier) and that the network is compatible. If you're scratching your head right now, get yourself a phone locally!

5 [ ] If you buy an imported computer, keep in mind that the keyboard layout may be a little different from what you're accustomed to. So what? Well, if you think you can learn to live without the "ç" or "ñ" keys, no big deal. Otherwise, think twice, or you may find yourself throwing the poor laptop out the window.

D ▶ 7.3 Listen, reread, and match photos a–e to the underlined words. Then match the highlighted words to definitions 1–5. What's the best tip, and which are irrelevant to you?

> I'd say tip 1 because it's the most general.

1	_____ noun [C]	a company that provides phone or Internet services
2	_____ noun [C]	the written promise to fix something for free
3	_____ verb	to put something on the market
4	_____ noun [C]	electronic problems in a device
5	_____ verb	to stop working

 a b c d e

E 🔴 **Make it personal** In pairs, complete 1–3 with the correct form of words from D, and then answer them. Any big differences?
1 Have you ever had to use the _____ for a product that doesn't work?
2 On a scale of 0 to 10, how happy are you with your cell phone _____? Why?
3 Have you ever bought a product a few days after it was _____? Did you have any problems or inital _____? Would you recommend it to a friend?
4 Have you ever been in a vehicle which suddenly _____ mid-journey?

🎵 Well somebody told me you had a boyfriend
Who looked like a girlfriend
That I had in February of last year
It's not confidential, I've got potential.

7.2

No, I guess I've just been lucky when I buy things.

2 Grammar Reported speech (1)

A ▶7.4 Listen and match the five dialogues to paragraphs 1–5 in **1C**.

B ▶7.5 Complete extracts 1–5 in pencil. Use your intuition! Listen to check.
1 The salesman said some of the keys _____ different.
2 He said that it _____ just as well as the famous brand.
3 The delivery guy told me I _____ mount it on the wall myself.
4 On the site, it said I _____ be able to use it in any country.
5 The store manager said it _____ just _____.

C Compare a–f in **1B** with 1–5 in **B** and circle the correct alternatives in the grammar box.

> **Reported statements**
> 1 If the reporting verb is in the past (*said, told*), the main verb often **moves one tense back / remains the same**.
> 2 "That" is **necessary / optional**.
> 3 *Said / Told* requires an object (*me, her, John*).
>
> ➡ Grammar 7A p. 150

⚠ **Common mistakes**
He said ~~me~~ he was sorry.

She told ~~to~~ me that she ~~will~~ buy it.

D ▶7.6 Change the underlined words in 1–5 into reported speech. Listen to the end of the dialogues to check. All correct? Are any of the phrases or situations familiar to you?
1 "You will learn fast." He said …
2 "I'm here every week, and I can get you video games, too." He told me …
3 "It's easy, and it'll only take 10 minutes." He said …
4 "Lots of people have complained." They told …
5 "These tablets usually sell pretty quickly." She said that …

E ▶7.7 Report what each person said in cartoons 1–4. Listen to check. All correct? Are any of the phrases or situations familiar to you?

1 tell / do well
2 say / dog / be / friendly
3 tell / party / be / informal
4 say / you / not / arrive late

F 🔴 **Make it personal** Think of a time you were told something untrue or wrong. Prepare your answers to 1–3. In groups, share your stories. Any similarities?
1 What was the situation?
2 What did the person say? How did you react?
3 What happened in the end?

When I was a kid, my parents convinced me that the tooth fairy really did exist. Well, …

People often use the traffic as an excuse for being late. For example, …

7.3 How much of your day is screen time?

1 Vocabulary Using touch screens

⚠️ **Common mistake**

This app was designed ~~by~~ for a teenager.

A Look at the photo. What do you think PleIQ might be? Who do you think it is designed for?

> PleIQ It looks like some type of …

B Read the description to check. Were you right? How does PleIQ work? What are the benefits?

Worried about your child's **screen time**?

Tired of seeing them aimlessly **swiping** left and right and **scrolling** through streams of pointless images? Look no further than PleIQ – a dynamic new app which transforms tablets and smart phones into educational tools.

PleIQ combines physical and digital aspects. The set contains eight cubes with letters, numbers, and other symbols, and an app. With augmented reality (AR), the symbols shown on the blocks are transformed into interactive, 3D cartoons. Children show a block to the screen, they **double-tap** on the icon they want to play with, and they can **zoom in** to see more details.

This invention, by Venezuelan innovator Edison Duran, attempts to improve screen time for children and reduce the educational divide by giving more children access to learning in their early years.

Parents have control. They can monitor their child's progress and add new items. Children can control how their app looks by **dragging and dropping** items into new locations.

With PleIQ, screen time is more constructive.

C ▶7.8 Cover **B** and match verbs 1–5 to the phrases. Listen and reread to check. Repeat the pink-stressed words. Then, in pairs, take turns miming 1–5 for the others to guess.

1 swipe   ☐ to see more details
2 scroll   ☐ through images
3 double-tap   ☐ left and right
4 zoom in   ☐ items into new locations
5 drag and drop ☐ on an icon

D 🔘 **Make it personal**   In pairs, answer 1–3. Any good tips to share?
1 What are the best kids' apps you know? Why?
2 Each describe a favorite app, how it works, and why it's good.
3 How have apps improved your life? What's easier than it was before?

> I love Evernote Scannable! You just zoom into the document or card or whatever, and the app converts it into a scan. Then you can just scroll through all of your saved documents.

2 Listening

A ▶7.9 Neide Sellin is a young inventor from Brazil. What do you think her invention is? Listen to check.

> I'm not sure. It could be a vacuum cleaner.

B ▶7.9 Listen again. Number these 1–7 in the order you hear them. In pairs, explain their significance.

> That's the number of Brazilians who can't …

☐ dog   ☐ 6.5 million   ☐ 100   ☐ 3,000
☐ airports ☐ 2020   ☐ 253 million

C 🔘 **Make it personal** 📡 In pairs, search online to find more inventions that have made the lives of people with disabilities easier.

> Stephen Hawking used a cheek-controlled communication system.

> And this meant he could speak through a computer.

♪ *The world I love, The tears I drop / To be part of the wave, can't stop / Ever wonder if it's all for you?*

3 Grammar Indirect questions

A Find how questions 1–4 are asked in ▶ 7.9 on p. 170. Complete the chart.

Original question	Indirect question
1 What is her latest development?	
2 How many guide dogs are there in Brazil?	
3 Is this really a more affordable option?	
4 How much does it cost?	

B Compare the two types of questions in **A**. Then answer 1–4 in the grammar box.

1. Which sounds more polite, the original question or the indirect question?
2. What is the word order for the subject and verb in indirect questions?
3. What happens to the auxiliary *do* in an indirect question?
4. If the answer to the question is *yes / no*, which word do you need to add?

→ **Grammar 7B** p. 150

Common mistakes

Excuse me, could you tell me where is the station?

Do you know where did he go?
went

C 🎙 Correct the questions about innovations. Then search online to find the answers.

1. Can you tell me when was Bluetooth first invented?
2. Do you know who did invent the first cordless vacuum cleaner?
3. I'd like to know how many years did it take to produce the first wireless earphones?
4. I wonder when will driverless cars come onto the market?
5. Could you tell me if will e-readers ever replace books?
6. Do you know when is the next iPhone coming out?

D ▶ 7.10 Read the review and complete indirect questions 1–5. Listen to check.

The Kenguru Car

❝ Tired of having to collapse your wheelchair?
Finally, a car designed with wheelchair users in mind!
Simply maneuver your chair straight into your car and off you go!
With a speed of 25 miles per hour and a range of 60 miles, you will be able to do your daily chores without any of the hassle.
The Kenguru currently costs $25,000, but with the incentive of clean, green energy, it's worth it! ❞

1	Who is it designed for?	Do you know _____?
2	How fast can it go?	I'd like to know _____.
3	How will it be helpful?	Can you tell me _____?
4	How much does it cost?	Could you tell me _____?
5	Can it travel very far?	I wonder _____.

E 🎤 **Make it personal** *Time to innovate!* In threes, choose a category and invent something to make life quicker, easier, and more efficient. Present it for the class to ask questions. Vote for the best idea.

Driving and parking   Studying   Shopping   Communications   Housework   Food and cooking

Use these questions to help you plan your presentation.
- What is your invention and how does it work?
- How will it be helpful in everyday life?
- How much do you think it will cost to make?
- How difficult / easy do you think it will be to produce?
- Is there anything else like it already? How is yours better or different?

Could you tell us whether it could work in any type of car?

Do you know if people with disabilities would be able to use it?

7.4 Are machines with personality a good idea?

1 Listening

A In pairs, brainstorm how you (or people you know) use phone voice command features. Who uses it the most?

I use it a lot. I can tell it who to call.   *I only use it to choose songs to play.*

Common mistake
~~well~~
It doesn't work very ~~good~~.

B 🔊 **Make it personal** In pairs, answer 1–3. Which of you likes voice recognition better?
1 Do you have any voice-activated devices at home / in your car? How well do they work?
2 What other devices / appliances should / could be voice-activated?
3 How "intelligent" do you think voice recognition will become in the future?

My GPS is voice-activated, but it's kind of stupid.   *Oh yeah? How come?*

C ▶7.11 Listen to Bruce and Ann comparing their cell phones. Whose is better at voice recognition?

D ▶7.11 Listen again and answer 1–4 using one or two words. Are you more like Ann or Bruce?
1 Who gave Bruce his new phone?
2 What's his voice-recognition software called?
3 Did he expect the phone to be so smart?
4 What's Ann's voice-recognition software called?

I'm definitely more like … because …

E ▶7.11 Young people often use *like* in informal speech. Study examples 1–3. Then listen again. How many times do you hear the word *like*?
1 The party was, like, so cool. (filler speech)
2 I was like, "What are you doing?" and he was like, "Nothing." (quotative)
3 It took, like, forever to get here. (to signal exaggeration)

F ▶7.12 Listen to Ann asking Bruce's phone 1–5. Did it understand (U) or misunderstand (M)? Is it funny?
1 Where am I?
2 Will the weather get worse?
3 Do you love me?
4 Please call me an ambulance.
5 Make me a coffee.

G 🔊 **Make it personal** *Machines with personality!*
Complete 1–4 with your opinion, then compare in groups.
1 In my opinion, this cartoon …
2 My computer / tablet / phone thinks I'm …
3 I think machines with personality …
4 I'd like my … to have a personality so …

I'd love to be able to talk to my fridge. It could suggest recipes, count calories, and help me stay healthy!

2 Pronunciation *-ed* ending followed by /h/

A ▶7.13 Listen and repeat 1–3 from the dialogue in **1C**. Choose the correct alternatives in the box.
1 He asked if he bored me.
2 I asked him if he was hungry.
3 I asked her to text someone.

When the final sound is /k/, *-ed* is pronounced: **/t/** / **/d/**
The /k/ sound in *asked* is: **strong** / **weak**
The /h/ sound in *him* and *her* is usually: **strong** / **weak**

B ▶7.14 *Dictation.* Listen and write Ann's five sentences. Then write them in direct speech.

🎵 *Cause she knew what was she was doin'*
When she told me how to walk this way!
She told me to walk this way, talk this way.

7.4

3 Grammar Reported Speech (2)

A Look at the examples in **1F** and **2B**. Are rules 1–6 true (T) or false (F)?

Reported questions, commands, and requests			
When reporting questions:		For commands and requests:	
1 use *do, does,* and *did*.	T / F	5 use *ask* for requests and *tell* for commands.	T / F
2 invert subject and auxiliary.	T / F	6 the main verb uses *(not)* + infinitive.	T / F
3 move one tense back.	T / F		
4 always use an object after *ask*.	T / F		

➡ **Grammar 7C** p. 150

Common mistake

~~for~~
She asked me ⌄ your contact details.

B Order the words to complete five "voice recognition disasters." Had any of your own?

Luke   I asked **my computer / read / to** my new email, and it started deleting messages instead!

Sue   I asked **it / rain / my phone / would / if** tonight and it said, "It's now 4 p.m."

Ron   The GPS told **to / turn / me** left, and I crashed into a tree.

Ian   The stereo asked **what / me / I / wanted** to listen to. I couldn't believe my ears!

Mitt   I asked **where / my GPS / I / was**, and he told **worry / me / to / not**. Can you believe that?

C Do you like autocorrect? Ever have problems with it? Last week it caused lots of problems for **Bruce** and **Ann**. Write their text conversations in reported speech.

I love autocorrect. That is, when it guesses correctly!

1
Why are you late?
I've just crashed my cat.
What do you mean?
No, no! Not my cat. The ___car___!
Hate autocorrect.

2
Are you hungry?
Yeah, I want vegetarian blood.
What?
OMG. What I meant to say was vegetarian _____!

3
Are you coming to the party?
Can't. I broke my uncle.
What?
I mean _____, but it's still serious.

D ▶ 7.15 In pairs, say what you think Ann and Bruce meant for 1–3 in **C**. Then listen to check.

You can crash into a cat, but you can't crash a cat, can you?

E 🙂 **Make it personal**   **Tech questionnaire** In pairs, follow the instructions.
1 Write six questions to find out about your classmates. For example:

How many remote controls do you have and actually use?
Do you ever think your phone knows what you're thinking?
Do you think you need to cut down on your screen time?

2 Ask as many of your classmates as you can. Make a note of their answers.
3 Report their answers back to your partner. Any unexpected answers?

Angelika said she hadn't changed her phone for three years!

Really? Paul told me that he'd changed his yesterday.

7.5 How often do you use a pen?

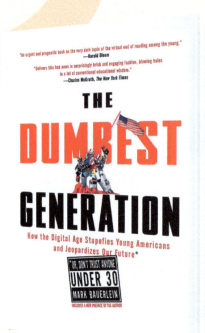

Skills Listening and note-taking

A Match words from the book cover to definitions 1–4. Who's the book about?

1	_____ verb	have confidence in
2	_____ adj.	most stupid
3	_____ verb	makes stupid
4	_____ verb	puts at risk

Common mistakes
It puts at risk the young people's futures.
People says this is true, but I disagree.

B ▶ 7.16 In pairs, answer 1–3. Listen to / Watch an interview to check. Would you consider reading a book like this?
1 How old do you think the author is? Why?
2 Which specific examples of digital culture do you think will be mentioned?
3 Which of these do you think American teens are becoming less interested in?

foreign affairs   leisure reading   partying   politics
social networking   studying for class   visits to museums

Many are becoming less and less interested in foreign affairs.

C ▶ 7.16 Read about note-taking. Then listen / watch again and complete the notes. Do any of 1–6 surprise or worry you?

> Note-taking is a useful learning skill to develop. When taking notes you should write as fast and economically as possible. Here are three ways to do that:
> • Focus on the most important information (facts, dates, numbers) + ignore less relevant details.
> • Omit articles, auxiliary verbs + prepositions—not usually important information.
> • Use figures for numbers (7 out of 10 = 70%), symbols (> = more than) + abbreviations (sts = students).

1 Digital culture doesn't open teens to _____, artwork, _____, _____ + foreign affairs.

2 Most popular sites for teens: social networking = _____%

3 Time spent reading + studying: < _____ / week. (_____% of sts.)

4 Time spent social networking: _____ / week.

5 Dying habits: Leisure reading, visits to _____ + _____.

6 Technology in teenage bedroom: _____, _____, video game console, _____ → interesting than Antony, Cleopatra, and Caesar!

D **Make it personal** Teens today. Are things changing? In groups, decide what's
1) similar and
2) different in your country. Cover these points:
• Do you mainly agree?
• Do any of the facts in **C** surprise or worry you? Why (not)?
• Are teenagers becoming less engaged? More isolated? More adventurous?
• What are the top three priorities among teens where you live?

It seems to me that teenagers are a bit different.

94

Do you enjoy a good argument?

7.5

ID in Action Expressing your views

A ▶ 7.17 A TV panel discussed *The Dumbest Generation*. Who do you think made the following points, and why? Listen to check. How many correct predictions?

💬 A GOOD ARGUMENT
TV PANEL SHOW
HOST: female, 50 years old
GUESTS: Tom, 32 and Barbara, 19

YOUNG PEOPLE ARE ...

1 reading less and less.
2 using different media to read.
3 not reading less because of the Internet.
4 ignorant despite the Internet.
5 becoming more intelligent.
6 becoming less sociable.

B ▶ 7.17 Match points 1–6 in **A** to the supporting arguments below. Listen again to check. In your opinion, which are the weakest arguments?

☐ My son thought Rome was a country.
☐ People's IQs have increased in the last century.
☐ Bookstores are closing down.
☐ Teens spend too long locked up in their rooms.
☐ People started to read less at least 30 years ago.
☐ I've got hundreds of digital titles.

⏱ Common mistake
My parents had a terrible ~~discussion~~.
argument

I googled no 4, about ignorance. One site said 20% of Americans believe the sun revolves around the earth!

No way! That's fake news!

I think the weakest arguments are the ones about Tom's son. I mean, who cares?

C Do you agree or disagree with the points in **A** 1–6? Why?

I think it's awful to say young people are ignorant. Of course we're not!

I know! We have access to so much information. How can we be ignorant?

D 📡 Are you convinced by the supporting arguments in **B**? Choose a point from **A** to research online. Report your findings to the class.

E ▶ 7.18 Complete the chart with these words. Listen and check, and then repeat.

can't   hold   more   on   point   points   totally   true

Stating an opinion	We ¹_____ deny that …
Holding the floor	²_____ on a second, let me finish.
Clarifying	Well, it depends ³_____ what you mean by …
Partially agreeing	That may be ⁴_____, but don't you think …? Well, you may agree or disagree, but he makes some valid ⁵_____.
Strongly agreeing	Yeah, I couldn't agree ⁶_____. My ⁷_____ exactly!
Strongly disagreeing	I ⁸_____ disagree.

Welcome to "Hot Topic"! Our guests tonight are ...

F 🔘 **Make it personal** *A good argument* In threes (host and two guests), choose a discussion topic and role-play a three-minute TV panel. First, think of your main points and supporting arguments. Take notes. What's your conclusion?

> Artificial intelligence will be used to replace teachers.
> We won't need to learn other languages because we will have translation technology.
> The Internet needs to be more strongly regulated.

🎵 *Yeah, we're just young, dumb and broke,*
But we still got love to give

95

Writing 7 A complaint email

*All I wanna do is (bang, bang, bang)
And a (kkkaaa ching!)
And take your money.*

A Julio Cruz recently bought an LED TV. Read his email. True (T) or false (F)?
1. He bought it at a shopping mall.
2. He's had problems with the TV since he bought it.
3. There are two problems with the TV itself.
4. He had two problems with the service.
5. He lost the receipt but still wants his money back.
6. He expects a fast solution.

To: customerservice@ledtv10.com
From: Julio Cruz
Subject: Refund

October 10th, 2013.

(a) _____ ,

1. I am writing to express total dissatisfaction with my purchase of a 42-inch-LED TV from your online store nearly a month ago. Unfortunately, your product has not performed at all well, and your service has been completely inadequate, to say the least.

2. Firstly, when I turned it on there were several spots on the screen, so I immediately called your service department, who told me the spots would soon go away. However, the problem has gradually been getting worse, and now it is almost impossible to watch any program comfortably.

3. Secondly, I am very disappointed because I've contacted your online support countless times, but they always seemed uninterested and unwilling to help. For instance, I was informed that they would send a technician to solve the problem, but this never happened.

4. Although you advertise top quality, both your product and your service are well below the standards I expected. As you can imagine, I am not satisfied. Therefore, to resolve the problem, (b) _____ . I attach a scanned copy of the receipt and must insist on receiving a full refund immediately or (c) _____ .

(d) _____ .

(e) _____ ,

Julio Cruz

B Match each paragraph to its purpose.
- ☐ action he wants to be taken
- ☐ reason for writing
- ☐ what happened when he used the product
- ☐ what happened when he complained

C Read *Write it right!* Then match 1–6 to gaps a–e in the email. There's one extra phrase.
1. Dear Sir / Madam
2. Yours sincerely
3. I would appreciate an immediate solution
4. Yours faithfully
5. I will be forced to take legal action
6. I look forward to hearing from you

✓ Write it right!

Start and end formal letters using:
- *Dear Mr. / Ms.* (+ last name) or *Dear Sir / Madam*, ...
- a closing sentence:
  I would appreciate a rapid response / I look forward to receiving your urgent reply.
- *Yours sincerely,* (if you know the recipient's name) or *Yours faithfully,* (if you don't).

To express dissatisfaction and demand action use **firm but polite phrases**:
- *I am writing to complain about ...*
- *I feel I am entitled to (compensation for all the inconvenience I have suffered).*

Avoid contractions or informal language.

D Underline the formal sentences in the email that correspond to 1–5.
1. Your service was horrible.
2. I've gotten in touch with you on the Internet.
3. Nobody wanted to help me.
4. You say your product's the best.
5. I want my money back.

E *Your turn!* Write a complaint email in 120–180 words.

Before	Choose a problem below and make notes for paragraphs 1–4 in **B**.
While	Follow the tips in *Write it right!* Use formal language.
After	Email it to a classmate to check before sending it to your teacher.

- You had a meal in a restaurant where the food and service was bad.
- You ordered an item of clothing online, but it is not as advertised on the website.
- You booked a holiday with a travel agency, but the hotel was not as advertised in the brochure.
- You took a long distance bus to a party. The bus left one hour late, arrived four hours late, and you missed the party.

7 The road NOT taken

1 Before watching

A Complete 1–5 with these words, and then match three of them to the photos.

| commuter | express | shocks | tow truck |
| transmission | | | |

1. ☐ A fast train that doesn't stop at every station is an _____.
2. ☐ A _____ moves a car that is broken down.
3. ☐ The _____ is the part of a vehicle that transmits the engine power to the wheels.
4. ☐ A _____ travels a long distance to work.
5. ☐ The _____ are the parts of a vehicle that absorb the energy from bumps in the road so the wheels run smoothly.

 a   b   c

B 🔵 Make it personal Has your vehicle ever broken down? If so, what did you do? Was it easy to repair?

Once I was on a bus that ran out of gas. The drivers behind us were furious.

2 While watching

A Watch the video and check the correct answer in 1–3.

1. What did August ask Rory and Daniel?
   ☐ He asked if they needed help.
   ☐ He asked if they needed him to pick up anything else.
2. What did Rory tell Daniel that Genevieve said?
   ☐ Her car had broken down.
   ☐ She decided not to have dinner with them.
3. What did Paolo tell Andrea and Zoey about the trains?
   ☐ He said they'd have to cross back over and go back the other way.
   ☐ He warned them their train was going express.

B Watch again. Who said each line?

1. Her car broke down on the expressway.
2. Dinner's going to get cold.
3. It'll just be a party for five.
4. They were expecting us twenty minutes ago.
5. But don't expect me for dinner.
6. This isn't our stop. We've missed it.
7. It passes our stop so we had to get off here.
8. You'll have to cross over to the other side.
9. We're not gonna make dinner.
10. That's so nice of you.

3 After watching

A Complete 1–5 with these verbs. There's one extra.

| asked | offered | complained |
| called | told | wondered |

1. August _____ if Rory needed anything else.
2. Genevieve _____ Rory to tell him that she wouldn't make dinner.
3. August _____ where they were and why they were late.
4. Genevieve _____ Andrea and Zoey that her car needed repairs.
5. Paolo _____ to wait for the train with Andrea and Zoey.

B Complete 1–4 with these times.

| 20 mins | 45 mins | 2 hours | a bit |

1. Genevieve said the tow truck guy would take at least _____.
2. Rory told Daniel it would take _____ for her car to get fixed.
3. Andrea told August she would see them in _____.
4. Andrea and Zoey had to wait _____ for the next train.

C 🔵 Make it personal In threes, share your experiences of planning things that didn't work out. Tell the class the best story.

Leo told us about a party he'd planned but no one came!

97

8

8.1 How important are looks?

1 Reading

A Is Photoshop a good thing? Have you used it? Would you use it?

> I use Photoshop to remove unnecessary objects from my photos – like trash cans!

> I've never used it. I like my photos to show reality.

B In pairs, take turns giving clues about the items in photos 1–5 until your partner guesses the item.

> It opens and closes.   Her eyes?   No, it's made of wood.   Is it red?

C ▶8.1 Listen and read the introduction to the article. In pairs, how do you think Photoshop has changed the world? Brainstorm five ideas. Then read and match photos 1–5 to a paragraph. Were all your ideas mentioned?

How Photoshop
HAS CHANGED THE WORLD

Adobe Photoshop is one of the most powerful image-editing tools in the world, and it has profoundly changed the art of photo retouching. What was once an expensive and time-consuming task is now a simple procedure with limitless possibilities. Here we take a look at how Photoshop has changed the way we view the world.

HOW WE THINK ABOUT IMAGES
"That must have been photoshopped!" [a _____] We even use "photoshop" as a verb to indicate that something doesn't look real.

HOW WE VIEW THE HUMAN BODY
A staggering 95 per cent of the human images we see are retouched. [b _____] The more camera-shy among us can photoshop away imperfections and it's great for simple things like removing red-eye. However, we are so used to photos being modified that seeing candid photos of celebrities, with all their imperfections, seems to shock us and many of these "un-photoshopped" images go viral.

HOW IT'S USED IN ADVERTISING
Look through any magazine and find an ad that hasn't been photoshopped. Good luck! Advertising has completely transformed since image manipulation. [c _____]

HOW IT'S USED IN THE TRAVEL INDUSTRY
Lots of vacationers wonder where the golden sand and blue skies are when they get to their destination. The sad fact is that travel companies doctor images. [d _____] This kind of manipulation only results in disappointed customers.

HOW WE VIEW HISTORY
Some of history's most iconic images were "photoshopped" before the software even existed! Photoshop has the power to alter the way we see history. [e _____] If not, they may be altered. With the recent craze of photobombing, politicians must be very grateful for Photoshop.

For better or worse, Photoshop is here to stay, and we are now so accustomed to seeing these images that often it doesn't even register that they've been photoshopped.

D ▶8.1 Complete the article with 1–5. Listen again to check. Has the article made you feel any differently about Photoshop?

1 Agencies can now just pay someone to make their ads for them without the need to take photographs!
2 As a result, Photoshop has changed our view of what is "normal."
3 For example, they might remove an ugly parking lot between your hotel and the beach.
4 Experts examine images in detail to make sure they give the right message.
5 These days, we are increasingly skeptical about the authenticity of images.

98

D **Make it personal** In groups, discuss 1–3.
1 Do you think Photoshop has had a positive or negative influence?
2 Do you think there should be more regulation of Photoshop in the media?
3 Has Photoshop affected your life in some way?

> *So you can keep me
> Inside the pocket of your ripped jeans,
> Holding me closer 'til our eyes meet,
> You won't ever be alone.*

> Well, I guess it depends on how you use it. If you work in the advertising industry, then it has had a positive influence.

2 Vocabulary Photography and photos

A Match the highlighted words in the article to the definitions.

1	_____	the red appearance of eyes in some photos
2	_____	to change something in order to deceive people
3	_____	describes someone who dislikes having his or her photo taken
4	_____	making small changes to a photo in order to improve it
5	_____	describes an image that has been manipulated by a computer program
6	_____	the activity of ruining someone else's photo by moving into view just before it is taken
7	_____	natural and informal

B Complete 1–7 with the correct form of the words from A.
1 Greta Garbo disappeared whenever a photographer appeared. She was incredibly _____.
2 _____ your vacation photos to make the weather look better is really easy!
3 My camera has a special flash mode to reduce _____.
4 The court discovered that the prosecution had _____ the image.
5 The photographer managed to get a _____ photo of the princess laughing.
6 The photo on the front cover had been _____ to make him look muscular.
7 Did you see that great photo from the Oscars a few years ago? Even celebrities are into this _____ craze.

> **Common mistake**
> Do you like ~~that people take your photo~~?
> having your photo taken

3 Listening

A ▶ 8.2 Look at James Fridman's Instagram account and answer 1–2. Listen to check. Were you right?
1 What is funny / unusual about the photos?
2 Who do you think James Fridman might be, and what does he do on social media?

B ▶ 8.2 Listen again and correct the errors in 1–5.
1 James Fridman is well-known for taking people's email requests for image alter*a*tions.
2 Most of his images are shocking and cruel.
3 Fridman encourages people to retouch their images to meet today's often unrealistic beauty standards.
4 One heart-warming example of James's work is a photo sent to him by a woman who was suffering from anxiety and low self-e*steem*.
5 She asked James to make her look younger.

C **Make it personal** In small groups, go online and each find a good photoshopped image by James Fridman (or someone else). Show and explain your choice. Create a caption for it. Which are the funniest / cleverest?

> Look at this one. It looks like the giraffe is photobombing them!

> The caption could be, "I'm much better looking than him!"

8.1

99

8.2 Do you like watching illusions?

1 Listening

A In pairs, share what you know about Michael Jackson. Have you seen this video? Any idea how he did the illusion?

I know he was in a group with his family before he went solo.

Maybe there was a metal pole in his jacket.

B ▶8.3 Listen to two people guessing how they did the illusion. Did they mention your ideas? Do you think they are right?

C ▶8.4 Listen to someone explaining how the illusion was really done. Were the speakers in **B** correct? Did you guess correctly?

D ▶8.4 Listen again and complete 1–6. If there's time, watch the video!
1 The illusion appeared in the music video for _____.
2 The dancers were able to lean at an angle of _____ degrees.
3 The lean was performed by wearing a _____.
4 It had an _____ opening in the _____. This attached to a _____ on the floor.
5 During a concert in 1996, Michael Jackson _____.
6 Someone bought the item for $_____.

E **Make it personal** Have you seen any spectacular performances by musicians?

Did anyone see Pink's Grammy performance? She sang while hanging from the ceiling on a ribbon!

2 Grammar Modal perfects

A Match the dialogue halves from **1B**. Then complete the grammar box.
1 How on earth did he do that?
2 Maybe it was something to do with his shoes.
3 Maybe he really could lean that far!
4 I guess his clothes were specially engineered.

a ☐ Yes, I suppose, he might have **put** magnets on them and on the floor.
b ☐ He was good, but not that good! He can't have **been able** to do that. It's impossible!
c ☐ Yeah, he may have **had** special pants made!
d ☐ He must have **had** wires attached to his jacket. It's the only explanation, surely!

Common mistake

have gone
He might ~~went~~ to a party.

1 Sentences a–d in **A** refer to the **present / past**.
2 The green verbs are the **simple past / past participle** form.
3 Check (✓) the modal verbs with the same meaning as the underlined words in a–c below.

	must have	can't have	might have may have
a I'm <u>almost sure</u> this happened.			
b <u>Maybe</u> this happened.			
c I'm <u>almost sure this did not</u> happen.			

➔ Grammar **8A** p. 152

100

B ▶8.5 Rephrase 1–6 using past modals. Listen to check.
1 You saw David Blaine live?! I'm certain the tickets were very expensive!
   The tickets must have been very expensive.
2 It wasn't possible for him to know my date of birth.
3 I don't know how he did that trick. Maybe he had the ring in a secret pocket.
4 I'm 100% sure he didn't levitate.
5 The illusion didn't work properly. Perhaps he didn't practice it enough.
6 I'm certain it wasn't comfortable in that block of ice!

> ♪ *It must've been love, but it's over now. It must've been good, but I lost it somehow.*

8.2

3 Pronunciation contractions

A ▶8.6 Contractions are the norm in fast spoken English. Listen and repeat the answers in **2B** with contractions. Notice the links between *n't* and *'ve* /təv/.
The tickets must've been very expensive.

B In pairs, go to ▶8.3 on p. 171 and practice reading the dialogue, changing the full forms to contractions using /mʌstəv/, /kæntəv/, and /maɪtəv/.

C In groups, speculate about events 1–6. Choose your best theory for each. Then compare with others. Who has the most interesting idea?

1 You find a wallet lying on the ground close to a gas station.	4 Your classmate is wearing gloves on a hot day.
2 Your laptop is sitting open on your desk where you left it, but the screen is smashed.	5 Your teacher has come to class wearing a dinner jacket / evening dress.
3 You arrive home, and the floor is soaking wet.	6 You arrive at work, and your boss is extremely angry.

> *The driver might've put his wallet on the car roof when he was opening the door.*

> *Yeah, I've done that with my phone!*

> *And then he must've forgotten about it and started driving. What do you think?*

D ▶8.7 Read about two illusions. In small groups, how do you think they were done? Listen to someone describing the tricks. Did you guess correctly?

One of **David Blaine**'s first tricks to be shown on TV was levitation. Blaine positioned himself with his back to the audience, raised his arms, and to the crowd's amazement, appeared to lift off the ground at least 30 cm! He stayed there for a few seconds before returning to earth.

David Copperfield's most famous trick was making the Statue of Liberty disappear. The trick was done in front of a live audience and on TV. Copperfield put a huge screen up in front of the statue. To prove it wasn't fake, the TV cameras were put in locked boxes, and a special radar screen showed the statue's position. When the screen was lowered, Lady Liberty had completely disappeared!

E ▶8.7 Listen again. T (true) or F (false)?
1 It doesn't really matter where David Blaine stands.
2 The trick is more effective in front of a large audience.
3 What Blaine wears will affect how well the trick works.
4 David Copperfield used distraction techniques.
5 The audience thought they were sitting still.
6 The trick was performed in partial darkness.

F 🟠 **Make it personal** 📶 In small groups, find out how other well-known tricks or illusions are done. Describe / Mime it for the class to guess how it must have been done.

> *I found a video where David Blaine pulls out a girl's teeth! Then her teeth reappear when he blows on them!*

8.3 Have you ever cut your own hair?

1 Listening

A In groups, answer 1–4. Do you all feel the same way about birthdays?
1. How do you like to celebrate your birthday?
2. What's your best birthday memory?
3. Which birthdays are significant in your country?
4. Have birthdays become too commercial?

I like to have a special meal out, blow out my candles, then go dancing.

B ▶8.8 Read the TV review. How do you think the critic rated the show? Listen and notice his tone of voice.

> *My Super Sweet 16* shows you all the fun, glamor, and excitement as kids prepare for their most important birthday celebration," says the MTV ad. OK. I get it. Your teenager is officially growing up. Fine. But there's nothing really sweet about *My Super Sweet 16* or *Quiero Mis Quinces*, its Latin version. Both shows are basically about a bunch of spoiled teens trying to look and act like adults as they prepare for their fifteenth or sixteenth birthday extravaganza. So don't waste your time. And be sure to keep your kids away from the TV—the show might give them some pretty expensive ideas.
>
> **BY JOEY MINOR**

C ▶8.9 Listen to Brandon telling Courtney about his birthday party. True (T) or false (F)?
1. His party was inspired by the show.
2. His mom suggested a movie party.
3. It'll be an outdoor party.
4. He liked the suit his father bought.

Wasn't Paris Hilton a little like that as a teen?

D ▶8.10 Listen to the second part and the activities 1–6. Do you know any teens like Brandon?

E ▶8.11 Match the two columns. Listen to extracts 1–6 to check.

1. Dad hired a fashion designer and
2. Your hair looks awesome! Tell me,
3. I spent four hours at the salon and
4. The pool's dirty and
5. Mom can't cook so
6. I'm exhausted!

☐ I **signed** all 200 invitations myself.
☐ we still need to have the cake **made**.
☐ we're going to have a new suit **made**.
☐ I got my nails **done**, too.
☐ Dad hasn't gotten it **cleaned** yet.
☐ did you have it **dyed**?

Hey, Courtney, awesome news. So, I'm having a party ...

F **Make it personal** In pairs, role-play Brandon and Courtney's dialogue. Read ▶8.9 and ▶8.10 on p. 172 and use the photos in **D** to prepare. Do you like feeling spoiled?

2 Grammar Causative form

🎵 *Now he's getting a tattoo, yeah, he's getting ink done. He asked for a "13" but they drew a "31."*

8.3

A Read the grammar box. Then answer 1–3.

> Use **have / get** + **object** + **past participle** to talk about services or actions that other people do for you.
> In causatives, **have** and **get** mean the same, but **get** is more common in spoken English.
> To emphasize that you did something without help, use a **reflexive pronoun**.
> • "Where did you get your hair cut?"
> • "Oh, I cut it *myself*, actually."
> • "We couldn't get anyone to redecorate, so we did it *ourselves*."
>
> ➔ Grammar 8B p. 152

a   b

1 Which preparations for the party did Brandon do himself?
2 Who did the other activities? Which do you think was the most expensive?
3 Match pictures a and b to the phrases.
  ☐ I had my photo taken with Zac Efron.
  ☐ I took a photo of Zac Efron.

B In pairs, remember the preparations for Brandon's party using the photos in **1D**. Then role-play **1D** again, switching roles. Be careful with causatives.

I can't remember. Did he have his hair dyed, or cut, or just dried?

Common mistakes

get my hair cut
I usually ~~cut my hair~~ at Hairway to Heaven.

have your eyes checked
Did you ~~check your eyes~~ last week?

had this tattoo done
I ~~did this tattoo~~ when I was 16.

C ▶ 8.12 Complete comments 1–5 from Brandon's very spoiled friends with the causative of these verbs. There's one extra. Listen to check. Do you know anyone like this?

| build | cover | do | get | make | redecorate |

Could you fix a broken faucet?

I'd probably try to do it myself. And then get someone to do it for me!

Really? I don't know how to. I'd have to get it fixed.

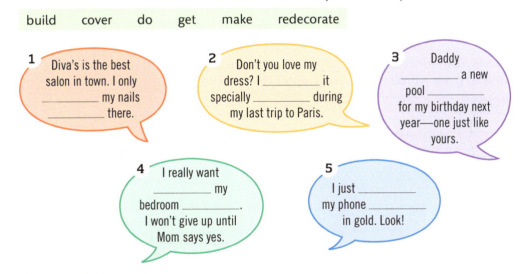

1 Diva's is the best salon in town. I only _____ my nails _____ there.

2 Don't you love my dress? I _____ it specially _____ during my last trip to Paris.

3 Daddy _____ a new pool _____ for my birthday next year—one just like yours.

4 I really want _____ my bedroom _____. I won't give up until Mom says yes.

5 I just _____ my phone _____ in gold. Look!

D 🟢 **Make it personal** In groups, ask and answer to find out who's the most self-sufficient. What would be different if you had a lot more money? Who would survive best on a desert island?

HOW SELF-SUFFICIENT ARE YOU?

Do / Could / Would you do these activities yourself?

Do / Would you get them done for you?

iron / clothes   fix / broken faucet   paint / house   build / home
change / flat tire   clean / bedroom   make / dinner   clean / windows
                         wash / car   grow / food

8.4 Do you have a lot of furniture in your room?

1 Vocabulary Furniture

A ▶8.13 Listen. Which bedroom is the designer describing? Match items a–k to these words.

☐ bookcase ☐ chair ☐ closet ☐ comforter ☐ dresser
☐ double bed ☐ lamp ☐ mirror ☐ nightstand ☐ pillow ☐ rug

B In pairs, use words in **A** to describe ten differences between rooms 1 and 2. If necessary, use a dictionary for the other items of furniture.

You can see a closet in room 1, but not in room 2.

C **Make it personal** Which bedroom do you prefer? Why? Is either similar to yours? What does each one tell you about its owner?

I imagine the first one belongs to a woman because ...

2 Listening

A ▶8.14 Listen to two friends talking about the second bedroom. What has happened?

B ▶8.15 Listen to the second part of the dialogue. Why did they do it?

C ▶8.15 Listen again. Check what they have done in the room.
☐ changed the rug   ☐ painted some furniture
☐ replaced the lamps   ☐ bought new pillows and a new comforter
☐ bought a new mirror ☐ had the bookcase made
☐ painted the walls   ☐ had the windows cleaned

> **Common mistake**
> much
> How ~~many~~ furnitures do you have?

D **Make it personal** In pairs, answer 1–4. Any surprises?
1 How would you feel if this were done to you?
2 Have you ever made a nice surprise for someone like this? Has anyone ever done it for you?
3 Which room in your house would you most like to change? How? Why?
4 What would your ideal bedroom look like?

I can't stand my living room. The paint is a horrible color. I'm going to have it repainted one of these days.

③ Grammar Tag questions

♪ *Well, I've heard there was a secret chord*
That David played and it pleased the Lord
But you don't really care for music, do you?

8.4

A ▶8.16 **Listen to the extracts and complete 1–6 with these phrases. There's one extra.**

did you?   don't you?   hasn't it?   isn't it?   was it?   won't he?   have you?

1   You haven't done anything crazy, _____?
2   It's great, _____?
3   He'll love it, _____?
4   You didn't do it all yourself, _____?
5   That rug wasn't there before, _____?
6   You know he's going to be over the moon, _____?

B **Look at A and complete rules 1–5 in the grammar box with these words.**

negative   ask for agreement   positive
check information   do   statement   verb

1   Use a tag question to _____ or _____.
2   A tag question goes at the end of a _____.
3   Use the same auxiliary _____ and tense in the tag question as the statement.
4   In statements without an auxiliary verb, use _____ in the tag question.
5   With + statements, use a _____ tag. With - statements, use a _____.

➡ **Grammar 8C** p. 152

> ⏱ **Common mistakes**
>
> *doesn't he*
> Your dad loves tennis, ~~no~~?
>
> You're not hungry again
> already, ~~do~~ you?
> *are*
> You were here yesterday,
> ~~was~~ you?
> *weren't*

④ Pronunciation Intonation in tag questions

A ▶8.16 **Read the information, then listen again and mark ↗ or ↘ in 3A.**

> Tag questions can have two different functions depending on your intonation.
> Rising ↗ intonation is usually a real question. It means "I'm not sure, so I'm checking."
> Falling ↘ intonation is more like a statement. It means "I'm not really asking. I just want you to agree."

B ▶8.17 **Listen to Tom's reaction. How many tag questions do you hear? Did he get upset?**

C ▶8.17 **In pairs, try to complete 1–4. Listen again to check.**

1   But _____ you'd be discharged tomorrow, _____?
2   You _____ about doing this, _____?
3   You _____ serious, _____?
4   That's the rug _____ in the department store, _____?

D **Complete 1–4 with tag questions and select the best answer for you.**

1 You really like **action movies**, _____?
   a Yeah, I love them.
   b They're OK, I guess.
   c Actually, I hate them.

3 You've never **been to the U.S.**, _____?
   a No, never.
   b No, but I'd love to.
   c Yes, I have.

2 You're **from the capital**, _____?
   a Uh-huh.
   b How could you tell?
   c Nope.

4 You didn't **go out last night**, _____?
   a No, I didn't.
   b I did, actually.
   c Why do you ask?

E ⏱ **Make it personal** **Replace the bold words in D with your own ideas. In pairs, ask and answer. Vary the verbs / tenses, and add follow-up questions. Share your best exchange with the class.**

You really like baseball, don't you?   *It's OK, I guess, but I prefer basketball.*   *Why's that then?*

105

8.5 Is your listening improving?

Skills Predicting

A In pairs, compare the logo makeovers. Do you prefer the old or the new versions?

I prefer the old iTunes logo.   *I don't know. I kind of like the new one.*

My guess is they won't mention ...

B ▶8.18 In pairs, guess what will not be discussed in a college lecture on logo makeover, and why. Listen to check. Were you right?

☐ why the logos changed   ☐ consumers' reactions   ☐ the cost involved

C ▶8.19 Read about predicting. Then look at 1–6, listen to the second part, and predict what the lecturer will say after each beep.

> Predicting what the speaker is about to say is a very useful listening strategy. Here are three clues to listen for:
> 1 Use of adverbs:
>   Dad was rushed to the hospital. <u>Fortunately</u> ... — You know it's good news.
> 2 Use of linking words:
>   The economy was good last year. <u>However</u> ... — You know it's a contrast.
>   Electric cars are greener. <u>In addition</u> ... — You know it's another point.
> 3 Intonation:
>   "Would I like to live abroad?" "Hmm ..." ↘ — You know the answer is probably no.

Common mistakes

they won't
~~I guess they're not going to~~ mention why.

Use *will* when it's just a guess / there's no evidence.

it's going to
Look at those clouds – ~~it'll~~ rain.

Use *going to* when it's probable / there's clear evidence.

Instagram
1 She'll mention something **positive / negative**.
2 She'll talk about **original / new** users.
3 She **likes / doesn't like** the logo transfor**ma**tion.

Starbucks
4 Customers **liked / didn't like** the new logo.
5 She'll give **her opinion / a suggestion**.
6 She'll **explain what she said / make a new point**.

D ▶8.20 In pairs, predict what happened to the Gap logo transformation. Use these questions. Listen to check.
1 How old was the logo?   3 Why did Gap want to change it?
2 How did people react?   4 What happened to the company president?

E ▶8.21 Predict how many words you will hear in gaps 1–3. Contractions count as two words. Listen to check. Order the four logos from most to least successful.
1 To mark the occasion, _____ thought: "Hey, let's create a new logo and drop the words 'Starbucks Coffee'."
2 However, Instagram was trying to attract new users—you know, people _____ visited the site before.
3 They _____ create something modern and contemporary, but, boy, were they wrong.

What's the hardest part of language learning?

8.5

ID in Action Expressing preferences

Awesome! I didn't know you could draw so well.

A **Logo Game!** Draw an authentic logo for 1–6. Compare in small groups. How many are the same? Score one point for each unique logo. Who's the class "Picasso"?

| 1 a sports clothing company | 3 a car manufacturer | 5 a TV channel |
| 2 a fast food chain | 4 a tech company | 6 a fashion label |

B In pairs, think of two companies for categories 1–6 in **A** and answer 1–3.
1 Which has a simpler logo?
2 Which is more famous? Does the logo help?
3 Do you prefer one company over the other? Why (not)?

I prefer Ray-Ban. Their designs are cooler.

C ▶8.22 Listen to two students leaving the lecture on logos on p. 106. Which logo(s) do they both like?

D ▶8.22 Try to remember the missing words. Listen again to check.

1 I love this class. It's really _interesting_ .
2 Which one do you like _____?
3 _____ are OK, I guess.
4 I think I like the old one better _____ the new one.
5 I don't really like _____ of them.
6 I actually prefer the second one _____ the first.

Common mistakes

~~more~~ better
I like ~~more~~ grammar than pronunciation.

to
I prefer English ~~than~~ French.

are
I think both channels ~~is~~ great. (both = they)

either
Pizza or pasta? I don't want ~~both~~ for lunch.

E Study *Common mistakes*, then correct 1–4. Do you agree with these opinions?
1 Both Facebook and Twitter has good logos, I think.
2 I like Chrome best than Safari.
3 Beyoncé or Shakira? Hmm … I don't like both of them.
4 I prefer cats than dogs. Actually, I can't stand dogs.

Let's see … First one … Yeah, I think so. I mean, they're so recognizable.

F 👤 **Make it personal** *English-learning preferences*. Interview three students and check (✓) their preferences. Use these words to help.

Which one are you better at: grammar or vocabulary?

easy   fun   good at   helpful   irritating   useful

Learner profile	1	2	3
grammar OR vocabulary			
listening OR reading			

Learner profile	1	2	3
pair work OR individual work			
speaking freely OR being corrected			

G 👤 **Make it personal** Report back to the class. Any major differences?

Two people in my group prefer grammar to vocabulary.

Well, here everybody likes vocabulary better.

🎵 I know someday you'll have a beautiful life,
I know you'll be a star
In somebody else's sky,
But why can't it be mine?

Writing 8 An opinion scholar

'Cause all of me loves all of you.
Love your curves and all your edges
all your perfect imperfections.

A Read Damir's opinion essay and check the best title for it.
☐ Beauty in the media   ☐ Beauty: the good and bad sides   ☐ Five steps to being more attractive

It is usually said that beauty is hard to define. At the same time, being beautiful, or at least being worried about the way you look, has become increasingly important in our society. Is this positive or are people getting obsessed with appearance?

On the one hand, taking care of your appearance has many advantages. In general, this leads both men and women to become more interested in a healthier lifestyle. For instance, they try to exercise and adopt better eating habits. All this, of course, has a positive effect on looks. In addition, these days it is much easier and cheaper to have beauty treatments that can boost your self-esteem and therefore make you feel happier.

On the other hand, some people are fanatical about having wonderful hair, the thinnest body, and the most attractive face. Many end up wasting a small fortune trying to do so. This false concept of perfection is usually imposed by the media, which makes us want to look like actors, sports stars, or supermodels. This image, of course, is not realistic for most people. So, the desire to look absolutely gorgeous can lead to stress, eating disorders, and even serious illness.

To summarize, I strongly believe that emphasizing perfection and physical attractiveness at all costs has extremely negative effects. It would be much better if people were more concerned about feeling good and taking care of their health.

B Which of structures 1–3 does Damir use to organize his opinion essay?
1 introduction + argument(s) for or against only + conclusion
2 introduction + one argument for + several arguments against + conclusion
3 introduction + argument(s) for + argument(s) against + conclusion

C Read *Write it right!* and match 1–6 to the highlighted conjunctions in the text.
1 Introducing arguments   4 Exemplifying
2 Contrasting   5 Summarizing
3 Adding   6 Expressing consequences

✓ **Write it right!**

In opinion essays, use a variety of conjunctions to organize and contrast your arguments.
- It's important to take care of your appearance. However, you should not become obsessed.
- Even though mass media, like TV, are important, they also have a negative influence, so be selective and don't just follow what others do.

Some conjunctions are followed by commas.
- However, / In addition to that, / Therefore,

Some mean the same.
- Although / Even though she looked great, she had plastic surgery.
- Despite his doctor's recommendations, he went on a radical diet.

D Match 1–5 to an equivalent expression.
1 It is usually said that   ☐ Moreover
2 So   ☐ In short
3 For instance   ☐ Therefore
4 In addition   ☐ For example
5 To summarize   ☐ People believe that

E Circle the correct option (a or b). Sometimes both options are correct (c).
1 _____ some models are dangerously thin, fashion magazines still use them.
  a Although   b However   c both
2 Fruit and vegetables are healthy. _____, they're sometimes cheaper than processed food.
  a In addition   b Moreover   c both
3 Doing aerobic exercises, _____ cycling and swimming, helps you stay in shape.
  a such as   b like   c both
4 Some people follow ridiculous diets. _____ they can get sick.
  a Therefore   b Although   c both
5 _____, feeling healthy is more important than being attractive.
  a To summarize   b In conclusion c both

F *Your turn!* Write an essay in 120–180 words entitled *You have to spend a lot of money to stay fit and healthy.*

Before	Note some arguments for and against. Choose a structure from **B** and organize your notes.
While	Write four paragraphs following the tips in *Write it right!* Try not to repeat any conjunctions. If you're writing on a computer, turn spell check off.
After	Ask a colleague to check spelling and formality or turn spell check on and see how many words you got wrong. Check conjunctions and punctuation before sending it to your teacher.

8 Small talk and smart phones

 Café

1 Before watching

A Match the get phrases to their meanings.

1 have a manicure
2 have a pedicure
3 permit someone a luxury
4 visit a barber / stylist
5 have your car serviced
6 complete a project
7 have a "2 for 1"

a get two things (done) for the price of one
b get something difficult done
c get your fingernails done
d get your hair done
e get a tune up
f get / be pampered (a spa day, a special dessert)

B 🔘 Make it personal Which of 1–7 in **A** have you done recently? How is / was your experience?

I got a pedicure done once. Never again! It really hurts.

I love being pampered. I get my nails done every week.

C Look at the photo. Guess five phrases from **A** you think you will hear.

2 While watching

A Watch up to 2:06 to check. What else did you pick up?

B Watch the video and complete 1–6 with the correct form of *get* or *get* + past participle. Watch again to check. Who said 1–6? What else did you hear?

1 You had to _____ that video _____.
2 It wasn't easy _____ all those martial arts shots.
3 This is heaven. I love _____ my nails _____.
4 I'm going to _____ my hair _____.
5 I should have _____ a tune-up long ago.
6 We never _____ to talk the other night!

C Watch the rest. How many voicemail messages are there? What good news does each of them get?

D Order the events 1–6. Watch again from 2:06 to check.
☐ Dr Moreno calls Zoey about her job application.
☐ Genevieve submitted a song for Daniel's TV show.
☐ Lucy changes her mind.
☐ Lucy says she doesn't want to ruin her nails.
☐ They all find out they got the jobs they applied for.
☐ Zoey and Genevieve listen to their messages.

E 🔘 Make it personal Do you still use voicemail? How often do you a) put off answering messages immediately? b) use flight mode? c) switch your phone off completely?

I sometimes put off difficult messages.

3 After watching

A True (T) or false (F)? Correct the false statements.
1 Lucy took Genevieve to a spa to thank her for her help.
2 Andrea and Paolo obviously don't like each other.
3 Zoey comes to the spa for a "two-for-one."
4 Genevieve put off getting a tune-up and got stranded at the mechanic's.
5 Zoey got a call about a job in the History department.
6 Lucy didn't want to answer her phone because she'd just gotten her nails done.

B Match 1–8 to their meanings a–h.
1 I owe you one.
2 They had on-camera chemistry.
3 That's putting it mildly.
4 It was a total disaster.
5 I should've gotten a tune-up.
6 I kept putting it off.
7 I ended up paying an arm and a leg.
8 It went from bad to worse.

a ☐ Everything went wrong.
b ☐ I delayed doing it.
c ☐ I spent too much money.
d ☐ It needed to be checked and fixed.
e ☐ It's not an exaggeration.
f ☐ They seem compatible on screen.
g ☐ It's my turn to help you.
h ☐ It started bad then became horrible.

C *Role-play.* In threes, create a "salon dialogue". Include at least two phrases from **1A** and **3B**. Role-play it for the class to spot which phrases you use.

Hi, Ale. What are you doing here?   *I'm getting my ...*

109

R4 Grammar and Vocabulary

A *Picture dictionary.* Cover the words and definitions on the pages below and remember.

pages	
87	8 phrasal verbs
88	5 common objects
89	4 reported speech stories
97	5 transportation words
99	7 photography words
102	6 party preparations
104	11 bedroom items
161	2 words for each sound in lines 3 and 4 of the consonants chart (not the picture words)

B In pairs, describe Sam Soccer's pre-match ritual. Which action is different? Why?

OK, so he has his uniform dry-cleaned before each match.

uniform / dry-clean

cleats / check

hair / cut and dye

photo / take

C *Role-play.* A: Interview Sam about his game day ritual. B: You're Sam. Be creative!

So, Sam. On game days, what time do you get up?

Well, for away games we normally sleep in a hotel. We get woken up at …

D ▶R4.1 Listen to the three tongue twisters. Which underlined ending is different? Listen again and practice saying the twisters.

1 a ask<u>ed</u>   b park<u>ed</u>   c start<u>ed</u>
2 a a<u>cc</u>use   b a<u>cc</u>ident   c e<u>x</u>cuses
3 a a<u>cc</u>elerate   b a<u>cc</u>ommodate   c e<u>x</u>periment

E ▶R4.2 Order the words in 1–7 to make sentences. Add the correct punctuation.
1 you / this / works / show / Can / how / me / phone / ?
2 you / this / stops / know / Do / where / bus / ?
3 I / if / tomorrow / it / will / wonder / rain
4 take / sugar / you / don't / milk / You / and / do / ?
5 forget / email / won't / will / You / to / you / send / that / ?
6 this / for / you / tell / me / Could / what / cable / is / ?
7 you / off / know / turn / Do / to / this / how / machine / ?

F In pairs, imagine what five pieces of news the people in photos 1 and 2 could have just received.

He might have gotten a message from an old girlfriend.

G In pairs, plan a surprise birthday party for a friend. Discuss what you need to do / have done and who is doing what.

Are we going to make a cake?

No, let's have one made.

H Correct the mistakes in each sentence. Check your answers in units 7 and 8. What's your score, 1–10?

Common mistakes

1 I asked to you don't turn on it. (3 mistakes)
2 Why you didn't say me hello? (2 mistakes)
3 Could you tell to me what does it say? (2 mistakes)
4 Do you know where is mall? (2 mistakes)
5 It depend of many things. (2 mistakes)
6 I don't know where is he. He might went to work. (2 mistakes)
7 I painted my nails at the salon. Don't they look great? (2 mistakes)
8 You should to cut on down screen time. (2 mistakes)
9 He likes more the cars than the motorbikes. (2 mistakes)
10 "I prefer rock than pop." "Really? I don't like both." (2 mistakes)

Skills practice

A Quickly reread the Photoshop text on p. 98. Then listen to ▶8.1, pausing every 12 seconds to write down the last five words you hear. Then reread to check.

B ▶R4.3 Listen to five extracts from ⓓ 3 and count the words in each. Contractions count as one word.

C ▶R4.3 Listen again and write the full extract. Check in pairs. Which words are hardest to understand?

D List eight electronic items you own. Order them from the most to the least important. In pairs, compare and explain.

> *I couldn't live without my refrigerator. It's too hot here not to have cold drinks.*

E In pairs, think of three things each person could be saying. Share the funniest with the class.

"I told you …"   "I thought you said …"

F Read the article opposite. True (T), false (F), or not mentioned (N)? Have you had a bad experience with builders?
1. Emreth installed the new items himself.
2. The bathroom cost more than he expected.
3. Emreth owns this small apartment.
4. Both the bath and the shower were dangerous.
5. When the bath fell it nearly killed Emreth.
6. Workers at WallsUp blame Emreth.
7. All the characters in the story are male.

G 🔘 Make it personal **Getting things done?**
Choose three verbs and write questions about the services people use. Ask four classmates and report the results.

clean	check	cut	(re)decorate
deliver	do	dye	iron	repair
renovate	service	test

> *When was the last time you had your eyes tested?*

> *She said she'd had them tested a month ago because she couldn't see the TV!*

♪ *I wonder, when I sing along with you, if everything could ever feel this real forever, if anything could ever be this good again.*

R4

H **Role-play.** Using smart phones
A: Imagine you're a Martian and have no idea what a smart phone is.
B: Explain three functions to the Martian. Then change roles.

> *Hello, human. What's that in your hand?*

I ▶R4.4 🔘 Make it personal **Question time!**
In pairs, listen to the 12 lesson titles in units 7 and 8. Pause after each one and guess what your partner's answer will be. Correct each other's wrong guesses. Any surprises?

> *Does technology rule your life?*

> *I think you'll answer, "No, I actually love technology."*

> *You're right! And your answer will be …*

Expensive bath

An L.A. **home**owner has learned the hard way that you have to be careful when you get home reno**va**tions done. Emreth Jones, 42, paid $15,000 for a new bathroom, and another $10,000 to fix the mistakes after a building ins**pec**tion. "It's terrible," he said. "I wanted to get a new bath and shower put in upstairs. I thought it would be simple."

The building ins**pec**tor noticed that the workers had seriously **weak**ened the floor when they installed the bath and shower.

"The bath might have come through the floor at any moment," said Jones. "If it had hit me, that would have been it."

The manager of WallsUp declined to comment, although an employee claimed it was Jones' fault.

"He asked us if we could do it cheaply. And he didn't tell us he would get an inspection."

111

9

9.1 Does crime worry you?

1 Vocabulary Crime and violence

A ▶9.1 Quickly match the text types to extracts 1–6. Then listen and read to check. Which type do you read the most?

I'm always tweeting.

☐ a tweet
☐ a discussion forum for students of English
☐ a newspaper article
☐ a discussion forum for travelers

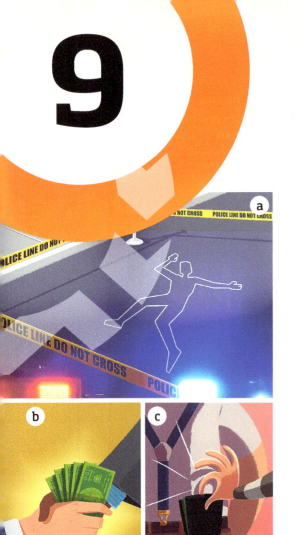

1. I spent four days in São Paulo. Lots of locals told me to be careful. I was, and it was cool. I heard a few crime stories, from credit card fraud to kidnapping. Maybe they're exaggerating. Anyway, enjoy your stay there. The food and nightlife are amazing!

2. Organized crime in Chicago has seen a fall. Statistics released recently show a 20% decrease in burglaries between June 2017 and 2018.

3. **Murder of millionaire shocks Jacksonville. Ex-husband main suspect.**

4. Got stopped for speeding. Actually thought about offering the cop $100, but remembered bribery is also a crime. Must slow down in future. #stupid
← Reply ⇄ Retweet ★ Favorite

5. 89-YEAR-OLD BOXING GRANDMA SENT TO PRISON FOR DOMESTIC ABUSE AND DRUG DEALING.

6. OK, I think I can help you. Theft is a noun, and it is when someone takes something from you without you knowing. So, for example, if you were walking down the street and I ran by and stole your purse, that would be theft. So, in a way, tax evasion and music piracy are forms of theft, too. Robbery is a noun, too, but that's different: it usually involves violence or fear. Steal is a verb. Someone steals something from you. Hope that helps! 😊

☐ a newspaper headline   ☐ a headline from a satirical news website

B ▶9.2 Match the highlighted words to pictures a–g. Listen to check.

C Complete 1–4 with other crimes from the texts. Then, in pairs, mime a noun from **B** or **C** for your partner to say it.

1 credit card f_____   3 tax e_____
2 domestic a_____   4 music p_____

Ha ha. That brilliant! A burglary.

D Complete 1–4 with the words below. There are two extra.

> burglary   robbery   robs   steal   stealing   thefts

1 There was an armed _____ at the gas station last night. Three men threatened the staff with guns and stole $6,000 in cash.
2 Unfortunately, we have had several _____ of personal property in the building recently.
3 They were so poor, they had to _____ food in order to feed themselves.
4 Many people install alarms to protect their houses against _____.

E 🎙 **Make it personal** Choose the three most and least serious crimes in **B** and **C**. In groups, compare your lists. Can you reach a consensus?

> *To me, credit-card fraud is the least serious crime.*

> *Well, it depends on the amount of money you steal, doesn't it?*

🎵 *Everybody wanna steal my girl*
Everybody wanna take her heart away,
Couple billion in the whole wide world,
Find another one 'cos she belongs to me.

9.1

⏱ Common mistakes

> *stealing*
> I saw you ~~robbing~~ my wallet!
>
> *stolen*
> Help! My cell phone was ~~robbed~~!
>
> *robbed*
> Have you ever been ~~stolen~~?
>
> *robbed*
> What? Your grandmother ~~stole~~ a bank?

② Listening

A ▶9.3 Listen and match short interviews 1–5 to the questions. There's one extra question.

Which of the crimes listed

☐ do you worry about the most?
☐ do you worry about the least?
☐ have / has affected someone you know?

☐ will probably increase in the next 10 years?
☐ would you like to eradicate for ever?
☐ shouldn't be considered a crime?

B ▶9.3 Listen again. True (T) or false (F)? Correct the false ones. Who do you empathize with?

1 He doesn't think people should pay for digital content.
2 People saw a robber in his neighborhood last year.
3 A middle-aged man broke into her neighbor's house.
4 The government is introducing new laws next year.
5 She has taught her kids to yell if a stranger approaches them.

> *Certainly not the first guy. I produce digital material myself!*

③ Grammar   Review of verb families

A Match the examples in 1–4 to the forms below, and name the four tenses. Then add a past example to each category, 1–4.

> English verbs fall into four categories:
> 1 Simple (states, habits, single actions): *I **study** English.*
> 2 Continuous (progress): *I **am studying** English.*
> 3 Perfect (links a point in time with a previous action): *I **have studied** English.*
> 4 Perfect continuous (progress before a point in time): *I **have been studying** English.*
>
> Knowing how each one works can help you make different past, present, and future verb combinations more easily.
>
> → **Grammar 9A** p. 154

> *Example 1 is in the ... tense.*

> *A past example for aspect 1 could be "I didn't study English at school."*

☐ S + *be* + *-ing*   ☐ S + *have* + *been* + *-ing*   ☐ S + *have* + past participle   ☐ S + *verb*

B Name the tense in audio extracts 1–4. Order them from easiest to hardest for you.

1 I've lived in this neighborhood for, what, two years …
2 You're simply downloading a song!
3 What has the government been doing to change things?
4 I don't see any way out.

C 🎙 **Make it personal** Use the survey in **2A** to interview two classmates. What are the most common answers?

> *Most students, four out of five actually, think credit-card fraud has increased.*

> *The crime everybody I asked would eliminate forever is …*

113

9.2 How could your city be improved?

1 Reading

I believe it's the second biggest city in Colombia.

A ▶9.4 In pairs, brainstorm what you know about Medellín. Listen and read the introduction. Then cover it. What can you remember?

Medellín Reinvented

Twenty years ago, if someone had said they were going on vacation to Medellín, Colombia, you'd have called them crazy. *Time* magazine once called it "the most dangerous city on earth." Civilized society had been destroyed, drug cartels ruled, and violence was part of everyday life. Fast-forward to the present and things couldn't be more different. Medellín is a city with plenty to celebrate and is fast becoming a hot destination! But why? Well, here are five things that I believe have brought a dramatic change to this fascinating city.

Maybe this cable car has made traveling much safer?

B ▶9.4 In pairs, look only at the photos and captions in the rest of the article to guess how each feature has helped reinvent Medellín. Then listen, read, and check. Were your guesses correct?

Public transportation

The public transportation network can take some credit for bringing peace to the city. MetroCable, the network of cable cars, connects poor and middle-class Medellín, both literally and symbolically, and this helped to reduce urban violence. Also, until 2011, the residents of Comuna 13, one of Medellín's poorest neighborhoods, had to climb 500 steps to get home. The commute has been reduced to five minutes thanks to outdoor escalators. These escalators gave people a sense of dignity and pride, which I think also had an impact on crime.

MetroCable

Innovation

Another reason I was impressed by Medellín is its urban development. It won the prestigious Lee Kuan Yew World City Prize award in 2016. This award is known as a kind of "Nobel Prize" for urbanism. It recognizes Medellín's transformation into a model of sustainable urban innovation. As well as the famous escalators and cable cars, Medellín's art galleries and public spaces were praised.

Art in Botero Square

Street art murals in Comuna 13

The arts

Medellín's art scene is also flourishing. Renowned artist Fernando Botero was born here and donated lots of his distinctive art to his home city. This also brings tourists to the area. Back in Comuna 13, previously the most notorious area, fantastic street art can be found. Local residents act as tour guides, giving them work and pride in their neighborhood. They explain with passion the personal stories told by the colorful murals. The tour really gave me an understanding of the history and transformation of Medellín.

Nature

Colombia is second only to Brazil for its biodiversity. It is home to 10% of the world's species! Protected areas are being expanded all the time. Some of these areas are accessible by MetroCable, including Arvi Park, where you escape urban life by walking, biking, and horse-back riding.

Arvi Park

Flower Festival

The "City of Eternal Spring"

Colombia is one of the world's biggest flower exporters, and billions of dollars' worth of flowers are exported every year. Medellín is in bloom all year round. The weather is a perfect 22–23 degrees Celsius whatever the season, and there are flowers everywhere you look all year round: on balconies, terraces, gardens, and parks. Thousands of tourists visit during "Feria de las Flores," and it was one of the most joyful and creative things I've ever seen. The festival will definitely be put on my list of favorite things to do in Latin America.

C **Reread and answer 1–5. Practice the pink-stressed words.**

1 How has public transportation helped to reduce crime in Medellín?
2 How does the flower festival help the economy?
3 Why was Medellín awarded the Lee Kuan Yew World City Prize?
4 How do the street art tours help visitors learn about the city?
5 How is Medellín protecting its biodiversity?

♫ *Sweet dreams are made of this, who am I to disagree? I travel the world and the seven seas ...*

9.2

D 🔘 Make it personal **In small groups, discuss 1–4. Any disagreements?**

For me, it was because the violence ended.

1 Which things do you think best explain Medellín's transformation?
2 Have any of the things in the article happened in your city?
3 Which other improvements could make your city better?
4 What would you put on your list list of favorite things to do in Latin America?

② Grammar Passive voice

A **Study the underlined phrases in 1C. Then read the grammar box and circle the correct alternative in rules 1–3. Is the form similar in your language?**

> Use the passive voice when the "doer" of a verb is unknown, unimportant, or obvious. It is often used to move important information to the front of a sentence.
> 1 The passive voice is formed with *have* / *be* + the **simple past** / **past participle**.
> 2 The verb *be* can go in **the present or past** / **any tense or form**.
> 3 *For* / *By* is used to show who did the action.
>
> → **Grammar 9B** p. 154

🕐 **Common mistakes**

Roses, carnations, and orchids
are ~~growing~~ in Colombia.
   grown

                    ignored by
This story has been ~~ignoring for~~
the press.

B **Complete the tweets about the article with these forms. There's one extra. Which are relevant where you live? In pairs, add a tweet of your own.**

will be	are being	can't have been	has been	should be	to be

@PedroH: Outdoor escalators! Wonderful idea. I really think they ¹_____ adopted as a model for lots of other cities!

@grumpyoldman: Places really can change! It's incredible how much crime ²_____ reduced because of things like this!

@donnamaria: It's amazing how the arts can help. Two new art galleries ³_____ built right now. Kids need art in their lives. #arttherapy

More natural areas need ⁴_____ protected. If Medellín keeps improving, the tourist industry will take over.

Honestly? I doubt these changes ⁵_____ sustained. These things take too much time and money.

C ▶9.5 **Complete the quotes about cities with the verbs in parentheses. Listen to check. In groups, choose your favorite. Which is the most popular?**

Our favorite quote is ... because ...

1 Buildings do not make a city. A city _____ (make) by the people who live there.
2 Cities are places where money _____ (make), but life _____ (lose).
3 By its nature, a city provides what otherwise _____ (could / give) only by traveling.
4 Villages and towns _____ (swallow up) by cities. Soon there will be no countryside at all.
5 The way you view the future _____ (change) by living in any big city.

D **Look at 2B on p. 113. Say 1–5 in the passive voice.**

Who's your favorite device made by?

E 🔘 Make it personal *Passive Favorites!* **In pairs, ask and answer full passive voice questions about your favorites in each square. Any coincidences?**

It's made by Samsung. It's my phone.

movie	dish	goal	perfume
directed by	made of	scored by	produced by
city	**device**	**celebrity**	**clothes**
invaded by	made by	married to	designed by
book	**song**	**car**	**drink**
written by	sung by	built by	made of

★ ★ ★ ★ ★ ★ ★ ★ ★ ★ ★ ★

115

9.3 Have you ever been to court?

POP CRIME?

Back in July, 22-year-old Chicago student Michael Lewis was driving home very late from a friend's house. He was listening to loud music in his car. Oh, with his windows down, naturally. The neighbors weren't happy, of course, and they called the police. Michael was **sent to jail** for the night, but was **released** the next day—free as a bird to terrorize the neighborhood again! A week later, more loud music at 2 a.m. This time, Michael was **charged with** disorderly conduct and **taken to court**, but there was no evidence against him, so Michael was **acquitted**. Free as a bird, again. Third week, more loud music. Trouble is, there was a police car patrolling the neighborhood. So Michael had to face the judge again, but this time things got serious: Michael was **convicted**. He was **sentenced to** three days in jail and had to pay a $1,000 **fine**. But, for some reason, the judge decided to give him an alternative. The judge asked Michael what his least favorite kind of music was. It turns out that Michael was not a fan of classical music. The judge's alternative was to listen to classical music for thirty hours. Easy choice, right? Not for Michael. After twenty minutes of Mozart and Beethoven, he chose the original punishment.

1 Vocabulary Crime and punishment

A In pairs, imagine the story in the pictures. Then read to check. Were you close?

> A guy was leaning on his car at night listening to loud music …

B ▶ 9.6 Match the **highlighted** words and phrases to the pictures. Listen to a dramatized version of the text to check. What kind of music would be a punishment for you?

> I'd hate to be forced to listen to …

C 🧑 Make it personal In pairs, use only the pictures to remember Michael's story. Take turns describing each scene.

2 Listening

A ▶ 9.7 In pairs, look at the punishments and guess the crimes. Listen to check.

B ▶ 9.7 Listen again and match the phrases to 1 and 2. Fair punishments?

- ☐ charged with
- ☐ sentenced to
- ☐ taken to court
- ☐ ordered to pay
- ☐ sent to jail
- ☐ released

116

C Complete extracts 1–11 with these prepositions. Then check in ▶9.7 on p. 173. How do you try to learn prepositions?

🎵 *Breaking rocks in the hot sun.*
I fought the law and the law won.

9.3

at	from	in (x2)	on	to (x4)	under	with

1 Thirty-two-year-old Shena Hardin was caught _____ camera driving on a sidewalk.
2 The judge sentenced her _____ an embarrassing punishment.
3 She was told to stand _____ a busy intersection.
4 Just to add _____ her humiliation ... she was ordered to pay $250 _____ court costs.
5 It was an ordinary morning _____ San Francisco's District Court.
6 Bring it _____ me now.
7 All 42 people present were charged _____ disturbing the peace.
8 All 42 people present were sent _____ jail.
9 The judge was permanently removed _____ office.
10 He said he had been _____ a lot of stress.

> *I memorize a personal example:*
> I work **in** Quito, **in** Bellavista, **on** Av. 6 September **at** number 347.

⚡ **Common mistakes**

of / about   *in*
Think ~~in~~ me when I'm ~~to~~ jail.

D 🔴 **Make it personal** 🔊 In pairs, search online for a crime story in the news. Figure out how to summarize it in simple English. Then tell the class.

> *A woman was caught on camera pushing someone else's car out of a parking space with her car so she could park there. She damaged the car and was charged with reckless driving!*

③ Pronunciation -ed

A ▶9.8 Listen how -ed links to vowels and consonants. Is the -ed sound clear or does it link? Listen again and repeat.

-ed = /ɪd/	clear	links
1 ... be arrested unless I get that phone now!		
2 ... decided to give him an alternative.		
-ed = /t/		
3 ... were released, of course.		
4 ... be sentenced to a week in jail.		
-ed = /d/		
5 ... no one confessed at all.		
6 ... was permanently removed from office.		

> **Remember:** The pronunciation of -ed depends on the last sound (not spelling) in a regular verb.
> - /d/ after a voiced consonant – lived /lɪvd/
> - /d/ after a vowel sound – studied /stʌdiːd/
> - /t/ after an unvoiced consonant – liked /laɪkt/
> - /ɪd/ after /t/ or /d/ – wanted /wɒntɪd/

B ▶9.9 *Celebrity gossip!* Write full sentences for 1–5. Listen to check. Do you know any similar stories?

1 Justin Bieber / arrest and release / bail for $2,500 / driving dangerously
2 Axl Rose / order / pay a huge fine after biting a man's leg
3 Lindsay Lohan / sentence / 10 days' community service
4 Michelle Rodriguez / send / jail / 18 days
5 Lauren Hill / confess and serve / three months in jail / tax evasion

> *Wasn't Josh Brolin arrested for fighting back in 2013?*

C 🔴 **Make it personal** In groups, decide on the right punishment for each crime. Do you all agree?

> **Man arrested for burglary after breaking into house to use bathroom**

> **Teen charged with kidnapping after taking girlfriend on surprise trip**

⚡ **Common mistake**

I think he should ~~to~~ do 100 hours' community service.

> **Elderly woman faces robbery charge after trying to rob a bank with a banana**

> **20-year-old hacks into college computers and changes own grades**

> *We've agreed the bank robber should be sentenced to at least five years.*

> *No, that's not fair. I mean, what if she dies in prison?*

9.4 Where will you be living ten years from now?

"You borrowed $27,000 over the years to study computer sciences. According to our files, you now owe us $1.83."

1 Listening

A ▶9.10 In pairs, look at the cartoon and answer 1–4. Then listen to part one of a radio show to check your answer to question 4. Were you right?
1. Who / Where are the cartoon characters?
2. Guess what happened to the man's debt.
3. What do you imagine will happen next?
4. Will cybercrime get better or worse in the future?

Hmm ... I don't know. It might've been a mistake.

B ▶9.10 Listen again and complete 1 and 2 with numbers.
1. The radio show host gives _____ examples of cybercrime.
2. He says it will be the world's biggest problem some time before _____.

C ▶9.11 Listen to part two. How worried is Deniz Kaya?

D ▶9.12 Using the photos, think of three reasons why cybercrime will get worse. Listen to part three to check. Any correct guesses?

Common mistake

~~By~~
~~Until~~ 2040 I'll be retired.

E ▶9.12 Listen again. True (T), false (F), or not mentioned (N)?
1. Deniz says some hackers are teenagers.
2. The Facebook Messenger virus starts when you watch a video.
3. It was created by Facebook.
4. Future e-devices won't need protection.
5. Cybercriminals often hack computers for fun.
6. Currently, 20 percent of all phones are under attack.

F Match the highlighted words to the definitions.
1. By 2025, cyber attacks will have become the world's top **threat**.
2. He'll be telling us if we should take these **warnings** seriously.
3. Cybercriminals will be **carrying out** attacks wirelessly, and we won't be protected.
4. They will have developed the ability to **spread** viruses across multiple devices very, very easily.
5. Cybercriminals will have **targeted** 20 percent of all the world's smart phones.

☐ to perform, conduct
☐ to try to attack someone or something
☐ to affect more items / to increase / to develop fast
☐ a person or thing that could cause serious problems
☐ messages that tells us about a possible danger

G 🔊 **Make it personal** In pairs, have you ever had a major cyber problem? How do you protect yourself from cyber attacks? Any novel ideas? Who's more careful?

A year ago, I lost all my data. The worst part was losing my photos.

I try to create really difficult passwords.

H ▶9.13 Listen to part four and Deniz's advice on how to protect yourself. Did he mention any of your ideas?

We'll be raising our hands, shining up to the sky
'Cause we got the fire, fire, fire,
yeah we got the fire, fire, fire.

9.4

2 Grammar Future perfect and continuous

A Reread 1–5 in **1F** and complete the rules in the grammar box with these words.

| be | have | continuous | perfect |

Use the future ¹_____ for an action completed before a point in the future.
Form: will / won't + ²_____ + past participle

Use the future ³_____ for an activity in progress at a point in the future.
Form: will / won't + ⁴_____ + -ing verb

→ Grammar 9C p. 154

B Complete 1–5 with the *future perfect* or *continuous*. What will you be doing in ten years?

FIVE CAREERS FOR 2030

PRIVACY MANAGER: If you think you've lost some of your privacy, get ready. By 2030, you ¹_____ most of it. (lose)

NANO MEDICS: Good news! In the next few years, you ²_____ nanotechnology to treat most of your health problems. (use)

BOOK-TO-APP CONVERTERS: In five years, you ³_____ paper books. Everybody will use an e-device. Just wait and see. (not read)

3D PRINTING ENGINEERS: By the end of the decade, the demand for 3D printing ⁴_____. (double)

TURBINE SPECIALIST: We ⁵_____ using electricity, but we will be getting more from green sources such as wind turbines, which need a lot of maintenance. (not stop)

> I won't be working in ten years. I'll have retired.

Common mistakes

I will graduate from college by 2022. *in*

When we celebrate our next anniversary, we will be married for 50 years. *have been*

I'll be studying this weekend while everyone else will be relaxing. *is*

C Match 1–5 to photos a–e. Write full sentences in the *future perfect* or *continuous*.

The Optimist's Guide to the Next 20 Years
1. ☐ soon / most people / work from home
2. ☐ we / stop / global warming / by 2040
3. ☐ scientists / discover / a cure for the common cold / by 2040
4. ☐ in next few years / most people / drive / electric cars
5. ☐ by / end / decade / all public places / install / free Wi-Fi

a
b
c
d
e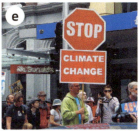

D 🟢 **Make it personal** In pairs, use the photos in **C** and the phrases below to make predictions.

I'm pretty sure (that) …   It's possible (that) …   I doubt (that) …

> It's possible that we'll all be driving electric cars by 2030.

> Really? I doubt that very much. I think lots of people will have stopped driving completely.

9.5 Do you watch TV crime dramas?

ID Skills Identifying sarcasm

A Quickly read the article and match 1–4 to the crimes in **1B** and **1C** on p. 112.

CRIME DOESN'T PAY. ESPECIALLY IF YOU'RE A DUMB CRIMINAL.

1 24-year-old Harry Zimmerman walked into the local convenience store with a gun and told the cashier to put all the money in a bag. On his way out, Zimmerman saw a bottle of Scotch behind the <u>coun</u>ter and told the cashier to put it in the bag, too, which the woman re<u>fused</u> to do because she suspected he might be under 21. So, <u>to prove his age</u>, Zimmerman, <u>a man of prin<u>ciples</u>, showed her his driver's license, took the bottle, and ran away. A few minutes later …

2 Forget "the dog ate my homework." Today's kids have <u>infinitely better ideas</u>. Like 22-year-old Brazilian student Susan Correia, for example, who was charged with reporting a false crime. One day, Susan called her mother in tears and told her that she'd just managed to escape from an old de<u>ser</u>ted house, where three armed men had held her <u>cap</u>tive for a whole day. <u>In de<u>spair</u>, her mother called the police</u>, who soon discovered that Susan had actually spent the day at a friend's house. At the police station, Susan admitted that …

3 Rashia Wilson of Tampa, Florida, was sentenced to 22 years in prison for buying a $70,000 sports car and giving her one-year-old son <u>a relatively ine<u>xpen</u>sive</u> $40,000 birthday party—you know, <u>just like the ones your parents used to throw</u>. Unfortunately, the self-pro<u>claimed</u> queen of fraud (yes, that's what she called herself – <u>subtle, huh?</u>) took lots of photographs revealing how she'd been using <u>tax</u>payers' money and, believe it or not …

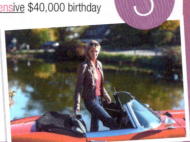

4 Today's <u>ultra-smart criminals</u> come from Iowa. Police had an easy time finding wanted criminals Joey Miller and Matthew McNelly. Before breaking into an apartment, these <u>masters of dis<u>guise</u></u> decided to hide their real identities. How did they do this? Well, <u>they covered their faces in permanent marker pen</u>. The thing about permanent marker pen is that … <u>it's permanent</u>.

B ▶ 9.14 In pairs, match the titles to stories 1–4 in **A**. Predict how they end. Listen to check. Did you guess them all?

☐ How to make your mark   ☐ Nope, it never happened
☐ Old enough to break the law ☐ Social media mistake

First one … Well, let's see. Maybe he left his driver's license at the store and went back to get it?

C Read the information. Then mark the underlined items in **A** sarcastic (S) or not sarcastic (N). Is sarcasm common in your community?

Well, my friends and I are sarcastic with each other. A lot!

De<u>tec</u>ting <u>sar</u>casm in writing, without intonation or facial expressions, isn't easy. Here are four tips:
• If a sentence looks sar<u>cas</u>tic, read it out loud. You might "hear" the sarcasm.
• Ask yourself, "Does it make sense in this context?" *"Thanks, American Air, for losing my bags again this year!"* is a clear example of sarcasm.
• Look for examples of exaggeration: *"Aren't you the greatest cook in the world?"*
• Consider the style. Informal writing usually contains more sarcasm.

Yeah, but when people don't understand you're joking, they can get upset.

D 🔘 Make it personal In pairs, answer 1–4. Any surprises?
1 In your opinion, who was the dumbest criminal?
2 What punishments should the people in **A** receive?
3 Have you ever committed a small crime?
4 What would you do if you were Susan's mom or dad?

I think all of them were pretty stupid, but the guy who showed his ID was the worst.

Are you good at making excuses?

9.5

 in Action Giving excuses

A In pairs, imagine the story behind the five headlines. Then change partners. Were any of your ideas the same?

> Maybe they thought the mayor was corrupt and wanted to access his computer to prove it?

- ☐ ARMED GANG BREAKS INTO MAYOR'S HOUSE
- ☐ BURGLAR FALLS ASLEEP IN VICTIMS' BED
- ☐ TERROR THREAT ON FLIGHT 207
- ☐ 70-YEAR-OLD ARRESTED FOR FLYING WITH SNAKE
- ☐ 14-YEAR-OLD DRIVER SCARES JACKSONVILLE

B ▶9.15 Listen and match the headlines to dialogues 1–3. There are two extra headlines.

Common mistake
say / tell them
He will ~~tell~~ he's sorry.

C ▶9.16 Guess each person's excuse. Listen to the dialogue endings to check. Were the excuses believed? Were any of the stories similar to yours in **A**?

> I think the burglar is going to say he entered the wrong house.

D ▶9.17 Complete 1–5. Listen, check, and repeat, copying the stress and intonation.

1	This is not what it looks _____.	4	It's not what it _____.
2	Just _____ me out, please!	5	_____, I can explain.
3	It's not what you're _____.		

E **Make it personal** *Not guilty!*
1 Brainstorm what's happening in each photo, and why. Which other people might be in each situation?
2 In pairs, choose and role-play a photo.

> Hey, what do you think you're doing?

> Just a minute! This is not what it looks like. I was just …

♪ I don't wanna close my eyes, I don't wanna fall asleep,
Cause I'd miss you, baby, And I don't wanna miss a thing.

Writing 9   A formal letter

♪ *Don't it always seem to go,*
That you don't know what you've got till it's gone;
They paved paradise,
And put up a parking lot.

A Read the headline from a local newspaper article and the letter written in response to it. Answer 1–4.

White Rose Park Set for Closure!
Town council seeking to sell land to construction company

1 Who's Melissa writing to?
2 Why's she writing and how does she feel?
3 Find six reasons she thinks it's a bad idea.
4 What are her two suggestions?
5 Who does she want to make contact with?
6 How does her home and place of work connect to the project?

Melissa Gil
23a White Rose Lane
Grangetown
melgil@electromail.com
202-555-0152

The Editor
The Evening Post
Mill Lane
Grangetown

Dear Editor,

Re: White Rose Park Set for Closure

1 I'm writing to you ¹_____ express my huge disappointment after reading your article.. The whole community must be saddened to hear about the possible closure of White Rose Park. What is the town council thinking? How can they close one of the few safe play spaces ²_____ the area simply in order to make quick, easy money by selling the land?

2 Closing the park would affect the entire community. White Rose Park has been used for sports and recreation by local children and families for generations. In the summer, it is used to host concerts and the very popular annual folk festival.

3 People are always complaining that children have far too much screen time. How are they supposed to spend time outdoors if there is nowhere to go? What will the younger members of our community be doing ³_____ five years' time with no safe space to play? My little nephew will be extremely sad when he hears about this.

4 Perhaps local residents could set up a charity organization to raise funds to maintain the park. We could also start a petition and get as many people as possible to sign it. We can then present this ⁴_____ the town council.

5 I'd be very interested to hear ⁵_____ other people who are interested in getting involved to help save the park.

Yours faithfully,

Melissa Gil
Melissa Gil
Second grade teacher, White Rose Elementary School

B Complete 1–5 in her letter with the prepositions.

| from | in (x2) | to | with |

C In which paragraph, 1–5, does Melissa:
- ☐ suggest possible solutions/ideas?
- ☐ ☐ describe her opinion on the news story and express her feelings with examples?
- ☐ request contact from other readers?
- ☐ refer to the news story and explain why she is writing?

D Read *Write it right!* Then find three style errors in the letter.

✓ **Write it right!**

When writing a formal letter to a newspaper:
- put your full name, address, phone number, and email address at the top of the letter.
- refer to the article you are writing about with the headline and date of publication.
- keep your letter short and to the point. Make sure it only contains relevant information.
- use a formal style, no contractions, etc.
- you can ask questions or make suggestions.
- end the letter in an appropriate way.

E 🎤 **Make it personal**   In pairs, read the headlines from a local newspaper. Brainstorm possible solutions and ideas for each story.

> Language center to close all evening and mid-week English classes. Now weekends only!

> Historical buildings to be demolished to construct downtown highway.

> Train and bus prices to double!

> No more nightlife! All venues must close at midnight, even on weekends!

F *Your turn!* Choose a headline from **E** (or one from a real local newspaper) and write a "letter to the editor". Write 120–180 words.

Before	Note ideas for your letter.
While	Follow the tips in **C** and the tips in *Write it right!*
After	Share with a partner to check formality, spelling, and punctuation, then send it to your teacher.

9 A knight at the museum

1 Before watching

A 🔵 **Make it personal** Which of these have you visited? List three items you'd expect to find in each. What's the most interesting exhibit you've ever seen?
1 an art gallery
2 a natural history museum
3 a planetarium

I loved the recent Da Vinci exhibit. It was awesome!

B In which of 1–3 in **A** would you expect to find an exhibit on the items below?

☐ armor ☐ gemstones
☐ black holes ☐ mammals
☐ bones ☐ mummies
☐ dinosaurs ☐ sculptures
☐ fossils

C Use the photo, lesson title and the information in **A** and **B** to guess where August and Rory are. What are they saying? Who do they meet? What might happen next?

Maybe they're … waiting to meet …

2 While watching

A Watch and check all you hear.
1 ☐ It's museum week and August was given two free tickets.
2 ☐ Rory has never been to the museum before.
3 ☐ Genevieve is not bringing anyone with her.
4 ☐ Rory has always been fascinated by dinosaurs.
5 ☐ Rory was given a tour of the museum.
6 ☐ Genevieve says mummies are "kind of creepy."
7 ☐ August's text to Zoey didn't reach her.
8 ☐ Zoey got lost and was rescued by Paolo.
9 ☐ Today is the last day the film on black holes will be shown.
10 ☐ Paolo works in the museum.

B Watch again and complete 1–6 with the *passive voice*. What else did you hear this time?
1 Rory   Well, I _____ always _____ by dinosaurs as a kid.
2 August   You know where all the different bears and mountain lion exhibits _____ _____.
3 August   Mummies! These mummies _____ recently _____ in …
4 August   Since you're a biologist and your studies _____ _____ on animals.
5 August   Next thing I knew she _____ _____ in the crowd.
6 Genevieve   She says when she came back, August _____ _____. And she _____ _____ a tour of the museum by Paolo!

3 After watching

A Answer questions 1–7.
1 What had Genevieve done before she got to the museum?
2 Whose studies were focused on mammals and biology?
3 Who was Zoey with after she got lost?
4 Who is "kind of like a knight in shining armor"?
5 Where else has August seen Paolo, and how does he feel about him?
6 What did August do to try to find Zoey?
7 In which exhibit room did August get distracted?
8 Why does Rory think Paolo might be wearing armor?

B Match the phrases 1–6 to the functions. Can you remember how each phrase ends and who said it?

Describing an experience	Making a suggestion
☐ ☐ ☐	☐ ☐ ☐

1 It's my first time at …
2 I was fascinated by …
3 Let's go see …
4 One minute I was … and the next …
5 Maybe we should …
6 Do you want to go see an exhibit on …?

C *Role-play.* In pairs, imagine you're art critics at a museum. Show each other photos from your phones or from this book and comment on them.

This is an amazing photo. The light and colors are really impressive.

Yes, and the composition is perfect, too. A work of genius!

123

10

10.1 What drives you crazy?

1 Vocabulary Moods

A ▶10.1 Read and match the **highlighted** words to photos a–h. Listen to check.

What is your temperament?

Cool as a cucumber, occasionally moody, or chronically short-tempered?

1	Do you ever wake up feeling grumpy?	Y | N
2	Do you have nervous habits, like biting your nails or scratching yourself?	Y | N
3	Do you ever get fed up with activities and people you actually like?	Y | N
4	Do you ever get annoyed by people who are constantly in a good mood?	Y | N
5	Do you ever swear when other drivers do something stupid?	Y | N
6	Do you sometimes go from smiling to crying to singing in a matter of hours?	Y | N
7	Do you ever yell at people for no serious reason?	Y | N
8	Do you ever have to count to ten and take a deep breath, or else you'll explode?	Y | N

CALCULATE YOUR SCORE

For each *Yes* answer, give yourself the same number of points as the question number, e.g., 1 point for a yes in question 1, 3 points for question 3, and so on.

27–36: Hey, calm down! Being this explosive can be bad for you!

18–26: You're temperamental, but not dangerous. Learn to recognize your anger and relax.

9–17: You have your moments of madness, but, in general, you're pretty easygoing. Well done!

0–8: You're the king / queen of cool. Nothing can upset you. Or … Are you simply hiding your true self?

B ▶10.2 Listen, read, and take the quiz. Calculate your score and read what it means. Do you agree?

I'm not convinced it's all true. I don't think that "nothing can upset me"!

C Match 1–4 to a **highlighted** word from **A**. Then write another example for your partner to match to the word.
1 "Keep your voice down. Do you want the whole building to hear you?"
2 "I love that you are always so happy. Nothing ever gets you down!"
3 "She was very calm and relaxed before her interview."
4 "Be careful, the tiniest little thing can make the boss angry."

Common mistakes

mood
My boss was in a bad ~~humor~~ again.
She has no sense of humor.

argue / fight
We respect each other and never ~~discuss~~.

D **Make it personal** Go back to your quiz answers. In pairs, ask follow-up questions to find out who is moodier? Any surprises?

♪ You're hot then you're cold, you're yes then you're no, you're in and you're out, you're up and you're down.

10.1

> You mean you're never grumpy? What's your secret?

> Life is short, and I'm just happy to be alive!

2 Listening

A ▶10.3 Listen to a couple talking about the quiz. Which three answers do they disagree on?

B ▶10.3 Listen again. True (T) or false (F)? Do they remind you of anybody?
1 Carlos thinks Gloria is short-tempered.
2 Gloria is thinking of taking yoga classes.
3 She used to like her job.
4 She finds her job repetitive.
5 She's looking for a new job.
6 Carlos has seen Gloria swear at other drivers.

> Carlos reminds me of my brother. A bit grumpy!

3 Vocabulary Binomials

A ▶10.4 Binomials are pairs of words connected by a conjunction or (e.g. *loud and clear*) a preposition (e.g. *step by step*). Try to complete 1–6, then listen to check. Are 1–6 true for you? Know any others?

1 I have my ups and _____, but I'm pretty stable.
2 Little by _____, I'm learning how to relax.
3 I'm sick and _____ of waking up early.
4 I need some peace and _____ in the morning.
5 I hate doing the same things again and _____.
6 Sooner or _____, I'll need to start looking for a new job.

> Not me. I'm much more emotional than that.

B Work in pairs. Take turns to say part of a binomial for your partner to complete.

> Peace and …   … quiet. Sooner or …   … later. More or …   … less. Again and …

C **Make it personal** Which of these items affect your mood the most? Choose your top three, and then share ideas in groups. What's the most influential factor?
- what you eat
- the weather
- exercise
- the time of day
- the day of the week
- the season
- other people's moods
- the news
- your workload

> I definitely have my ups and downs, but I'm usually in a better mood in winter, when it's cooler.

125

10.2 What do you love to hate?

1 Grammar Gerunds and infinitives

A Read the definition. Does the example annoy you? Do you have a pet peeve?

> Pet peeve *noun [C]* — something that annoys you very much or makes you extremely angry. One of my pet peeves is people eating with their mouths open.
>
> Yes! When someone talks during a film and then asks, "Who's he?" "What happened?" etc.

B ▶10.5 Complete 1–10 with a–j. Listen to a radio show to check.

a interrupting you
b playing with
c ringing the bell
d to put their trash
e being the first
f to call you
g to pick
h knocking first
i using the word
j not returning

PEOPLE'S TOP PET PEEVES
We asked and you voted! Here are the results:

1 People who are addicted to _____ their phone.
2 _____ to arrive at a party.
3 When someone uses a finger _____ their teeth.
4 People who are too lazy _____ in the trash can.
5 People who promise _____, and then they don't.
6 Friends who honk instead of _____ when they come to pick you up.
7 Bad phone habits, like _____ texts or phone calls.
8 People who keep _____ "like."
9 When people keep _____ when you talk.
10 People who suddenly open the door without _____ first.

C In pairs, match 1–10 in B to the rules in the grammar box.

Use a gerund	Use an infinitive
• as the subject of the sentence: ☐	• to express purpose: _____
• after certain verbs: ☐☐☐	• after adjectives: _____
• after prepositions: ☐☐☐	• after certain verbs: _____
Form the negative by adding *not* before the gerund.	Form the negative by adding *not* before the *to*.

→ Grammar 10A p. 156

⚠ Common mistakes

of not
Dad's afraid ~~of don't~~ finding a new job.

to
Students who are too lazy ~~for~~ do their homework.

not to
I asked you ~~to not~~ keep interrupting.

not to
We told you ~~to not~~ chew gum.

D Complete 1–5 with the gerund or infinitive form of the verbs in parentheses.

1 _____ (not know) who a text message is from is really annoying.
2 I get really mad when I find it difficult _____ (sleep).
3 People who use social media _____ (show off).
4 I don't like people who avoid _____ (make) eye contact.
5 People telling you _____ (not use) your phone and then theirs rings!

E In pairs, compare your feelings about the pet peeves in B and D. Which are your top three?

F 🟢 Make it personal In groups, brainstorm more pet peeves. Use 1–5 to help. Choose your group's favorite.

1 People who _____ without / after / before _____.
2 People who try to _____ by _____.
3 _____ing in the middle of the night / early in the morning.
4 People who keep / enjoy / avoid / insist on _____.
5 People who are too _____ to _____.

> People who change the TV channel without asking.
>
> Yeah, and taxi drivers who keep talking about themselves!

I can't stand ...
I don't like ...
I don't mind ...
... doesn't bother me.

🎵 *'Cause we were just kids when we fell in love*
Not knowing what it was
I will not give you up this time

10.2

② Listening

A ▶10.6 Listen to an anger management group and match the four people (Jim, Mia, Julia, and Vince) to the pet peeves in **1B**.

B ▶10.6 Listen again and circle the correct alternative.
1. Julia **is / isn't** new to the group.
2. Mia **agrees / disagrees** with her employers' opinion of her.
3. Jim's girlfriend says he is too **sociable / aggressive.**
4. Jim responds to Vince's criticism **sincerely / sarcastically**.
5. The coach wants to **change the subject / use the argument as an example.**

③ Vocabulary Common expressions with *for* and *of*

A ▶10.7 Listen and repeat extracts 1 and 2. Notice the stress and the weak forms, then circle the correct alternative in the box.

> /əˈfreɪdəv/   /wɑnə/   /fər/
> 1 I'm afraid_of losing my job.   2 I want_to thank you for being so honest.
> The prepositions *of*, *for*, and *to* are usually **stressed / unstressed** and the *o* is pronounced /ə/.

B ▶10.8 Try to complete extracts 1–6. Listen to check. Then repeat.
1. She accuses me _____ _____ aggressive.
2. I'm sick and tired _____ _____ that kind of English.
3. I apologize _____ _____ your sensitive ears!
4. There's just no _____ _____ bad grammar.
5. Remember there are ways _____ _____ with this.
6. We are responsible _____ _____ our anger.

My Spanish teacher used to say that a lot.

C Complete the mind maps with the examples from **B**.

```
            ADJECTIVE
            VERB ─── FOR
thank (you)
            NOUN
```

```
afraid
            ADJECTIVE
            VERB ─── OF
            NOUN
```

D ▶10.9 Guess what they are saying. Listen to compare. Were you right? What would you have said / done?

I'd have told him to forget the wedding!

You should apologize …
I'm sick and tired …

I'm afraid …
There's an easy way …

⚠️ **Common mistakes**
of
I'm afraid ~~about~~ flying.
for helping
Thank you ~~to help~~ me with my project.

E 🔵 **Make it personal** In groups, role-play your own anger management session. Choose your pet peeves and elect the coach. Who's the angriest student?

Mario, welcome to the group. What brings you here?   *Well, I'm sick and tired of …*

127

10.3 How assertive are you?

1 Listening

A In pairs, answer 1–3. Any disagreements?
1. What mistake has the teacher made?
2. Why does no one want to tell him?
3. Can we train people to be more assertive?

> Yeah, I think so. A friend of mine took a course like this once.

"Not ME. YOU go tell him it's misspelled."

B ▶10.10 Listen to the first part of a training course on assertiveness. Answer 1–2.
1. What is their definition of assertiveness?
2. What are the benefits of being assertive?

C ▶10.11 Listen to the whole course and complete the notes. Is it all good advice?

Assertiveness

- Assertiveness is a way of ¹_____
- It's difficult to tell the difference between ²_____
- Assertive people are good at ³_____ because they can reach a compromise
- You shouldn't expect other people to ⁴_____
- You can control your own actions, but you can't ⁵_____
- It's important to ⁶_____ when confronting people you disagree with
- You have to learn to say ⁷_____
- Try saying "I will" instead of ⁸_____

> **Common mistake**
> ~~tell~~
> I can't ~~say~~ the difference between X and Y.

2 Grammar Verb + gerund or infinitive

A Look at the highlighted items in ▶10.11 on p. 175. Underline the gerunds and circle the infinitives after *stop*, *try*, and *remember*. Then complete the grammar box with *-ing* or *to*. Does your language make this distinction?

> **Common mistakes**
> ~~chatting~~
> Please stop ~~to chat~~ on your phone at lunch. Turn ~~it~~ off ~~it~~.

Gerund and infinitive after *stop*, *try*, and *remember*

If you use two verbs together, the second one can be either a gerund or an infinitive. Sometimes there's no difference in meaning:
- I **began** to study / studying English when I was six.
- I **like** to listen to / listening to classical music while I'm driving.

But there are a few important exceptions.
Stop + _____: Not do something anymore.
Stop + _____: Interrupt what you're doing in order to do something else.
Try + _____: Make an effort to do something.
Try + _____: Do something and see if it works.
Remember + _____: Remember that you did something in the past.
Remember + _____: Remember that you should do something.

→ **Grammar 10B** p. 156

128

B ♪ 10.12 **Read a questionnaire from the training course. Match a–h to 1–8 and circle the correct alternative. Listen to check and practice the** highlighted **words.**

♫ *I am not afraid to keep on living*
I am not afraid to walk this world alone **10.3**

a   stop **talking** / **to talk** to her
b   try **staring** / **to stare** at them
c   try **crying** / **to cry** or something
d   stop **standing** / **to stand** there politely

e   stop **showing** / **to show** up for these family dinners
f   he'll probably **trying** / **try** to find a way to get the money
g   instead, you write a "Remember **calling** / **to call** Jane" note
h   hey, I remember **lending** / **to lend** you some money a while ago

TEST YOUR ASSERTIVENESS

1 An uncle you meet regularly at family dinners is very critical of you and your career. You:
☐ say nothing and be friendly. Who wants conflict in the family?
☐ [1]_____. Forever. And tell everyone why.
☐ ask your uncle why he keeps criticizing you.
☐ [2]_____. Maybe a little drama will work. Who knows?

2 A close friend has just broken up with her boyfriend. She needs some emotional support. The phone rings, and you see her number. You're finishing an urgent report at work. You:
☐ don't pick the phone up. [3]_____.
☐ [4]_____. The report can wait.
☐ say you're busy and can only talk for five minutes.
☐ are tough. Tell her she should stop crying and forget about him. Then hang up.

3 Your cousin borrowed $1,500 and promised to pay you back by April 30. It's October, and you still haven't heard from him. You:
☐ say nothing and accept the fact that you'll never see that money again.
☐ want to talk to him, but you keep putting it off. Give him a few more months. [5]_____.
☐ explain why you need the money and negotiate a payback plan and a new deadline.
☐ call him and, in the middle of the conversation, say "[6]_____," as if you'd just remembered.

4 You're standing in line at the bank, and someone cuts in front of you. You:
☐ smile and say, "Excuse me, perhaps you didn't realize there is a line."
☐ [7]_____—perhaps they'll notice how annoyed you are.
☐ just stay where you are. A few more minutes won't make any difference.
☐ [8]_____—push back in front of them.

C In pairs, choose the most assertive reaction to 1–4 in **B**. What would your personal response be? Are your answers similar?

In the first one I'd probably stop going to those family meals.

D 🔊 Make it personal **In groups, say what you would do in situations 1–5. Who's the most assertive? Is it possible to be too assertive?**

1 The passenger next to you is playing a loud video game. The flight attendant has already asked him to turn it off.

2 You find out that someone at work / school has been spreading rumors about you.

3 The waiter brings your food after a very long wait, and, when it finally arrives, it's cold.

4 You have a friend who is consistently 15 to 20 minutes late when meeting you.

5 A coworker / classmate you interact with for hours and hours has bad breath.

I'd start _____ing / to _____.

I'd stop _____ing / to _____.

I'd try _____ing and see if it worked.

I'd try to find a way of _____ing.

I'd _____.

129

10.4 How similar are you to your friends?

I must admit a couple of my friends sometimes drive me crazy.

Me too. I have a friend who's a terrible gossip.

① Listening

A ▶10.13 ▶ Do all your friendships make you happy? Why (not)? Imagine what "a toxic friend" is. Listen to / Watch the start of a vodcast to check.

B ▶10.13 ▶ Listen / Watch again and check all the points you hear. Imagine what you will hear in the next part.

1 ☐ In a relationship, both people's needs have the same importance.
2 ☐ Friends and significant others should try to make you happy.
3 ☐ Toxic relationships take away our energy.
4 ☐ Sometimes even close friends can be toxic.
5 ☐ Toxic relationships can impact all aspects of our lives.
6 ☐ The program will suggest ways to escape from toxic relationships.

C ▶10.14 ▶ Listen to / Watch the rest of the vodcast and match the two columns.

Antitoxic step	Main idea
1 Diagnose the relationship.	☐ Establish certain limits and be firm.
2 Recognize your role.	☐ Ask other people for advice.
3 Build boundaries.	☐ Stay away from people who treat you badly.
4 You can't change other people.	☐ Respect yourself, and others will respect you.
5 Get a second opinion.	☐ Ask yourself how this person makes you feel.
6 Look out for yourself.	☐ Do you put other people before yourself?

D In pairs, summarize the video's advice from the pictures.

Some relationships can take away our energy and ...

DON'T WORRY ABOUT ME. I'M NOT IMPORTANT!

E 🔶 **Make it personal** What are the most important things in a friendship? Write your top five. Compare with a partner. Agree on three.

Sharing the same sense of humor has to be one of them.

⟳ **Common mistakes**

relationship
I'm in a stable relation.

look out for / look after / take care of
You have to look for yourself.

130

2 Vocabulary Phrasal verbs

A Complete the definitions with the highlighted phrasal verbs. How many are literal meanings?

Friends are supposed to give you energy and lift you up when you're down.

How do you know if a friend is bringing you down? Well, in much the same way that you know you're coming down with a cold.

If a friend or partner is stealing your sunshine, you need to figure out what you're doing to allow them to do this.

Are they constantly bossing you around? Once you know the boundary that you want to set, stick to it! Draw your line in the sand.

1 _____ sb _____: tell somebody what to do
2 _____ sb _____: make somebody feel happier
3 _____ sb _____: make somebody feel sad
4 _____ sb / sth _____: find the answer, understand
5 _____ sth: continue, not change your mind
6 _____ sth: become sick with something

B 🎙 Make it personal Complete 1–4 with verbs from **A**. In pairs, ask and answer. Any surprises?

WHEN WAS THE LAST TIME …
1 you couldn't _____ how to use a machine without reading the manual?
2 you missed school / work because you _____ a cold?
3 negative feedback (from a teacher, boss, or friend) _____ you _____?
4 you made a resolution? How long did you _____ it?

3 Grammar Separable and inseparable phrasal verbs

A Read the grammar box, and then write separable (S) or inseparable (I) next to 1–6 in **2A**.

When a phrasal verb needs an object, sometimes you can separate the verb and particle (you can split them up), and sometimes you can't.
1 Most phrasal verbs with one particle are separable. If you use a pronoun, it always goes in the middle: Turn on the TV. / Turn the TV on. / Turn it on.
2 But some common phrasal verbs with one particle are inseparable: I'm looking for a job. If you're not sure, say it out loud, separating the verb and the particle. If the verb is inseparable, the sentence will sound really strange! I'm looking a job for (!)
3 Phrasal verbs with two particles are usually inseparable: She cut down on sugar.

➡ Grammar 10C p. 156

🖊 **Common mistake**
When you buy new shoes, try on ~~them~~ first.
      them^

B Reread the questionnaire in **2B** on p. 129. Underline six phrasal verbs and mark them S or I.

C Complete 1–6 using it / them and the particles below. Do you like tests like these?

with (x3)   to   up (x2)

FRIENDSHIP TEST
1 I never argue with my friends. I have never fallen out _____.
2 If one of my friends is feeling sad, I know how to pick _____.
3 I consider some of my friends to be like family. I get along so well _____.
4 If I make a promise to a friend, I will stick _____.
5 If the phone rings and it's a friend, even if I'm really busy, I'll always pick _____.
6 I don't see some of my friends often enough. I'd like to hang out _____ more often.

D 🎙 Make it personal In groups of four, ask and answer the friendship test. Add follow-up questions, too. Any unusual stories or perspectives?

Do you ever fall out with friends?   Hardly ever, but there was this one time …

10.5 What do you find hardest about English?

That's not me at all. I find writing hard, especially spelling.

For me, it's speaking. The most difficult thing is pronunciation.

I'm bad at listening. It's really hard to understand native speakers.

Common mistakes

~~pronouncing~~
I have difficulty ~~to pronounce~~ new words.

trouble / difficulty using
I have ~~a problem to use~~ the present perfect.

find it easy
I ~~have facility~~ to remember new expressions.

Skills Proofreading

A Mark 1–6 with S (same as / similar to me) or N (not like me). In groups of four, compare ideas. What's the most difficult skill?

Easy		Difficult	
1	I think I'm good at grammar	4	I find it hard to read fast
2	I have no trouble remembering new words	5	I have trouble expressing my ideas
3	I'm comfortable writing in English	6	I have a lot of difficulty understanding native speakers

B ▶10.15 Now write 1–6 from **A** in the gaps in the messages. Then listen to check.

C In pairs, read each message, ignoring the blanks for now, and find …
1. two unnecessary words (cross them out).
2. two missing words (insert them).
3. a missing *s* in a word (add it).
4. a misuse of *-ing* (correct it).

Feeling frustrated with your English? Worried you might not be making enough progress? Wondering what the best way forward is? Send us your message, and we'll try to help you in next week's podcast.

1 My name's Bruna, I'm have twenty-three years old, and I'm from Bucaramanga, in Colombia. I've studied English four years, and some things are easy, but others are very hard! For example _____ (I love rules!), but when I have to interact with other people, _____ and I hesitate a lot. My teacher says that I'll get better, she say it's only a matter of time. But sometimes I thinking I never to become fluent.

2 I'm Byung-Sang, from Seoul. I have studied English since I was a little boy, but, to be honest with you, I don't like English. I can communicate well, _____ (especially emails), but listening is nightmare. _____. Once I spent two week in London, and I am felt really lost. Do you know about if there anything I can do to improving my listening?

3 When I read, I try understand each and every word on the page, but people saying this is a bad habit. I have a friend who she is a teacher, and she told me do not worry about all the new word. But, honestly, _____, for general comprehension. What do you think? There's another problem: How can I use the new vocabulary? _____, but it's hard for me to use them. Any suggestions? Omar, from Istanbul.

D **Make it personal** Complete 1–4 with the phrasal verbs in the correct form. Then discuss them in pairs. Are you good proofreaders?

pick up   figure out   look up   put off

1. I _____ all of the mistakes in **B**.
2. I always _____ words in the dictionary if I'm not sure of the spelling.
3. I proofread my work immediately. I never _____ (it) until later.
4. I always check my grammar and _____ any mistakes myself.

Are you going to take an English exam?

10.5

ID in Action Making recommendations

A In pairs, list two ways to improve your listening, speaking, reading, writing, grammar, vocabulary, and pronunciation. Share with the class.

To practice listening, watch TV first without subtitles, then again with subtitles to check.

B ▶10.16 Listen to the podcast. Check the two recommendations the teacher makes to each student. Do you agree?

BRUNA
1. ☐ Spend some time abroad.
2. ☐ Don't worry too much about mistakes.
3. ☐ Find someone you can practice with.
4. ☐ Think carefully about what you want to say.

BYUNG-SANG
1. ☐ Watch both easy and difficult videos.
2. ☐ Increase your vocabulary.
3. ☐ Don't use subtitles.
4. ☐ Improve your pronunciation.

OMAR
1. ☐ Vary your reading strategies.
2. ☐ Take a reading course.
3. ☐ Use a monolingual dictionary.
4. ☐ Learn expressions, not isolated words.

C ▶10.17 Match the two columns. Listen to check and repeat.

Making recommendations	
1 Try to focus …	☐ learning "make an effort" instead of "effort"?
2 Have you thought …	☐ of practicing is watching Internet videos.
3 A good way …	☐ consider giving pronunciation a little more attention.
4 You should …	☐ reading slowly all the time.
5 Try to avoid …	☐ on expressing your ideas fluently.
6 How about …	☐ about asking a friend to practice with you?

D Paircheck. A: Cover the first column and remember the full sentence. B: Check. Then change roles.

E Role-play the recommendations for the students as a dialogue.
A: You're a student. B: You're the teacher.
Change roles and suggest extra ideas.

So, Bruna, are you pleased with your progress?

Well, yes and no. I still have difficulty speaking. What do you suggest?

F 🎯 **Make it personal** Think about your English, and note your strengths and weaknesses in two columns, plus any action ideas. Compare in groups, make more recommendations, and note down the best ideas.

I'm only human. I make mistakes. I'm only human. That's all it takes. Don't put your blame on me.

I'm OK with grammar—especially verb tenses. But I find pronunciation hard, like the "th" sound.

Have you thought about using a pronunciation book with audio to practice? Or finding some pronunciation videos on YouTube?

133

Writing 10 A forum post

Go, go, go
Figure it out, figure it out, but don't stop moving
Go, go, go
Figure it out, figure it out, you can do this

A Read the forum post, ignoring any mistakes. What advice does Lara ask for? Does she get a good response?

LaraVenice

Good English school in the center of Edinburgh? — Sep 5th, 19:02

Hi, I'm planning to come to the UK for learning (to learn) English during four weeks. I'm not sure which city would be a good place to stay. I'm thinking about Edinburgh. What do you suggest? Also, if you was me, what would you do about accommodations? Do you think it's better stay with a host family or in a hostel or an apartment?
Could you suggest a good school in Edinburgh? Is a good city for students? I'm 23 years old.
What do you advise me doing?
Thanks in advance.

CatCrazy21

Re: Good English school in the center of Edinburgh — Sep 6th, 07:31

Have you thought about to contact the British Council? They are the country's cultural ambassadors. They have offices all over the world and will help you figure out where to go. You should have a look at schools on ARELS (Association of Recognized English Language Services), too.
IMO Edinburgh is a great place for study! There's a university and lots of things to do and places to explore. You ought to contact the University. They probably have courses and plenty of informations for overseas students. As far as accommodation is concerned, how about stay with a host family? You'll learn much more about the culture and also get used to the Scottish accent faster! 😊 Good luck!

B Reread, find, and correct
 1 five more mistakes with the use of gerunds and infinitives.
 2 five more common mistakes.

C Underline five phrases used for asking for advice and circle four phrases for giving advice.

D Match the sentence halves.

1 You ought	☐ about speaking to your tutor?
2 You shouldn't	☐ leave the door unlocked.
3 How about	☐ go to bed early tonight?
4 Have you thought	☐ hiring a bicycle?
5 Why don't you	☐ to call your mother.

E Read *Write it right!* Then find examples of indirect questions in the forum posts.

> ✓ **Write it right!**
> - Internet forums are useful places to share / get information.
> - Forums have rules, so make sure you check and follow them.
> - **A**cronyms such as OP (original poster) and TBH (to be honest) are often used to make communication faster. These are informal.
> - Use indirect questions when asking for information to sound more polite.
> - You can use more direct questions when you are familiar with the person you are chatting to online.

F What do you think the acronyms in 1–5 mean? Use these words to help you.

as (x2)	at	by	in	laugh	loud
moment	my	opinion	out	possible	
soon	the (x2)	way			

 1 BTW, have you thought about asking your tutor?
 2 I'm a bit busy ATM. I'll call you later.
 3 IMO, the Scottish accent is difficult to understand.
 4 I'll think about it and let you know ASAP.
 5 That's the funniest photo ever! LOL.

G 👤 **Make it personal** In pairs, what advice would you give to someone coming to study language in your hometown?

H *Your turn!* Write a forum post asking for advice on one of the following topics.

> Help! I'm giving a class presentation.
> Nice places to walk my dog
> Best restaurant for a family celebration

Before	Decide what advice you want to ask for.
While	Follow the tips in *Write it right!*
After	Use more direct questions when you are familiar with the person you are chatting to online.

134

10 Mad men

1 Before watching

A Match 1–6 to their definitions a–f.
1. brood and mope around
2. knock some sense into people
3. watch chick flicks and cry your eyes out
4. work your fingers to the bone
5. yell like Tarzan
6. stereotyping

a ☐ to work incredibly hard
b ☐ to cry a lot watching a rom-com-type movie
c ☐ to make someone behave more logically
d ☐ to label something as "typical" in a negative way
e ☐ to express anger or emotion in a loud, primitive way
f ☐ to obsess about what makes you unhappy

B 🔘 **Make it personal** In pairs, share your experiences of 1–7.

When her boyfriend doesn't call, my sister broods and mopes.

2 While watching

A Watch to 2:00 and answer 1–4. Check all you hear.

1. According to the guys, on a girls' day out, they ...
   ☐ cry their eyes out.   ☐ shop.
   ☐ watch a "chick flick."   ☐ sit in a spa.
   ☐ complain about men.   ☐ gossip.
   ☐ get their nails done.   ☐ laugh at men.
   ☐ do their hair.

2. What really annoys August the most?
   ☐ that he's tired of competing
   ☐ that Paolo is always the "hero"
   ☐ that he's scared
   ☐ that he's not a knight in shining armor

3. Seeing a shrink means you have to
   ☐ sit in an office.   ☐ talk about your life.
   ☐ work out your problems.   ☐ pay unnecessarily.

4. What makes Rory angry?
   ☐ losing a game   ☐ cooking for other people
   ☐ sitting on the bench   ☐ having no confidence

B Watch the video again and order what happened, 1–10.
☐ The guys talk about how to solve their problems.
☐ Rory wonders what a "girls' day out" is all about.
☐ August complains about Paolo's heroic behavior.
☐ Daniel says he's pretty happy and confident.
☐ Daniel explains what he thinks women do when they are out together.
☐ August reminds Rory about how cooking was a disaster.
☐ Daniel recommends that August talk to a therapist.
☐ Rory realizes that Daniel is right.
☐ Rory thinks that stereotyping is a bad idea.
☐ They end up relaxing by playing video games.

C Complete the excerpts. Who says them? Watch again to check.

beating	boxing	brooding	chasing
competing	complaining	experiencing
jumping	moping around	using

1. What if the science foundation starts _____ my ideas without my permission?
2. Rory, you're mad because of the time you wasted _____ after Genevieve.
3. I've seen you both _____ the extremes of emotions. Some days practically _____ for joy, other days _____ and _____.
4. _____ stinks!
5. Stop _____.
6. Yep, nothing's ever so bad that a little _____ can't cure.
7. _____ you two at video games makes me feel the number one winner.

3 After watching

A True (T) or false (F)? Correct the false statements.
1. August needs to build up more muscles and more confidence.
2. Daniel tells Rory and August to stop complaining.
3. Daniel thinks video games are a bad solution.
4. August says that yelling like Tarzan is a great therapy.
5. Rory tried punching an avatar to deal with stress.

B 🔘 **Make it personal** Do you use video games to relax? In groups, share suggestions for working out anger or stress. Which works best for you?

Dancing is a great way to de-stress.   *Hmm ... For me, yelling and exercising is much better.*

C 🔘 **Make it personal** Which ID Café characters do you like the most and the least: Andrea, August, Daniel, Genevieve, Lucy, Paolo or Zoey?

I really like Genevieve. I'd love to be a musician, and she seems really confident.

135

R5 Grammar and Vocabulary

A *Picture dictionary.* **Cover the words on the pages below and remember.**

pages	
112	7 crimes
116	Michael's story
118	3 cybercrime risks
119	5 optimistic predictions
124–125	8 mood words and phrases
127	6 expressions with *of* and 6 with *for*
130	4 pieces of advice from the video
131	6 phrasal verbs from the definitions
161	2 words for each sound in lines 5 and 6 of the consonants chart (not the picture words)

B **Rewrite 1–6 using the *passive voice*. Do you remember which units of ⑩ 3 refer to them?**

1 Millions of Americans watch late night talk shows.
2 Technology is killing our creativity.
3 Dyson invented the first cordless vacuum cleaner.
4 Disney gave the cast of *Avengers: Infinity War* fake scripts.
5 Do you think our voices will operate more technology in the future?
6 Brandon is holding his party outside.

C **Complete signs 1–6 with *to*, *for*, or *of*. In pairs, think of two places where you might see each of them.**

1 **All thieves will be taken _____ court.**

2 **If you're afraid _____ change—give it to me.**

3 **Thank you _____ not smoking.**

4 **Tired _____ being single?**

5 Ticket machine under maintenance.
We apologize _____ any inconvenience.

6 **Not responsible _____ personal items left in vehicles.**

The first one looks like it's in some kind of store.

D 🔊 **Make it personal** **Circle the correct alternative. In pairs, ask and answer. Any surprises?**

1 How many times do you stop **to have** / **having** a break at work / school?
2 Do you worry about **to be** / **being** robbed online?
3 Can you remember **to learn** / **learning** to ride a bike?
4 Have you ever tried **to camp** / **camping**?
5 Do you always remember **to wash** / **washing** your hands before **to eat** / **eating**?

I stop maybe three or four times a day.

And what do you do on your break?

E ▶ **R5.1** **Listen to three dialogues and match verbs 1–7 to the particles. Listen again and find one more phrasal verb in each dialogue.**

1	get	☐	with
2	figure	☐	down
3	stick	☐	into
4	lift	☐	out
5	come down	☐	to
6	bring	☐	up
7	boss	☐	around

F **Make ➕ or ➖ predictions about these topics 20 years from now. Compare in pairs. Any different opinions?**

climate change   colonize the moon
discover time travel   end poverty   over-population
pandas disappear   use house phones

I guess we'll be starting to colonize the moon.

Really? I don't think we'll have started by then.

G **Correct the mistakes in each sentence. Check your answers in units 9 and 10. What's your score, 1–10?**

✏️ **Common mistakes**

1 *They tried to steal the shop but didn't rob anything. (2 mistakes)*
2 *This photo was took secretly and has been showing on the Internet. (2 mistakes)*
3 *Hurry up! By the time we get the theater, the movie will start. (2 mistakes)*
4 *People shouldn't to go in prison for theft. (2 mistakes)*
5 *Do you worry with not to pass the final exams? (2 mistakes)*
6 *Remember locking the doors after to leave. (2 mistakes)*
7 *I like the people who are smiling all the time. (2 mistakes)*
8 *Do you want to go with me out to a party this night? (2 mistakes)*
9 *I'm good with speaking but I have difficulty to understand. (2 mistakes)*
10 *Is it easy for to use correctly prepositions? (2 mistakes)*

Skills practice

Hey, Jude, don't make it bad
Take a sad song and make it better
Remember to let her into your heart
Then you can start to make it better

R5

A Listen again to the four stories ▶9.12 on p.120 one at a time. After each one, reread and underline any words that were difficult to hear. Are they:
- a unfamiliar?
- b words with unexpected pronunciation?
- c words which "disappear"?
- d difficult for another reason?

B 🎧 **Make it personal** In groups, which do you think is the worst, and why?

	a	b	c
1	bribery	tax evasion	music piracy
2	Mondays	rainy days	getting up early
3	preparing food	washing dishes	ironing
4	big hands	big feet	big head
5	being tired	being thirsty	being hungry

C Read and order the paragraphs in this article.

Cup of History

☐ In 1966, the Jules Rimet was on display in London, ahead of the World Cup there. On Sunday, March 20, the security guards noticed that the cabinet [1]_____ (open) and the trophy [2]_____ (steal). The police [3]_____ (start) an investigation, but the trophy [4]_____ (find) a week later by a man walking his dog.

☐ In 2018, the World Cup [5]_____ (hold) in Russia, a historic first for the "new" trophy! It [6]_____ (win) by France for the second time, making them one of only six teams to [7]_____ (win) it more than once.

☐ Italy won the competition in 1938 and so the trophy [8]_____ (display) in Rome. When the country [9]_____ (occupy) by the German army, an Italian FIFA official [10]_____ (hide) the cup in a shoebox under his bed to keep it from the Nazis.

☐ Since the World Cup started in 1930, there [11]_____ (are) two trophies. The original, the Jules Rimet, [12]_____ (give) permanently to Brazil in 1970, after they won their third tournament. This cup has many interesting stories around it.

☐ In 1983, the cup was stolen again, this time in Rio de Janeiro. It [13]_____ (never / find) to this day.

D Complete **C** with the correct form of the verbs in parentheses. Past or present? Active or passive? Simple or perfect?

E Complete 1–5, then share in pairs. Any similarities?
1 I'm sick and tired of _____.
2 _____ is getting better, little by little.
3 Most _____ have its / their ups and downs.
4 I go to _____ when I need some peace and quiet.
5 It annoys me when I have to _____ again and again.

I'm sick and tired of this weather. When will it change?

F ▶R5.2 Order the story, 1–5. Listen to check.

G ▶R5.3 **Dictation.** Listen and write six extracts from **F**. Listen again, and repeat.

H ▶R5.4 🎧 **Make it personal** Listen to these pet peeves and react in pairs. How do they make you feel?

Oh, I really hate it when people do that.
Really? It doesn't bother me much.

I Role-play. In pairs, choose a pet peeve.
A: You are doing this action.
B: You are annoyed by it. Complain to **A**.

PLAYING LOUD MUSIC	ENTERING WITHOUT KNOCKING
CELL PHONES AT THE MOVIES	BITING NAILS	EXCESSIVE PESSIMISM
CHEWING WITH MOUTH OPEN	SINGING OFF THE BEAT

J ▶R5.5 **Question time!**
In pairs, listen to the 12 lesson titles in units 9 and 10. Pause after each one and tell each other the **opposite** of your normal answer. Ask follow-up questions, too, for fun.

Does crime worry you?
No, not at all. I love it when people rob me.

137

Grammar **Unit 1**

1A Review of present tenses

Simple present

Subject	Verb	Time phrase
I / You / We / They	hang out	on weekends.
He / She / It	meets up	twice a week.

Use the **Simple present** for habits and states:
- *Johann and Melina usually **meet** for dinner once a month.*
- *She often texts during dinner. It **annoys** her boyfriend.*
- *I **hate** going to parties by myself. I always **take** a friend.*

Note: adverbs of frequency come before the verb.

Present continuous

Question	Auxiliary	Subject	Verb phrase
What	are	you	doing here?
Where	is	he	going?

Use the **Present continuous** for:
1 actions in progress.
- *I'm **chatting** to my mom.*
2 future arrangements.
- *She **isn't coming** tonight.*

Note: do not use stative verbs in the Present continuous.
Do you understand me? NOT ~~Are you understanding me?~~

Present perfect

Subject	Auxiliary	Past participle
I / You / We / They	have / 've have not / haven't	hung out there before. gone there before.
He / She / It	has / 's has not / hasn't	spent time with him. been too hot today.

Form: *have / has* + past participle (for irregular participles list, see p. 158–159).

Use the **Present perfect** for:
1 past experiences without a specific time.
- *I've never **been** here before.*
2 completed actions from a past point in time to now.
- *We've just **eaten**.*
3 unfinished past: actions / states that began in the past and continue until now.
- *She's **had** three dates **since** she started speed dating.*

Yes / No questions	Short answers
Have you (ever) been on a meet-up?	Yes, I have. No, I haven't.
Have they (ever) broken up before?	Yes, they have. No, they haven't.
Has she (ever) lost her cell phone?	Yes, she has. No, she hasn't.

For short answers, do not contract the subject with the auxiliary.
Yes, I have NOT ~~Yes, I've.~~

1B Review of question forms

Yes / No questions

Auxiliary	Subject	Verb + object
Are	they	your workmates?
Do	you	know Natalie?
Have	you	been to London?
Can	you	play the piano?

Questions ending in prepositions

Question	Auxiliary	Subject	Verb phrase	Preposition
Who	do	you	want to speak	to?
Who	did	they	go to the party	with?

Object questions

Question	Auxiliary	Subject	Verb + object
What	do	you	want to eat?
Where	did	he	park the car?

Subject questions

Question (+ subject)	Verb + object
Which boy	won the prize?
Who	likes lemonade?

1C Emphatic forms

Subject	Auxiliary	Verb	Object
I	do	love	the sound of her voice.

Use auxiliary + verb to emphasize agreement / disagreement.
- *"You don't seem to like him."*
- *"That's not true. I **do** like him."*

Use adverbs before the verb to emphasize an opinion or agreement / disagreement.
- *I **really** don't think he's going to show up!*
- *I **definitely** want to meet him sometime.*

Note: emphatic auxiliaries and adverbs are more common in speech than in writing.

Unit 1

1A

1 Complete 1–6 with the *Simple present* or *Present continuous* of the verbs in parentheses.
1. He _____ with his friends this weekend. (travel)
2. Mara always _____ impatient when she _____ in long lines. (get / stand)
3. They _____ every night because they _____ classes. (not go out / have)
4. Ben and Amy _____ right now—I think they often _____. (not get along / argue)
5. You really _____ bored by this TV show. (seem)
6. So, how _____ him? (you know)

2 Use the phrases to describe each picture a–c. Try to use the *Simple present, Present continuous,* or *Present perfect*.

a Museum
guide works
is explaining
has never seen

b Eating competition
participating in an eating competition
has to
already eaten

c Skateboard park
hang out every Saturday
has started
is waiting

3 🟢 **Make it personal** Describe where you've been lately, what you do every weekend, and what you're planning to do next weekend.

I always go to the same restaurants every weekend, so I have decided to try new places.
I've been to that new restaurant that's just opened. The Japanese place. And next weekend my friends and I are visiting a Turkish restaurant.

1B

1 Write *yes / no* questions for these answers.
1. He likes this city.
2. They are good at soccer.
3. She can drive a truck.
4. The baby is awake.

2 Circle the correct preposition.
1. What were you waiting **to / for**?
2. Who are you so angry **with / of**?
3. What is she spending all her money **in / on**?
4. Which line are you standing **in / at**?

3 Write one subject and one object question for each sentence.
1. Joanna loves taking photographs.
2. The kids went into the yard.
3. Chris has lost his keys.
4. Marie likes George.

4 Order the words in 1–5 to make questions.
1. time / in / which / city / some / would / spend / like / you / to / ?
2. talking / what / been / about / the / gossip magazines / have / ?
3. learning / a / you / find / language / do / easy / ?
4. starred / who / watched / last / film / you / in / the / ?
5. you / talk / last / best / friend / to / when / did / your?

1C

1 Complete 1–6 with an emphatic auxiliary.
1. You know, she _____ look a little bit like Emma Stone.
2. Come to think of it, I _____ feel a bit tired.
3. Well, they couldn't make it to our party, but they _____ send us a card.
4. If I _____ seem stressed, it's only because of the thunderstorm.
5. It _____ sound too good to be true, doesn't it?
6. We _____ have to pay something to use this site—it's not free, you know.

2 Complete 1–5 with the best adverb below.

absolutely   certainly   definitely   really   sure

1. Are you _____ going to wear that orange shirt with those pants?
2. Well, she _____ told me she was getting the afternoon flight.
3. They _____ look as if they're having fun.
4. He _____ is a quiet sort of guy, isn't he?
5. I'm telling you, I'm _____, 100 percent certain I've seen him before!

139

Grammar Unit 2

2A Adjectives from verbs and nouns

- *I only use recharge**able** batteries in my devices.*
- *She bought a very space-**efficient** apartment.*
- *This software is really user-**friendly**!*

Form adjectives by adding *-able*, *-efficient*, and *-friendly* to verbs and nouns.

-able means "can be done:" *drinkable, breakable, doable*.
Verbs ending in *-e* ➤ cut *-e* + *-able*.
- reuse ➤ reusable
- recycle ➤ recyclable
- love ➤ lovable

Exception: *rechargeable*

Use a hyphen between nouns and *-efficient* or *-friendly*.
- *She bought an energy-efficient washing machine.*
- *We took our nephews to a child-friendly restaurant.*

2B Present perfect continuous

Subject	have / has	been + -ing
I / You / We / They	have / haven't	been sitting here for hours.
He / She	has / hasn't	been waiting for the bus since 8:30.
It	has / hasn't	been raining all afternoon.

Form: *have / has* (not) + *been* + verb + *-ing*.
Use contractions: *have = 've / haven't, has = 's / hasn't*

Question	have / has + subject	been + -ing
What	have I / you / we / they	been talking about?
How long	has she / he / it	been doing it?

Use the **Present perfect continuous** with:
- *since* to indicate a point in time: *1989, eight o'clock, yesterday = a moment*
- *for* to indicate a period of time: *a few hours, six months, 20 years = a duration*

2C Present perfect vs. Present perfect continuous

You can often use **Present perfect** or **Present perfect continuous** interchangeably.
- *I've lived here since 2010.*
- *I've been living here since 2010.*

Present perfect

Use the **Present perfect** to describe activities that have or haven't been completed from a past point in time until now.
- *Agatha's written ten books in ten years.*

Present perfect continuous

Use the **Present perfect continuous** to emphasize the time a process or series of events took. It can also be used to describe an activity that is unfinished or temporary.
- *They've been hanging around with Mary lately.*
- *Agatha's been writing books since she was in her 20s.*

Don't use the Present perfect continuous with a stative verb (e.g. *be, have, know, understand*).

2D Simple past vs. Present perfect simple / continuous

Simple past

Subject	Past tense of verb	Object
I / You / He / She / It / You / We / They	traveled	to the North Pole.

Use the **Simple past** for completed actions in the past.
- *Jordan Romero **reached** the top of the Everest when he was only 16.*

Present perfect

Use the **Present perfect** to connect the past and present and to describe how much has been completed.
- *The explorer **has climbed** a lot of mountains in his life.*
- *The polar ice caps **have melted** over the past 30 years.*

Present perfect continuous

Use the **Present perfect continuous** to describe how long something has been happening.
- *He's **been exploring** exotic environments since he graduated from school.*
- *The polar ice caps **have been melting** since the 1980s.*

"According to this, you haven't been waiting long enough for treatment."

Unit 2

2A

1 Cross out the incorrect adjective in 1–5.
1 She always brings **recycling** / **recyclable** bottles to the store.
2 He likes the **usable** / **user-friendly** features of his new dishwasher.
3 We have **energy-efficiency** / **energy-efficient** lights in our house.
4 I only use **natural-friendly** / **nature-friendly** detergents.
5 **Disposing** / **Disposable** batteries are bad for the environment.

2 Describe photos a–d. Use adjectives from verbs and nouns.
Well, I guess it's child-friendly but ...

2B

1 Complete 1–5 with the correct form of *have*.
1 _____ he been saving money for a new car?
2 What _____ you been doing all day?
3 Where _____ they been storing all those recyclable cans and boxes?
4 _____ you been listening to the news today?
5 _____ it been raining here?

2 Complete 1–5 with the *Present perfect continuous* of these verbs.

| buy | collect | live | swim | work out |

1 How long _____ you _____ watches?
2 They _____ in their new heated pool.
3 I _____ every day for the past three weeks.
4 Mario _____ next door for six years.
5 My mom _____ eco-friendly products since I was a kid.

3 🟢 **Make it personal** Describe what you've been doing lately at work / school / home.
I've been working out at the gym twice a week, but I haven't been running since I hurt my knee.

2C

1 Circle the correct option in 1–5.
1 She has **walked** / **been walking** to and from school every day since she was ten.
2 We've **tried** / **been trying** three different products and we still can't get this shirt clean.
3 He's never **traveled** / **been traveling** on a luxury cruise ship before.
4 They have **used** / **been using** energy-efficient appliances in their house recently.
5 I haven't **done** / **been doing** my housework as often as I should.

2 Complete the dialogues with the correct form of the verb in parentheses.
1 A: Where _____? There is mud all over your shoes. (walk)
  B: Oh, I _____ the garden and it _____ my shoes wet. (water / get)
2 A: I'm absolutely exhausted. I _____ since 8 a.m. (drive)
  B: Wow. You should let me drive for a while. I _____ at all. (not drive)
3 A: You _____ yourself enough time to get ready for work this morning. (not give)
  B: This old alarm clock _____ the right time for years! (keep)

2D

1 Order the words in 1–5 to make questions.
1 have / how / you / long / been / the / phone / using / you / that / bought / new / ?
2 flooding / has / any / been / there / you / where / live / ?
3 government / doing / to solve / has / the / been / problems / environmental / our / what / ?
4 know / the North Pole / did / that / global / you / has / warming / caused / at / melting / ?
5 since / the laws / enforced / been / about / pollution / have / they / made / were / ?

2 🟢 **Make it personal** Write your responses to the questions in **1**.

141

Grammar Unit 3

3A Past perfect

Subject	Auxiliary	Past participle
I / You He / She / It We / They	had / 'd	never been to Hong Kong before.
		already left by the time the suitcases appeared.
	had not / hadn't	had anything to eat for nearly 24 hours.
		ever been abroad until this trip.

Form:

⊖ and ⊖ = Subject + *had* (*not*) + past participle.

Use *'d* contractions for ⊖ and ***hadn't*** for ⊖ sentences.

❓ = *Had*(*n't*) + subject + past participle?

▸ ***Had*** you ***taken*** medicine before you flew?

▸ ***Hadn't*** you ever ***seen*** that before?

▸ What ***had*** you ***eaten*** before you got sick?

Note: when the main verb is *have*, *had* will appear twice, either together or separated by an adverbial expression.

▸ *We **had** already **had** lunch when they called.*

▸ *Before I met her, I **had had** serious problems in my relationships.*

Use the **Past perfect**:

1 for actions that happened before another past action.

▸ *I didn't start studying English until after I'**d finished** high school.*

2 to express past wishes and expectations.

▸ *My birthday party was better than anything I'**d expected**!*

▸ *The movie was more thrilling than they'**d hoped**!*

Expressions like *already, before, by the time, never, until recently*, etc. indicate the duration of the event or when it happened.

▸ *When the electricity went out, they'd **already** gone to bed.*

▸ *She'd never met a celebrity **before**.*

▸ ***Until recently**, I hadn't used that website.*

3B Past perfect continuous

Subject	Auxiliary	*been*	Verb + *-ing*
I / You He / She / It We / They	had / 'd	been	living there for a long time.
	had not / hadn't		standing in line for several hours.

Form:

⊕ and ⊖ = Subject + *had* (*not*) + *been* + verb *-ing*.

Use *'d* contractions for ⊕ and ***hadn't*** for ⊖ sentences.

❓ = *Had*(*n't*) + subject + *been* + verb *-ing*?

Use the **Past perfect continuous** to emphasize the duration of an action that was in progress before another past action.

▸ *It **had been raining** for hours before the game started.*

▸ *We'**d been walking** in the park when we encountered our old friend.*

Note: don't use the Past perfect continuous with stative verbs.

3C Narrative tenses

Simple past

Use the **Simple past** to talk about past actions and states.

▸ *I **graduated** from high school and then I **went** to college.*

Past continuous

Subject	*was / were*	Verb + *-ing*
I / He / She / It	was / wasn't	getting ready to go out.
You / We / They	were / weren't	listening to me.

Use the **Past continuous** to talk about actions in progress at a point in the past.

▸ *I **was working** at a summer camp for three months.*

Use the **Simple past** to talk about actions that interrupt actions in the **Past continuous**.

▸ *I **was walking** home when I **saw** Julia.*

Past perfect

Use the **Past perfect** to emphasize that one action happened before another in the past.

▸ *He made breakfast after he **had taken** a shower.*

If the sequence is clear, use the **Simple past**.

▸ *He made breakfast after he took a shower.*

Past perfect continuous

Use the **Past perfect continuous** to emphasize the duration of an action that was completed in the past.

▸ *We'**d been studying** all afternoon before the examiner arrived.*

▸ *How long **had you been dating** before you got married?*

142

Unit 3

3A

1 Complete the dialogues with the *Past perfect* or *Past simple* of the verbs in parentheses.

1 A: How was your trip to Italy? _____ you ever _____ there before? (be)
   B: It was great. I _____ there before. It was my first time. (be)
2 A: _____ you _____ Italian before you went there? (study)
   B: Yes, but I _____ more than a few words. (not learn)
3 A: _____ you _____ in time to see the festival? (arrive)
   B: No. By the time I got there, it _____ just _____. (end)

2 Describe the events in each of a–c in two or three sentences. Use the *Past perfect*.

3B

1 Complete 1–5 with the *Past perfect* or *Past perfect continuous* of the verbs in parentheses.

1 We _____ video games for almost two hours before the outage. (play)
2 Imagine if dinosaurs _____ because of climate change. (not die out)
3 She _____ for long when the lightning suddenly woke her up. (not sleep)
4 They _____ on coming to the party with us, but they had a family emergency at the last moment. (plan)
5 The tigers were pacing their cage because they _____ yet. (not eat)

2 Correct the mistakes in 1–5.

1 The manager had been warning him twice to stop using his cell in the theater.
2 They were towing our car because we had been parking in a tow-away zone.
3 She was still feeling confused even after the officer had gave her directions.
4 The law that all dogs must be on a leash had be in effect for thirty years.
5 Her wedding wasn't as perfect as she's hoped.

3 **Make it personal** Describe five "first times", or things you had never done before. Use the topics from the box, plus any others you can think of.

(buy) your own computer, phone, or car (drive) a car
plan a party (ride) a horse or a bicycle travel by plane

I had been living on the farm for one month but I hadn't ridden one of the horses ...

3C

1 Circle the correct alternatives to complete the anecdote.

Last Sunday, I ¹ **went / was going / had gone** to the cinema with my sisters. We ² **didn't drive / weren't driving / hadn't been driving** for very long when suddenly a small dog suddenly ³ **ran / was running / had run** out in front of us. It ⁴ **happened / was happening / had been happening** too fast, and I ⁵ **wasn't seeing / hadn't seen / hadn't been seeing** the dog before it ⁶ **ran / was running / had been running** out. We ⁷ **stopped / were stopping / had stopped** the car and ⁸ **got / were getting / had gotten** out. We ⁹ **were all feeling / had all felt / had all been feeling** very upset. We ¹⁰ **looked / was looking / had looked** under the car. Luckily, we ¹¹ **hadn't hit / weren't hitting / hadn't been hitting** the dog at all. It ¹² **hid / was hiding / had been hiding** under the car! We were very relieved!

2 **Make it personal** Describe a time when you thought something bad had happened, but it ended happily.

143

Grammar Unit 4

4A *too / enough*

Use:

- *too* before an adjective when something is more than necessary.

- ▸ *Some students are **too** proud to ask for help.*
- ▸ *You're never **too** old to learn something new.*

- *enough* after an adjective / adverb, but before nouns when something is the necessary amount.

- ▸ *I didn't get to class early **enough** to get a good seat.*
- ▸ *There wasn't **enough** time to get everything done.*

Note: don't use *too* with adjectives + noun to mean *very*. *Her family are very nice people.* NOT *Her family are too nice people.*

Use:

- *too many* before plural **C** nouns.

- ▸ *They have **too many** problems to deal with.*

- *too much* before **U** nouns.

- ▸ *There's **too much** pressure to get a high score on the exam.*

Note: when **U** nouns have a plural meaning or with *types of / kinds of*, use *too many*.

- ▸ *There are **too many** types of fish in this aquarium!*

4B *should have*

Use *should have* + Past participle:

1 to express a regret.

- ▸ *You **shouldn't have left** your drink near the computer.*

2 to speculate about the past.

- ▸ *We **should have known** there would be a test today.*

3 to give / ask advice about a past event.

- ▸ *What **should** I **have done** instead?*

Form:

Subject + *should (not)* + *have* + past participle.

Note: we often use the contraction *'ve* in spoken English.

- ▸ *She should**'ve** called to tell me she wasn't coming.*
- ▸ *I should**'ve** realized you would be late.*
- ▸ *You should**n't've** gone cycling without a helmet.*

4C First and second conditional

First conditional

If	Subject	Simple present	Subject	*will / won't*	Infinitive
If	I	have time,	I	will	buy some bread on the way home.
If	you	don't listen,	you	won't	know what to do.

Use the **First conditional** to talk about real and possible future situations.

Second conditional

If	Subject	Simple past	Subject	*will / won't*	Infinitive
If	I	could be anything I wanted,	I	would	be a lawyer.
If	they	didn't study so hard,	they	wouldn't	get such good grades.

Use the **Second conditional** to talk about "unreal" or imaginary situations.

The *if* clause can come first or second. Use a comma separating the clauses when the *if* clause comes first.

- ▸ *I'll buy some bread on the way home if I have time.*
- ▸ *They wouldn't get such good grades if they didn't study so hard.*

We can also use *when* or *as soon as* with the same sentence structure as with *if*.

- ▸ ***When** I get there, I'll call you.*
- ▸ *I'll call you **as soon as** I get there.*

We can use *can / could / may / might* instead of *would*.

- ▸ *If you studied a bit harder, you **might** get a higher score.*

144

Unit 4

4A

1 Circle the correct alternative in 1–5.
1. The print was **too / enough** small for her to read.
2. They've canceled the class because there weren't **too few / enough** people signed up.
3. The school was criticized because it didn't have **enough / too many** teachers.
4. Students complained that they were under **too much / enough** pressure to get good grades.
5. The educators thought the exams were **too / enough** hard for most students.

2 Complete 1–5 with *too much* or *enough*.
1. I don't have _____ time to read my notes before the test begins.
2. He has _____ time on his hands—he just plays video games all day.
3. Kindergarten children seem to get _____ homework.
4. I've got _____ money saved to buy a new tablet!
5. He hasn't done the dishes in days, so there aren't _____ cups for all of us.

3 🔘 **Make it personal** Describe these things. Use *too* and *enough* in your sentences.

apps on my phone   space in my room
free time   friends on Facebook   work
homework   hours in a day

I don't have enough free time!

"If you ask me, he's come too far too fast."

4B

1 Correct the mistakes in 1–6.
1. He should had organized his time better.
2. We should to have taken the bus instead of the subway.
3. They should have not given out their phone number.
4. You should listened to your father's advice.
5. It should've be easy to find his house with your GPS.
6. You should haven't left your wallet at the restaurant.

2 Order the words in 1–4 to make sentences. Then match 1–4 to a–d.
1. for / have / she / studied / should / more / exam / the / .
2. we / taken / road / that / should / have / not / .
3. pin / written / have / I / down / should / number / the / .
4. alarm / set / clock / have / should / they / their / .

a ☐ We got lost.
b ☐ I couldn't take out any money.
c ☐ They were late for class.
d ☐ She failed her test.

3 🔘 **Make it personal** Describe things you shouldn't have done or should've done differently.

I should've started learning English earlier. I still find it difficult.
I shouldn't have gone out last night. I'm exhausted.

4C

1 Check the correct ending for the sentences.
1. If you saw your favourite movie star,
   ☐ what will you do?
   ☐ what would you do?
2. If you are in trouble,
   ☐ I'll always help you.
   ☐ I'd always help you.
3. I'll see you later
   ☐ if you go to the party.
   ☐ if you went to the party.
4. I'd lend you my phone
   ☐ if you take care of it.
   ☐ if you took care of it.
5. If I knew the answer,
   ☐ I'll tell you.
   ☐ I'd tell you.
6. What would you do
   ☐ if you fail your exams?
   ☐ if you failed your exams?

2 🔘 **Make it personal** Complete the sentences so that they are true for you.
1. If I had one week left to live …
2. If I go out this weekend …
3. If I have enough money …
4. If I could go anywhere in the world …

Grammar Unit 5

5A Third conditional

If Clause			Result Clause		
If	I / you / he / she / we / they	had been on time,	I / you / he / she / we / they	would've	gotten a seat.
		'd read the book,		might've	understood the lecture.
		hadn't called,		wouldn't have	come to the party.

Use the **Third conditional** to express past wishes or possible past events and their probable results.
- *If you'd had more time, **what** would you have done?*
- ***How** would the world be different today if we'd had computers 100 years ago?*

Form:
If + subject + had (not) + past participle + subject + would have + past participle + phrase.
Note: use **might / could have** when the result is less sure.
- *If I'd lost some weight, I could have won the race.*

"Mom, would you have married Dad if you had seen him in high definition first?"

5B Modals of possibility / probability

Use **can / can't** or **could / couldn't** to show possibility.
- *You **can't** be serious.*
- *I thought you **could** do it.*
- *He **can't** be hungry again!*
- *It's midnight! Who **could** it be at the door?*
- *It **can't** be the kids! They're all in bed!*

Use **might** or **must** to show degrees of certainty or uncertainty.
- *I **might** go to the party tonight, but I'm not sure.*
- *You **must** be tired after your long flight.*
- *Yeah, I **may** just call in for half an hour.*

Note: you can use **may** instead of **might** or **could**.

5C Adjective order

- *It's a very **effective herbal** remedy.*
- *That **talented Spanish** actress is their new spokesperson.*

Fact adjectives follow this order:

size	age	shape	color	material	purpose	+ noun
little	old	square	red	brick	elementary	school

- *It was a **little, old, square, red, brick elementary** school.*

Note: try not to use more than three adjectives together.
- *He's a very **nice, smart, young** guy.*

Opinion adjectives (*amazing, friendly, good, interesting, nice, pretty,* etc.) usually come before fact adjectives (*American, metal, tall, young,* etc.).

A nice young man NOT ~~A young nice man~~

Note: add a comma after each consecutive adjective.

Opinion	Fact	Noun
a delicious	square chocolate	brownie
a funny	new stand-up	comedian
an ugly	old plastic	bag

You can change the position of fact and opinion adjectives for emphasis. Put the most important adjective next to the noun.
- *It's a **boring, old** story.* → *It's the same **old, boring** story.*
- *He had an **ugly, large** bag.* → *He had a **large, ugly** bag.*

"Brilliant! A 3-D, holographic, pop-up annual report. Hopefully, no one will notice what a lousy year we had."

Unit 5

5A

1 Match *If* clauses 1–6 to result clauses a–f.
1. If the alarm hadn't gone off,
2. If the Internet had been working,
3. If it had been an easier test,
4. If the sign hadn't been hidden,
5. If my phone hadn't run out of battery,
6. If we'd planned better,

a ☐ she wouldn't have missed the turn.
b ☐ there would've been enough food.
c ☐ I would've called you.
d ☐ he would've checked the schedule.
e ☐ more students might have passed it.
f ☐ you would've been really late.

2 Correct the mistakes in 1–5.
1. If you hadn't procrastinated, you'd had enough time to study.
2. I would've tell him if I would've seen him.
3. If you had bought a lottery ticket, you might win a lot of money.
4. We could been in the race if we'd sent our applications in on time.
5. If I hadn't found her when I did, she would lost.

3 🅰 **Make it personal** Describe what would have happened *if* …

… you'd learned another language.
… you'd found some buried treasure.
… you'd been born the opposite gender.
… you'd been a professional athlete.

If I'd been a professional athlete, I would've been a soccer player.

5B

1 Match 1–5 to comments a–e.
1. I walked five miles to get here.
2. He hasn't eaten very much today.
3. Sorry, sir, you don't have enough money in your account.
4. There's no sound from the TV.
5. I heard thunder in the distance.

a ☐ He might be hungry. Offer him something.
b ☐ You can't be serious! How could that be?
c ☐ There may be a storm coming.
d ☐ You must be tired!
e ☐ It could be the speakers.

2 Circle the correct alternative in 1–5.
1. Studies show that lack of exercise **can / might** not lead to obesity.
2. Sugar-free chewing gum **can't / might not** be so good for your teeth.
3. He didn't realize that his car **could / must** get such good mileage.
4. It **might not / could** be so easy to find a replacement for that device.
5. It **can / must** be a really long wait for a table at this restaurant.

3 Complete 1–5 with *can't* or *must* and these verbs.

believe   imagine   keep   realize   think

1. I _____ _____ listened to her entire story again!
2. You _____ _____ that this is a controversial subject.
3. She _____ _____ how you got him to talk about it.
4. My friends _____ _____ I'm crazy to go out with him.
5. Don't tell her—she _____ _____ a secret.

5C

1 Order the words in 1–5 to make sentences.
1. wearing / long-sleeved / he / blue / was / a / T-shirt / cotton / .
2. new / we / car / washed / shiny / red / our / sports / .
3. the road / put / a / big / cone / plastic / the / construction / on / crew / orange / .
4. for / you / look / should / small / gray / house / wooden / old / a / .
5. scary / dressed up / monster / green / huge / a / like / he / .

2 Describe each photo using as many adjectives as you can.

3 🅰 **Make it personal** Describe what you are wearing. Use as many adjectives as you can.

I'm wearing a beautiful, blue and white cotton skirt.

Grammar Unit 6

6A Restrictive relative clauses

Restrictive relative clauses identify the word(s) they refer to. They are essential for meaning and don't need commas.

Sentence 1	Sentence 2	Subject of relative clause
A guest sang last night.	The guest was Rihanna.	The guest *who* sang last night was Rihanna.
The class is meeting now.	It's in room 3.	The class *that* is meeting now is in room 3.
The man's dog is so smart.	He lives next door.	The man *whose* dog is so smart lives next door.

Sentence 1	Sentence 2	Object of relative clause
We bought a new apartment.	It's in Dubai.	The new apartment *that* we bought is in Dubai.
She's in love with a movie star.	He's Will Smith.	Will Smith is the movie star *that* she's in love with.
I met a man.	His sister is in my class.	I met a man *whose* sister is in my class.

Use relative clauses to connect two ideas with a relative pronoun.
▸ *Shh! The game show **that** we're all addicted to is on now.*
▸ *The contestant **who**'s winning is from Atlanta.*

Relative pronouns

	Subject	Object	Possessive
People	who, that	who, whom	whose
Things	that	that	

Note: *that* can only be used in restrictive relative clauses. It is optional when it refers to the object of the sentence.
▸ *The soap opera she's addicted to is Another World.*

6B Non-restrictive relative clauses

Non-restrictive relative clauses are not essential. They add extra information and need commas.

Subject	Non-restrictive clause	Phrase
Calvin Harris,	who is from Scotland,	is my favorite DJ.
My favorite band,	(which is) One Direction,	is from the UK.
The party I went to,	which was last Saturday,	was really fun.
The girl in my class,	whom I had never met before,	was from Argentina.
Shakira,	whose voice is amazing,	is a world-famous singer.

Use non-restrictive relative clauses to give additional information.
▸ *Lady Gaga, who sang at 9 p.m., was unable to leave the theater.*

Form non-restrictive relative clauses with **who / whom**, **whose**, and **which**.
The non-restrictive clause always comes between two commas or a comma and a period.

Note:
- do not use *that* in a non-restrictive clause.
- do not repeat the subject or object pronoun in the clause.

Miami, which is one of the most exciting cities in the world, is an expensive place.
NOT ~~Miami, that is one of the most exciting cities in the world, it is an expensive place.~~

The movie that we want to see is playing at 9 p.m.
NOT ~~The movie that we want to see it is playing at 9 p.m.~~

"The editor who turned down the first Harry Potter book, say hello to the publisher who took a pass on Stephen King."

Unit 6

6A

1 Complete the dialogue with *who*, *that*, or *whose* when necessary.

A: So tell me about the concert ¹_____ you went to yesterday.

B: It was great! There were two performances ²_____ were perfect.

A: Really? Wow! Who performed?

B: The first singer ³_____ I heard was Bruno Mars! He's awesome.

A: I love him! Isn't he touring with ... oh, what's the name of that band ⁴_____ lead singer is from New Jersey?

B: That's Bon Jovi. They're the band ⁵_____ Bruno sang with! There were lots of people in the audience ⁶_____ were amazed by their performance.

2 Which gaps, 1–6 in **1**,

a) could also be *which*?

b) are correct with no relative pronoun?

3 Combine the two sentences with *who*, *that*, *which*, or *whose*.

1 I'm sick of that talk show host. She complains too much.

2 We always watch the international news. It's on at 6 p.m.

3 Meghan's not interested in the guy. His ex-girlfriend just broke up with him.

4 *Star Trek* is a sci-fi show. It has been popular since the 1960s.

5 There are a lot of movies. They are based on superheroes.

6B

1 Correct the mistakes in 1–5.

1 This movie, that is based on a novel by Virginia Woolf, won many awards.

2 My favorite author, which I've liked since grade school, is J.K. Rowling.

3 They speak a language, that is called Basque, we hadn't heard before.

4 I saw Emma Stone, who's latest movie was brilliant, in the mall this morning.

5 He loves dancing to "Gangnam Style," that is a popular music video from South Korea.

6 Tom Cruise who's one of world's richest actors, he has three children and three ex-wives.

2 Match columns A, B, and C to make non-restrictive relative clauses.

A

1 The first book I read,

2 Cardi B,

3 That TV show,

4 My first teacher,

5 The time machine in *Back to the Future*,

B

☐ which was set in 1985,

☐ which was canceled after three episodes,

☐ who I remember well,

☐ which I really loved,

☐ whose real name is Belcalis Marlenis Almánzar,

C

☐ performed for a huge audience.

☐ was Mrs. Rodriguez.

☐ was called *Zero Hour*.

☐ was a Delorean.

☐ was *Harry Potter*.

3 Order the words in 1–5 to make relative clauses. Remember to use commas in the non-restrictive clause.

1 the movie / saw / which / that / I / Academy Awards / two / favorite / won / my / is / .

2 known for / has / shows / which / Canada / great / is / its / locations / popular / TV / a lot of / .

3 one of / famous / Johnny Depp / is / who / actors / in his fifties / most / Hollywood's / .

4 is / J.K. Rowling / who / the / of / crime / author / the / novel / Robert Galbraith / really / is / .

5 last / superheroes / *The Avengers* / movie / which / about / is / was / summer / released / a / .

4 🔘 **Make it personal** Describe your favorites in these five categories. Use non-restrictive relative clauses to give additional information.

movie   movie star   movie character   novel
TV show

My favorite TV show is Brooklyn Nine-Nine, which is set in New York, I think it is really funny.

Grammar Unit 7

7A Reported speech

Direct speech	Subject	Reporting verb	Reported speech
I **go** there every day.			he / she **went** there every day.
I **am working** here.	I		he / she **was working** there.
We'll **travel** tomorrow.	You		you / they **would travel** the next day.
I **would try** if I **could**.	He She	said (that) told (me, him, her, etc.)	he / she **would have tried** if he / she **could have**.
They **went** to the U.S.	We		they **had gone** to the U.S.
I **was talking** to her.	They		he / she **had been talking** to her.
We **had done** this before.			you / they **had done** that before.

Use **Reported speech** to report what someone said / told (you).
Form:
- a Simple past reporting verb (*said, told*, etc.).
- the main verb moves one tense back.
In reported speech, also remember to change:
- pronouns (*I* ➜ *he / she; we* ➜ *they*)
- place and time expressions (*this* ➜ *that; here* ➜ *there, tonight* ➜ *that night; yesterday* ➜ *the day before*, etc.)
The most common reporting verbs are: *describe, emphasize, explain, mention, observe, recommend, report, say, speculate, state, suggest, tell (someone).*
Note: use an object (*you, me, her, John*, etc.) with *tell*.
She told me she was traveling. NOT *She told she was traveling.*

7B Indirect questions

Expression	*if* *whether* *wh* word	Statement
Do you have any idea	if	I could leave my luggage here?
	whether	there's free Wi-Fi in the lobby?
Do you know / remember	what / which	payment methods I can use?
	when	the restaurant opens?
Could you tell me	where	the restroom is?
	why	I can't get my keycard to work?
Can you tell me	how	to get to the nearest bank?
	who	is in charge here?

Use indirect questions to sound more polite.
For *yes / no* questions, use *if* or *whether*. *Whether* is more formal.
Form:
Indirect question expression + *if / whether / wh* word + inversion of auxiliary and subject.
Note: don't use a question mark with the indirect question expressions *I wonder* or *I'd like to know*.

7C Reported questions, commands, and requests

Reported questions

Use expressions like *He asked me* and *They wanted to know* to report questions.
- ▸ *"Do you know the answer?"* ➜ *I asked him if he knew the answer.*
- ▸ *"What time does the flight leave?"* ➜ *They wanted to know what time the flight left.*
- ▸ *"Where did I leave my purse?"* ➜ *She wondered where she had left her purse.*

Form:
- as in reported speech, the main verb moves one tense back and there are changes to pronouns and place and time expressions.
- use the same word order as a statement.
They asked us who the man was. NOT *They asked us who was the man.*
- reported questions end with a period, not a question mark.
Note: use an object with *ask*.

Reported commands and requests

Use *ask* when reporting requests and *told* when reporting commands.
- ▸ *"Can I see your passport, please?"* ➜ *He asked to see my passport.*
- ▸ *"Place your bags on the X-ray machine."* ➜ *She told me to place my bags on the X-ray machine.*

Form:
- commands and requests are usually reported using *(not) + to + infinitive*.
- ▸ *"Please remember! Don't forget the homework!"* ➜ *He told us not to forget the homework.*

- *ask* and *tell* are followed by an object.
- ▸ *She asked / told them to help her.*

Unit 7

7A

1 Correct the mistakes in 1–7.

1 He said he doesn't know where was the parking lot.
2 She mentioned that she won't be back in time for the party.
3 She said she not know where was David.
4 They never told us where is the party.
5 He explained why there will be an extra charge on the bill.
6 He said me that he wasn't going to Lima.
7 They told they would be late.

2 Complete 1–5 with the correct form of these verbs.

be   learn   locate   mention   not know

1 The teacher promised that we _____ Spanish in three weeks!
2 He told us he _____ if he could fix the Internet connection.
3 We wondered where the restrooms were _____.
4 She _____ that the concierge would not be back until 1 p.m.
5 The manager said that the elevators _____ broken.

7B

1 Complete 1–5 with the words below.

what   when   whether   where   who

1 Do you know _____ the changing rooms are?
2 I'd like to know _____ or not the flight will be on time.
3 Could you tell me _____ the Internet is going to be working again?
4 Do you have any idea _____ he was trying to say?
5 Could you tell me _____ I have to contact to solve this problem?

2 Match 1–5 to a–e to form indirect questions.

1 I wonder if you can
2 Could you please
3 Do you happen to know
4 Could you tell me whether
5 Do you have any idea what

a ☐ what time the train leaves?
b ☐ this button on my phone is for?
c ☐ this bus is going downtown or not?
d ☐ tell me where I put my keys.
e ☐ remind us when the next flight leaves?

3 You're a polite tourist in a hotel. Prepare indirect questions to ask about five of these things.

ATM   cheap stores   free parking   free Wi-Fi
good restaurant   gym   restroom   safe
swimming pool

Could you tell me where the restroom is?

7C

1 Order the words in 1–6 to make sentences.

1 asked / knew / if / he / get / to / repair / how / shop / I / to / a / .
2 she / me / take / Main Street / left / a / to / told / on / .
3 not / for / late / the / told / they / us / to / be / lecture / .
4 actor / reporter / asked / what / was / favorite / the / his / movie / the / .
5 her / asked / instructor / what / in / time / hand / could / she / the / paper / the / .
6 soccer player / the / time / training / what / started / new / asked / the / coach / the / .

2 Complete 1–4 with reported questions.

1 A: Excuse me, is there an ATM nearby?
  B: Sorry, what did you ask me?
  A: I asked _____.
2 A: What's your rate for a single room?
  B: Excuse me, I didn't understand what you said.
  A: I asked _____.
3 A: Do you know where the bus station is?
  B: Pardon me? I didn't catch what you said.
  A: I asked _____.
4 A: Did you talk to your girlfriend about it?
  B: What did you say?
  A: I asked _____.

3 Report the instructions using *You told us (not) to.*

1 Don't blame me.
2 Keep calm and carry on.
3 Don't worry, be happy.
4 Enjoy yourselves but don't go crazy!

Grammar Unit 8

8A Modal perfects – *must have, can't have, might / may have*

Use **Modal perfects**:
1 to speculate about the past.
▸ You **must have** been really upset when that happened.
▸ It **can't have** been easy to give up chocolate!
2 to express possibility or uncertainty.
▸ They **might have** left the party early ... I don't see them!
▸ Do you think the area **may have** flooded?

Form:
Subject + modal + *have* + past participle.
Note:
must have = we're sure something **did** happen
can't have = we're sure it **didn't** happen

8B Causative form

Use the **Causative** form to talk about services / actions that other people do for you.
▸ Do you know where I can **have my car fixed**?
▸ She doesn't **get her hair styled** by a professional.
▸ You **got your teeth whitened**, didn't you?
▸ Are you **getting your computer fixed**?
▸ We're going to **have a class photo taken** at school tomorrow.

Form:
Subject + *get* / *have* + object + past participle.
Remember: *get* / *have* can be in any tense.
Note: when other people do bad things to you, it's more common to use *have* instead of *get*.
▸ He **had** his car stolen last night.
(He didn't ask / pay anyone to do it = not a service.)

8C Tag questions

Tag question	
➕ Statement	➖ Question tag
We're crazy to be doing this,	aren't we?
She has already traveled to Europe,	hasn't she?
I think Chris and Sue went to the beach,	didn't they?
He had planned on coming over,	hadn't he?
I'm sure you'll be fine,	won't you?
➖ Statement	➕ Question tag
She didn't do this correctly,	did she?
You have no idea what I'm talking about,	do you?
They weren't married, I think,	were they?
I haven't told her anything,	have I?
He would never ask her out,	would he?
We've got nothing to lose,	have we?

Form:
- Subject + ➕ statement + comma + ➖ auxiliary + subject?
- Subject + ➖ statement + comma + ➕ auxiliary + subject?
- Keep the tenses the same.

Use:
- rising intonation to check information that you are not sure about.
- falling intonation to state your opinion and invite the other person to comment.

Note:
- a **question tag** is the "mini-question" after the comma.
- a **tag question** is the whole sentence, plus the "mini-question."
- even when the verb in the statement is ➕, if its meaning is ➖ because of words like *never, no, nothing, nobody*, etc., the **question tag** should be ➕.
▸ You never enjoyed sports at school, **did you?**

"But in your business, being laughed at is *good*, isn't it?"

Unit 8

8A

1 Complete 1–5 with *can't have, may have, must have,* and the past participle of the verb in parentheses.
   1 You drove from Chicago to L.A.! That _____ a long time! (take)
   2 I don't know why the traffic is so slow. There _____ an accident. (be)
   3 That loud sound _____ all the animals. (scare)
   4 "What was that noise?" "I don't know, it _____ a cat or something." (be)
   5 Well, she _____ too hard for her keys. They're on the table! (look)

2 Prepare at least two sentences about each photo a–d, using *must have / might have / can't have* to apologize, criticize, or sympathize.

A: *Excuse me, but this bill can't have been calculated correctly. It's too expensive.*
B: *Sorry, but you might have forgotten this is a French gourmet restaurant.*

8B

1 Complete 1–5 with the correct form of *have / get* of these verbs.

break   change   check   install   rebuild   steal

   1 Do you go to Dr. Smith to _____ your teeth _____?
   2 This neighborhood is getting dangerous. Joe _____ his car _____ last night.
   3 Their kitchen looks really nice now, after they _____ it _____.
   4 My car sounds a little strange. I think I need to _____ the oil _____.
   5 Grandpa _____ his house _____ into, so he _____ an alarm _____ and now he feels more secure.

2 Describe two things you can get done by these people.
   a a beauty technician
   b a mechanic
   c a doctor
   d a construction worker
   e an artist
   You could get your nails done by a beauty technician.

8C

1 Complete 1–6 with the correct tag.
   1 This coat doesn't make me look overweight, _____?
   2 You were going to say "yes," _____?
   3 I'm not very good at managing these files, _____?
   4 That's absolutely incredible, _____?
   5 They haven't gone home yet, _____?
   6 She got her car fixed before the trip, _____?

2 Look at photos a–d and make tag questions using the words in parentheses.

He / can't   You / not like

You / not study   It / hot

3 Correct the mistake in these tag questions.
   a That boy's too young to drive, isn't it.
   b Lots of kids don't eat enough vegetables, don't they?
   c You'll never speak English if you don't practice, won't you?
   d There are too many plastic bottles in the world, aren't they?

153

Grammar Unit 9

9A Review of verb families

Time \ Family	Simple	Continuous	Perfect	Perfect continuous
Present	⊕ He **studies** English. ⊖ They **don't work** together. ❓ **Does** she **live** near here?	⊕ I'm **writing** an essay. ⊖ She's **not working** today. ❓ **Are** you **kidding** me?	⊕ I've **lived** here since 1998. ⊖ You **haven't seen** her for a long time. ❓ **Has** she **bought** anything since then?	⊕ Global warming **has been getting** worse recently. ⊖ We **haven't been waiting** for long. ❓ How long **has** she **been working** here?
Past	⊕ We **danced** all night long yesterday. ⊖ I **didn't go** to Mary's party. ❓ **Did** you **hear** what she said?	⊕ They **were fighting** again. ⊖ She **wasn't crying** because of you. ❓ **Were** they **talking** about her?	⊕ I'd **left** by the time they arrived. ⊖ They **hadn't arrived**. ❓ **Had** they **called** you before you left?	⊕ We'd **been trying** that before she called. ⊖ They **hadn't been talking** to each other. ❓ **Had** he **been living** with her before she moved to the U.S.?

9B Passive voice

Simple passive

Present	am / is / are (not)		The chefs here **are known** for their amazing dishes.
Past	was / were (not)	Past participle	These sweaters **were made** in Ireland.
Future	will / won't		**Will** the construction **be completed** by 2030?

Perfect passive

Present	have / has (not)			**Has** the bank **been authorized** to send money?
Past	had / hadn't	been	Past participle	I wanted to buy that painting but it **had already been sold**.
Future	will / won't have			It **won't have been built** by next month.

Continuous passive

Present	am / is / are (not)			How cool! You**'re being followed** on Twitter. The website **is being watched** by the authorities.
Past	was / were (not)	being	Past participle	In January 2019, Facebook **was being used** by over 2.25 billion people.

In the active voice, the subject does the action and the object receives the action.

In the passive voice, the receiver is the subject and the "doer" is optionally included as the object.

Active: *Tony washed the dishes.*
Passive: *The dishes were washed (by Tony).*

Use the passive voice:
1. to emphasize that receiving the action is more important.
2. if you don't know (or don't want to mention) who does the action.

9C Future perfect and continuous

Future perfect

Use the **Future perfect** to talk about a future action that will be finished before another future time or action.

▸ *By next week, we'll **have been** together for six months!*

Form: ***will (not) have*** + **past participle** + phrases like *by the time, by the year (2030), in (hours)*.

Future continuous

Use the **Future continuous** to talk about an action in progress at a certain future time.

▸ *By this time tomorrow, **we'll be lying** on a beautiful beach.*

Form: ***will (not)*** + ***be*** + verb + *-ing*.

Unit 9

9A

1 Complete 1–6 with *Present* or *Past*, *Simple* or *Continuous* form of the verbs in parentheses.
1 We _____ our time this morning. There's no need to rush. (take)
2 I _____ at the light when the bike ran into my car. (wait)
3 She _____ to download that file but her laptop froze halfway through. (try)
4 Students always _____ new words on that language website. (pick up)
5 We _____ in dangerous areas at night. (not walk)
6 _____ you _____ TV when I texted you? (watch)

2 Complete the dialogues with the correct form of the verbs. Use contractions where possible.
1 A: What _____ ? (you / do)
   B: Well, I _____ this show about the history of crime. It's so interesting. (watch)
2 A: Really? I _____ you _____ into history. (not know) (be)
   B: Yeah, I guess I _____ . _____ the story of Al Capone? (be) (you / hear)
3 A: Oh, yeah! _____ he the guy who _____ alcohol back in the 20s? (be) (sell)
   B: Yep, that _____ him. He _____ one of the most notorious criminals in history, until he _____ in 1947. (be) (be) (die)

3 Describe pictures a and b. Use as many verb tenses as you can.

a

b

9B

1 Complete 1–6 with *has / have / had + been*.
1 We're sorry. The phone number _____ changed.
2 I tried to download the song, but the site _____ shut down.
3 Lately it seems like books _____ replaced by digital texts.
4 The movie _____ nominated for three awards, but didn't win any.
5 They _____ (not) _____ notified of the flight's cancellation and are still waiting at the airport!
6 Excuse me, ma'am. _____ your passport _____ stamped?

2 Correct the seven mistakes.

Welcome to the ALCATRAZ NATIONAL PARK. Our website is designing to help you understand the history of Alcatraz.
Our visitors' center has just being renovated and guided tours being given every hour. Alcatraz prison is built in 1933 and have been one of the most famous federal prisons in the U.S.
The National Park Service is being dedicated to keeping the park up to date, clean, and accessible for all visitors. The park will be not held responsible for cancellation due to weather.

9C

1 Complete 1–5 with the *Future perfect* or *Future continuous* of the verbs in parentheses.
1 The new student center building _____ by the time school starts. (not finish)
2 I really don't know what I _____ next week. (do)
3 By next June, I _____ in this town for five years. (live)
4 I think the government _____ this problem for years to come. (debate)
5 Don't worry, they _____ the exhibit before you see it. (not take down)

2 🟢 **Make it personal** Describe what you think will be happening or have happened in the future to at least five of these.

extinction of animals   genetically-modified food
new forms of transportation   growing old
living in space   soccer players' salaries

By 2050, I think people will be living on Mars.

155

Grammar Unit 10

10A Gerunds and infinitives

Use **gerunds**:

1. as the subject of a sentence
2. for an activity in progress
3. after prepositions or adjective + prepositions
4. after specific verbs

- *Listening to music always calms him down.*
- *I really don't like looking at your mess.*
- *She never asks before using my computer!*
- *We are sick of standing here and waiting for tickets.*
- *She got angry without knowing the whole story.*

Verb + gerund

admit	deny	imagine	regret
adore	dislike	keep	risk
advise	enjoy	mind	spend (time)
avoid	fed up with	miss	suggest
can't help	feel like	practice	understand
consider	finish	quit	waste (time)

Use **infinitives**:

1. to express purpose
2. after adjectives
3. after specific verbs

- *I'm studying hard to get good grades.*
- *It will be impossible to finish this on time.*
- *I was stupid not to tell the truth.*

Form: *must have* = we're sure something **did** happen
can't have = we're sure it **didn't** happen

Verb + infinitive

afford	demand	offer	remember
agree	expect	plan	seem
appear	fail	prepare	stop
arrange	forget	pretend	wait
ask	hope	promise	want
decide	manage	refuse	wish

10B Verb + gerund or infinitive

Using the gerund **G** or infinitive **I** after *forget, remember, stop,* and *try* changes the meaning.

Forget

I not do something that you should do / have done.	I forgot **to bring** my ID!
G a planned activity that is canceled.	Well, you can forget **coming** to my party! I'm uninviting you.

Remember

I remember something you should do.	He never remembers **to lock** his car.
G remember an event or action in the past.	I remember **seeing** her at the party.

Stop

I interrupt an activity to begin another.	She was lost so she stopped **to get** directions.
G interrupt or quit something.	She stopped **smoking** last year.

Try

I make an effort to do something.	He'll try **to go** to your party, but he's very busy.
G do something and see if it works.	I'll try **talking** to her about it. She might change her mind.

After certain verbs, there is little change in meaning.

- *She doesn't like talking / to talk about her problems.*
- *I prefer working / to work alone.*

Verb + gerund or infinitive

begin	continue	like	prefer
choose	hate	love	start

10C Separable and inseparable phrasal verbs

Separable phrasal verbs

Most phrasal verbs with one particle are **separable** and can take a direct object (*the book, your friend*) between the verb and the particle or after the particle. If the object is a pronoun, it **must** go between the verb and the particle.

- *Mike was afraid to ask Julie out, but he finally called her up.*
- *We tried to cheer the team up by taking them out.*

Mike finally called her up. NOT ~~Mike finally called up her.~~

Inseparable phrasal verbs

With **inseparable phrasal verbs**, objects (and pronouns) cannot come between the verb and particle.

She turned into a princess. NOT ~~She turned a princess into.~~

Verbs with more than one particle are usually inseparable and the object follows the second particle.

- *I know what you're going through. It's a really hard time.*
- *Let's catch up when we're not so busy.*
- *You know he's not easy to get along with.*

Separable	Inseparable
Don't **throw** the bottles **away**.	I'm **looking forward to** it.
Can I **try** your glasses **on**?	Will we ever **run out of** oil?
Can you **turn** the heat **up**?	If I make a plan, I **stick to** it.
Switch your phone **off**!	I'm sorry, we've **sold out**.
Plug it **into** the wall socket.	This sofa **turns into** a bed.
I **cut** salt **out** of my diet.	What's that statue **made of**?
I'm cooking. Please **keep** the cat **away**.	My car **broke down** on the highway.
Please **hear** me **out**!	The office was **broken into**.
Stop **putting** it **off**!	Nick hasn't **showed up** yet.

156

Unit 10

10A

1 Complete 1–5 with the correct form of these verbs.

avoid   call   like   promise   wake up

1 I _____ last night to ask for your advice.
2 She _____ answering texts or calls when she's having dinner.
3 I've never _____ playing video games.
4 We often _____ feeling too tired to work.
5 She always _____ to help me tidy up, but she never does.

2 Correct two mistakes in each of 1–6.

1 I don't mind to drive you for the train station.
2 She's not interested on listen to his problems.
3 It's a very interesting subject for talking about.
4 They got fed up with hear to neighbor's noisy party.
5 I hope you seeing again one day soon.
6 I usually prefer watch movies to read books.

10B

1 Circle the correct alternative in 1–5.

1 Lee's so afraid of **making** / **to make** a mistake that he doesn't try.
2 You can try **change** / **changing** my mind if you want, but it won't work.
3 After joining www.stopthejunk.com we stopped **to get** / **getting** spam.
4 Alex hadn't thought about **to do** / **doing** anything special for her birthday.
5 I can't stand people who bump into me on the street without **to apologize** / **apologizing**.

2 Match 1–5 to a–e to make sentences.

1 I'm looking forward to
2 They've planned on
3 We prefer not
4 She hopes
5 Don't forget

a ☐ to sit near the aisle.
b ☐ to turn on the security system when you leave.
c ☐ to graduate next year so she can get a job.
d ☐ seeing you next weekend! We'll have a great time.
e ☐ visiting the art museum this Saturday.

3 Describe photos a–d using *forget*, *remember*, *stop*, and *try*.

In the first photo, I hope she doesn't forget to pack her passport.

10C

1 Complete 1–6 with the correct separable or inseparable phrasal verb and an object.

cut down on   grow up   look at   pick up
run into   run out of

1 Jose _____ in a beautiful neighborhood of Buenos Aires.
2 Yumi needed bread but forgot to _____ after work.
3 They're mad at Jeff and hope they don't _____ at the party.
4 Lu eats too many sweets. She's trying to _____.
5 The pop star walked by and he couldn't stop _____.
6 My car's _____ so I can't drive you to the station.

2 Order the words in 1–5 to make sentences.

1 with / wants / she / boyfriend / break / her / to / up / .
2 put / can't / up / noise / I / all / on / weekend / with / that / the / .
3 that / should've / tried / you / sweater / on / .
4 he / can / he / call / any / time / up / us / wants / .
5 away / best / when / seven / was / my / I / old / moved / years / friend / .

3 🔵 Make it personal Correct the mistakes in 1–5. Then prepare questions for 1–5.

1 When I learn a new word, I try it on with my friends.
2 Tom is going to ask out her on a date.
3 It's difficult to figure it out what new words mean.
4 He always forgets to turn the lights before he goes to bed.
5 She'd been making a cake when she ran out eggs of.
How do you remember new words?

Verbs

Irregular verbs

Irregular verbs can be difficult to remember. Try remembering them in groups with similar sounds, conjugation patterns, or spellings.

Simple past and Past participle are the same

Base form	Simple past	Past participle
bring	brought /brɔt/	brought
buy	bought	bought
catch	caught /cɔt/	caught
fight	fought	fought
teach	taught	taught
think	thought	thought
feed	fed	fed
feel	felt	felt
keep	kept	kept
leave	left	left
mean	meant /mɛnt/	meant
meet	met	met
sleep	slept	slept
lay	laid	laid
pay	paid	paid
sell	sold	sold
tell	told	told
send	sent	sent
spend	spent	spent
stand	stood /stʊd/	stood
understand	understood	understood
lose	lost	lost
shoot	shot	shot
can	could	could
will	would	would
build	built /bɪlt/	built
find	found /faʊnd/	found
hang	hung	hung
have	had	had
hear	heard /hɜrd/	heard
hold	held	held
make	made	made
say	said /sɛd/	said
sit	sat	sat
swing	swung /swʌŋ/	swung
win	won /wʌn/	won

Base form and Past participle are the same

Base form	Simple past	Past participle
become	became	become
come	came	come
run	ran	run

No changes across the three forms

Base form	Simple past	Past participle
cost	cost	cost
cut	cut	cut
hit	hit	hit
let	let	let
put	put /pʊt/	put
quit	quit /kwɪt/	quit
set	set	set
split	split	split

Special cases

Base form	Simple past	Past participle
be	was / were	been
draw	drew /dru:/	drawn /drɔn/
fly	flew /flu:/	flown /floʊn/
lie	lay	lain
read	read /rɛd/	read /rɛd/

Simple past + -en

Base form	Simple past	Past participle
beat	beat	beaten
bite	bit	bitten
break	broke	broken
choose	chose	chosen
forget	forgot	forgotten
freeze	froze	frozen
get	got	got / gotten
speak	spoke	spoken
steal	stole	stolen
wake	woke	woken

158

Verbs

Simple past + -en

Base form	Simple past	Past participle
beat	beat	beaten
bite	bit	bitten
break	broke	broken
choose	chose	chosen
forget	forgot	forgotten
freeze	froze	frozen
get	got	got / gotten
speak	spoke	spoken
steal	stole	stolen
wake	woke	woken

Base form + -en

Base form	Simple past	Past participle
drive	drove	driven /drɪvən/
eat	ate	eaten
fall	fell	fallen
give	gave	given
ride	rode	ridden /rɪdən/
see	saw /sɔ/	seen
shake	shook	shaken
take	took	taken
write	wrote	written /rɪtən/

Base form ending in o + -ne

Base form	Simple past	Past participle
do	did	done /dʌn/
go	went	gone /gɔn/

i - a - u

Base form	Simple past	Past participle
begin	began	begun
drink	drank	drunk
ring	rang	rung
sing	sang	sung
swim	swam	swum

ow - ew - own

Base form	Simple past	Past participle
blow	blew /blu:/	blown
grow	grew	grown
know	knew	known
throw	threw	thrown

ear - ore - orn

Base form	Simple past	Past participle
swear	swore	sworn
tear /tɛr/	tore	torn
wear	wore	worn

Common stative verbs

Thinking / opinions

(dis)agree	imagine	realize	suppose
believe	know	recognize	think
depend	matter	remember	understand
guess	mean	seem	

Feelings / emotions

feel (=have an opinion)	(dis)like	prefer	wish
	love	promise	
hate	need	want	

Senses

see	taste	feel
hear	smell	

Others

belong	have	involve
contain	include	own

Use stative verbs:

▸ to describe states / opinions, not actions.
   I believe in God. I hate spiders.
▸ in the simple form, even for temporary situations.
   Sorry, we don't understand. NOT ~~We aren't understanding.~~

Note:

▸ Some verbs which are usually stative can be actions:
   I think that's a good idea. (opinion).
   It's lunchtime, so I'm thinking about food. (action)
   We're having a 10-minute break.
▸ A few, especially *like* and *love* are increasingly used in speech as "actions":
   I'm liking this burger.
   I've been loving you for so long …

Sounds and usual spellings

S Difficult sounds for Spanish speakers
P Difficult sounds for Portuguese speakers

▶ To listen to these words and sounds, and to practice them, go to the pronunciation section on the Richmond Learning Platform.

Vowels

/iː/	three, tree, eat, receive, believe, key, B, C, D, E, G, P, T, V, Z
/ɪ/	six, mix, it, fifty, fish, trip, lip, fix
/ʊ/	book, cook, put, could, cook, woman
/uː/	two, shoe, food, new, soup, true, suit, Q, U, W
/ɛ/	pen, ten, heavy, then, again, men, F, L, M, N, S, X
/ə/	bananas, pajamas, family, photography
/ɜr/	shirt, skirt, work, turn, learn, verb
/ɔr/	four, door, north, fourth
/ɔ/	walk, saw, water, talk, author, law
/æ/	man, fan, bad, apple
/ʌ/	sun, run, cut, umbrella, country, love
/ɑ/	hot, not, on, clock, fall, tall
/ɑr/	car, star, far, start, party, artist, R

Diphthongs

/eɪ/	plane, train, made, stay, they, A, H, J, K
/aɪ/	nine, wine, night, my, pie, buy, eyes, I, Y
/aʊ/	house, mouse, town, cloud
/ɔɪ/	toys, boys, oil, coin
/oʊ/	nose, rose, home, know, toe, road, O

160

Sounds and usual spellings

□ Voiced
□ Unvoiced

Consonants

/p/	pig, pie, open, top, apple
/b/	bike, bird, describe, able, club, rabbit
/m/	medal, monster, name, summer
/w/	web, watch, where, square, one
/f/	fish, feet, off, phone, enough
/v/	vet, van, five, have, video
/θ/	teeth, thief, thank, nothing, mouth
/ð/	mother, father, the, other
/t/	truck, taxi, hot, stop, attractive
/d/	dog, dress, made, adore, sad, middle
/n/	net, nurse, tennis, one, sign, know
/l/	lion, lips, long, all, old

/s/	snake, skate, kiss, city, science
/z/	zoo, zebra, size, jazz, lose
/ʃ/	shark, shorts, action, special, session, chef
/ʒ/	television, treasure, usual
/k/	cat, cake, back, quick
/g/	goal, girl, leg, guess, exist
/ŋ/	king, ring, single, bank
/h/	hand, hat, unhappy, who
/tʃ/	chair, cheese, kitchen, future, question
/dʒ/	jeans, jump, generous, bridge
/r/	red, rock, ride, married, write
/j/	yellow, yacht, university

161

Audioscript

Unit 1

▶1.1 Notice the word and sentence stress and the connections.

M = Mika   C = Carlos

M How's_it going? Settling_into your new home? How's the new job?

C It's going_OK, thanks! I've met_a few new people through work, but it'll be nice to make some more friends.

M Of course. I'm_sure you'll_start meeting people soon. It's_early days. Got_any plans for tonight?

C Yup, I'm going on a "meet-up"! It's the first one I've ever been on, actually?

M You're going_on_a what?

C You know, a meet-up. It's like a social group for people who want to make new friends_and network, that kind_of thing. I've organized_it through an_app. You download the_app or go_on the website, register, and write_a profile about yourself. Upload pictures_and stuff. The_app then matches you with people who you've got things_in common with. Then you go_on meet-ups. It could be a restaurant, museum, sports_activity ... anything!

M Oh, I see. I haven't heard about_that. It sounds like_a great_idea, though! Especially when you're new_in town. So, what happens when you've registered and been matched with people?

C Well, then you can chat_online and get_to know people_a bit there first. Then you choose_a meet-up to go to. I've met some nice people_online so far. I guess I'll see how the meeting-up_part goes! We're going_ on_an organized walk_on Sunday and the organizers_encourage you to prepare some questions to_ask to help get_to know people.

M Really? Like_an interview. So, uh, what kind_of people_are you hoping to meet, then?

C Um, I'm just hoping to make some new friends who_are_into the same things_as me and can show me_around the city a bit. It would be good_to meet some new_work contacts, too. Networking_is_always good!

M Really? So, you're going_on this meet-up to make work contacts?

C No, not really. You know, I just want to meet some cool people and if_I meet someone who can help with business, that's_a bonus!

M Always thinking_about work, aren't you?

C Well, sure, that's why I moved here. But I'm ready to make some new friends, too. What_about you? What's_going_on with ...?

▶1.2 Notice /w/, the connecting /w/ (caused by two vowel sounds connecting), and silent /w/.

C = Carlos   J = Jenny

C Hi ... I'm Carlos. It's really nice to meet you. You are ...?

J Hi, Carlos! I'm Jenny. We chatted online a bit. Great to meet you in person!

C Oh yes, we did chat online, didn't we? I remember now.

J So, have you been to one of these things before? I remember you said you were new in town.

C No, I haven't. I've just moved here recently, so this is the first one. I'm feeling a bit nervous, to be honest!

J Don't worry. It's only natural. It can be a bit scary meeting lots of new people at once, can't it?

C It really can be! So, how ... er ... how ...

J Shall we have a look at our questions? Did you prepare some? That will give us something to talk about while we walk.

C Ah, yes. Good idea. I did prepare some.

J Great. I've still got mine, too. I bring them to every meet-up I come to. It might seem a bit strange, but it's a really good way to get to know someone.

C OK then! Why don't you go first?

▶1.3 Notice the intonation. ↗↘

C = Carlos   J = Jenny

J How long have you lived here? ↘ Do you have a favorite part of town? ↘

C Ah, that's a difficult one. I've only been here for two months so it's difficult to say. I love the square—what's it called? ↗ Queen's Square. It's really pretty.

J Yes, there are some really nice bars and shops there. I'm going there tomorrow evening, actually. I'm meeting some friends for coffee. You're welcome to join us if you like. Anyway, your turn ...

C Ah, thanks. That's really nice of you! So ... er ... tell me about your friends ... Who do you spend the most time with? ↘

J Well, I'm working so much at the moment, I spend most of my time with my cats! I've got three.

C Three cats! I have to admit, I'm more a dog person. I prefer dogs to cats.

J Well, I like dogs, too, but cats are easier to take care of.

C True.

J My turn. What about your parents? ↘ Who are you closer to—your mom or your dad? ↗

C Mom. Definitely. I haven't had any contact with my dad in years ... I don't want to talk about that if you don't mind.

J Oh, I'm sorry. Of course not.

C No need for you to be sorry. So, what are you doing this weekend? ↘

J This weekend, I'm visiting a friend for her birthday.

C That sounds like fun.

J It will be. OK. My turn. What celebrity would you enjoy having dinner with? ↘

C Hmm ... Let me think. I'd have to say Emma Stone ...

J Oh, me, too! She's the best. I've seen all of her movies.

C Really? Isn't she fantastic? ↗ So ... speaking of movies, what was the last movie that made you cry? ↘

J That's a good question ... Well, probably A Street Cat Named Bob. You know I love cats, and that cat was just amazing.

C No way! I cried like a baby watching that one, too.

J What's the first thing you do every morning? ↘

C That's easy! I throw my alarm clock on the floor. I hate the noise it makes!

J I see! Not a morning person, then. I love early mornings! It's the best time of day. Carlos, here's another question. What's the one thing you're most afraid of? ↘

C Promise you won't laugh? ↗ ... The dark.

J The dark? ↗ Oh, that's kind of cute.

C You think so? ↗

J Look at you! You're turning red! Are you a little bit embarrassed? ↗

▶1.5 Notice the silent /t/ and the connections with vowels.

I first met_Adam two years_ago. I used to walk my dog_in the park next_to my house and he was_always there walking his dog, too. We just used to smile and say hello. Anyway, I was_attracted to him immediately. He has this really beautiful smile and ... one morning the dogs started playing together and he said something lame about the weather_or something and we started chatting and we got_along really well so we swapped numbers. Then we went_out together a few times, you know, just for coffee and stuff. I thought he was funny and charming_and interesting. We started hanging out a lot more, going to restaurants and meeting each other's friends. We talked_about everything and got to know_each other really well. Things were great for about the first six months and then, you know, it was little things at first. I was working a lot at the time and he couldn't understand why we weren't spending as much time together. We argued a lot and fell out_over stupid things like not returning each other's messages. It just wasn't working and eventually we broke_up. I got so angry with him that he couldn't understand how important my career was to me. We were both really upset. After a few more months, I started to miss him, so I called_ and we talked_about stuff. He promised to be more understanding and I promised to make more time for him. Then we got back together! I think_I ... I think I've fallen for him again! How weird is that? But who knows what_our future will bring!

▶1.7 Notice the false starts, repetitions, and uh pauses.

Kathy I think be realistic that you, our expectations sometimes are so high ... But most of marriage is lived in between the ups and the downs... And that it's hard work. And not all the time, but it's hard work.

Gene Uh, I think one of the pieces of advice that my dad gave me is, "Gene, always communicate. Always talk, talk things out." And I really believe that communication is so essential ... And that uh, you need to work out many different areas before you get married. Uh, I think you need to talk about money matters. I think you need to talk about child rearing. I think religion is important. I think sex takes care of itself ... Pretty much ... At least initially. But I really do think there are some topics or some areas that need to be hashed out, otherwise, it's conflict.

Karl You gotta learn to uh, give more than you take, or you'll never make it and uh, that's, that's the bottom line.

Bonnie And you need, you need to, you know, grow together, uh, in what, in what you do ... Try new things, you know. Go out and start skiing if you haven't done it, do it as a couple. Do things together, you know, or as a family if you have a family. I think those are important things, too, you know. Don't you have your own hobbies and your husband or spouse have their own hobbies. That's not a real good way ...

Bill Every time, if you have a disagreement or a problem, you correct it before you go to bed. And uh, then, you never wake up, and uh, with a carry-over. And uh, that has—to me—always been good advice. I'm not sure that Kay and I have always followed that, but uh, you know, most of the time we have.

162

Audioscript

Kay I'd have to say those who play together stay together, instead of going your own separate ways and doing your own things.

▶ 1.9 Notice /ə/ and sentence stress.

Professor Robin Dunbar is an anthropologist and evolutionary psychologist at Oxford University. He is famous for calculating "Dunbar's Number", which is an estimate that the number of relationships humans are able to manage is 150. He believes that this number has been almost the same throughout human history. From small villages in the past all the way up to the modern age of international travel and social media. Dunbar's Number came from research Professor Dunbar did with primates in the 1990s. He discovered that there was a connection between the size of these animals' brains and the social groups they belonged to. By using the data he collected in his studies of primates, he estimated that humans should be able to handle only 150 relationships at any one time.

In order to build relationships, we need to remember details about people's lives, etc., so the size of our brains is an important factor. According to Dunbar, our brains can only hold enough information to maintain about 150 relationships. This number can be seen in lots of different situations: the size of villages, remote tribal groups, the number of Christmas cards we send, and the average number of Facebook friends we have.

Of course, within these 150 relationships, there are different levels. The first is made up of about five very close friends, the next 15 are good friends, 50 friends we see reasonably often, and then the remainder is acquaintances. This number is based on averages, so it's possible to have more or fewer people in your social circles. However, if we have more, it will be difficult to manage and the quality of the relationships will suffer. It seems that 150 is the best number. With this many people, we can maintain stable, honest relationships.

▶ 1.10 Notice /θ/, /ð/, and /d/.

J = Jamie   A = Alison

J   That's a nice picture! Are they your colleagues?
A   Yes, they are. They're a great bunch. Luckily, we all get along really well.
J   When did you take that one?
A   That was taken at the Christmas party last year!
J   Looks like you had fun! What about this one? Who's that?
A   That's Lucy. She's my sister's best friend. She's a musician.
J   Does she play professionally?
A   Yes, she does. We often go to watch her.
J   Can she play any other instruments?
A   Sure! She's really talented; one of those people who can play anything!
J   Oh, what a nice shot! Who took this one?
A   My dad took it, I think. This is Dominic. We've known each other since kindergarten. He's great. The kind of person you can always depend on.
J   So, out of all these lovely people, who are you closest to?
A   Hard to say really. I love them all!

▶ 1.12 Notice the spellings of /k/.

A = Anna   B = Betty

A   So, who are you following on Insta these days? I want to find some new accounts to follow. Any good ones?

B   Yes, sure. I've added some really cool ones recently. Do you want to see?
A   OK, let's have a look.
B   Right, well, I like to follow accounts that I find inspiring, funny, cute, etc. For example, travel accounts. Look at this one. This couple is traveling the world together. They take amazing photographs and they really inspire me. Each photo is so creative! I mean, who doesn't want to do what they're doing?!
A   Oh, I see! Look at that picture. Wow! They sure look like they're having an amazing time. Where is that? Vietnam?
B   I think so. They certainly are worth following, I think.
A   OK, I'll add them! What else?
B   I don't know about you, but I just love anything with cute animals, so I follow a few of these accounts. Look at this one! I mean, these instantly put me in a good mood.
A   "Animal Addicts". Oh, look at the puppies! So cute!!
B   And then there's this one. These guys rescue mistreated animals. It's so moving and inspiring.
A   Ah, yeah. That one's definitely for me. I'll add it. Why would anyone ever want to hurt those animals? It's so touching to see those people with them!
B   I know. I do love this one. It's one of my favourites. Want to see some more?
A   Sure, this is fun!
B   OK, I also like following accounts that post motivational quotes. Look, this one's called "Secret to Success". It's quotes from famous people.
A   "Don't watch the clock. Do what it does. Keep going." I like that!
B   It does make perfect sense.
A   I'll follow that one, too. Thanks! I've got some great ones to follow now.

▶ 1.15 Notice the intonation. ↗↘

K = Kelly   R = Roberto

K   So ... How did it go last night?
R   You mean the date? ↗
K   Yep. The one you met on that player.me app, right?
R   Yes, that's the one. Well, we arranged to meet at Starbucks on 57th. You know, the cozy one, great coffee ...
K   Uh-huh.
R   I got there a bit late because of the traffic and ... Well, anyway, I opened the door and, to my surprise ...
K   Go on ... ↘
R   I spotted her immediately. Sitting right in front of me, drinking coffee. It was obvious it was her even though I had no idea what she looked like. She was just perfect, you know?
K   Hold on a sec. You mean you hadn't seen her photo?
R   No! You see, she hadn't put a picture of herself on her profile. Just an image of the character she likes playing.
K   No way! ↗
R   Yeah, but I knew straightaway she was the girl I'd been chatting to on the app! I just knew.
K   What happens next? ↘
R   Our eyes meet, we shake hands and, you know, try to break the ice, talk about the coffee, the weather, the traffic ...
K   And then ...
R   She gets up and leaves.
K   What do you mean "leaves"? ↘

R   She says, "Look, I don't think this is going to work out," leaves her share of the bill on the table, and walks away.
K   Just like that? ↗
R   Just like that.
K   Are you serious? ↘
R   Yep. So there you go, one more disastrous date for my collection. How about that?
K   Oh, dear. Well, don't let it get to you, Roberto. You know, you'll meet someone else.
R   Yeah, yeah ... Oh well.

Unit 2

▶ 2.4 Notice the silent letters.

It started out as an experiment. I wanted to see if I could leave no impact on the environment for an entire year, and I asked myself, "Was it possible I could become a happier person by reducing my impact on the environment?" And the answer I found out is a resounding "yes." So, I started by cutting out garbage, taxis, throw-away coffee cups ... I eliminated tomatoes in the middle of January, A/C in the dead of August, bottled water from France, and new clothing from who knows where. I saved money, lost weight, gained energy, improved my health, spent more quality time with my family and friends, renewed my relationship with my wife, and discovered an overall sense of freedom. I learned that, yes, sometimes less is more.

▶ 2.7 Notice the silent *h* and the /ə/ in the *How long* questions.

1 **M**   Guess what! I go to the gym twice a week now! [beep]
   W   Really? How long_have you been going there?
2 **M**   I live near the park now, you know? [beep]
   W   Really? How long_have you been living there?
3 **M**   Susan's going out with Paulo. Can you believe that? [beep]
   W   Really? How long_has she been going out with him?
4 **M**   John's learning how to recycle glass. [beep]
   W   Really? How long_has he been learning that?
5 **M**   Rick plays the guitar really well. [beep]
   W   Really? How long_has he been playing it?

▶ 2.9 Notice the short (/) and long (//) pauses.

1 The Earth is getting hotter, / not the sun. // In fact, / a number of independent measures of solar activity / indicate that the sun has cooled by a few degrees since 1960, / over the same period that global temperatures have been increasing. // Over the last 35 years of climate change, / sun and climate have been moving in opposite directions.
2 Some people say, / "Well, we've had ice ages and warmer periods, / so climate change is natural! / It's got nothing to do with us!" // This is like saying that forest fires have happened naturally in the past, / so any recent forest fires can't be caused by humans. // It just doesn't make sense.
3 Climate researchers have been publishing papers for years / saying that climate change is happening right now. // We can see the evidence in flooding and droughts all around the world. // We need to start making changes / immediately. // Around 97% of researchers agree on this. // There is no "Planet B".

163

4 Climate change deniers say the planet has been cooling down since a peak in 1998. // However, experts have shown that in a climate being warmed by man-made carbon emissions, / it is possible to have long periods of cooler temperatures. // This does not mean that climate change isn't happening. // In fact, / globally, / the hottest 12-month period ever recorded / was from June 2009 to May 2010.

5 A large number of ancient mass extinction events have been linked to global climate change. // Because the world's climate has been changing so rapidly, / the way species typically adapt / (for example, migration) / is, / in most cases, / simply not possible. // This, / along with poaching, etc., / does not help the world's threatened species.

▶ 2.12

1 Notice /ɪ/ and /iː/.

L = Lorna B = Beth

L Hi Beth! You're looking well. Have you been on vacation?

B Hi! I wish. No, I haven't. Thank you, though.

L What have you been doing, then? I mean, you've obviously been doing something. You look great! You're really glowing!

B Well ... actually ... I've been trying this new dietary supplement.

L Ah, not another one of these "superfoods"?! They are such a load of nonsense!

B Yes, it is ...

2 Notice the **letters that disappear** in speech.

Z = Zach P = Pedro

Z Hey Pedro, I tried to call you, like, five times. Dude, where were you?

P Ah, Zach. Sorry bro. Not my fault. It's this thing I bought ...

Z ... one of those green models?

P Yeah, but, uh, I'm taking it back to the store first thing tomorrow.

Z Oh yeah? How come?

3 Notice the /t/, /d/, and /ŋ/ endings.

B = Bruce T = Tom

T Are you still working for TechStars?

B I quit last month.

T Bruce! No! You loved that place.

B Yeah, I worked there for over ten years. But, like, you see, I ... I just couldn't handle the stress ...

T I know what you mean, sure. So, uh ... Have you found a job yet?

B Nope.

T So, like, let me try a different question. Have you been looking for a job?

B No ... You see, I spent the whole month away from Chicago ... just meditating, relaxing, and trying to find some peace of mind, you know?

▶ 2.13

1 Notice /s/ and /z/.

L = Lorna B = Beth

L Ah, not another one of these "superfoods"?! They are such a load of nonsense!

B Yes, it is. Moringa, have you heard of it?

L Mor ... what? No, I haven't. What is it?

B It's the leaves of the Moringa tree. They call it the "Miracle Tree". It's meant to be one of the healthiest things around.

L Well, it does seem to be working on you. What do you do with it?

B You just add it to drinks and food. It's really easy to use and I have to say, I've really noticed the benefits. I've got more energy, I'm sleeping

better, and I'm not catching as many colds. It's really worth it!

L I can see. Let me know where you buy it. I'm definitely going to try it!

2 Notice the spelling of /uː/, /ʊ/, and /aʊ/.

Z = Zach P = Pedro

Z Oh yeah? How come?

P I've been trying to call you back for about an hour, and I haven't been able to get through. This thing is useless!

Z No kidding! It just doesn't connect to the network?

P No, it just keeps dying after an hour. What a waste of money! To think I threw away the old phone! I had my old Samsung for three years, and sure, it wasn't "green", but the battery life was much better.

3 Notice /ŋ/ and /n/ + consonant.

B = Bruce T = Tom

B No ... You see, I spent the whole month away from Chicago ... just meditating, relaxing and trying to find some peace of mind, you know?

T Wow! But where exactly did you go?

B I went to a meditation retreat up in the mountains. I was there for about a month, you know?

T And ...?

B I'm a brand new man.

T No way!

B Yeah. Never been happier.

▶ 2.17 Notice the silent /r/.

Our planet has some amazing species, but too many of them face extinction. Here are some of the rarest animals on earth. Perhaps the most famous rare animal is the giant panda. In 2014, scientists found fewer than 2,000 pandas in the bamboo forests of China, and there are only 300 pandas in our zoos, too. Imagine the world without pandas!

Next, one of the rarest marine animals. The Hawaiian monk seal only lives in the ocean around the beautiful islands of Hawaii, and fewer than 1,000 of these magnificent creatures remain.

OK, next up is the adorable golden lion tamarin from the Atlantic forests of Brazil. There are only around 3,000 of them left in the wild, although at least this number is now up from just 200 in 1980. Way to go, Brazil, keep up the great work!

It's not such good news for the mountain gorilla. They are under threat from poaching, war, and loss of habitat through deforestation. These gorillas were only discovered about 120 years ago, and now there are only about 800 left in the African mountains.

Another ocean mammal in extreme danger is the North Atlantic right whale. Mostly found along the Atlantic coast of North America, they are one of the most endangered of all large whales. Despite over 70 years of protection from hunting, fewer than 400 of these extraordinary creatures are still alive.

A similar sad story is the Javanese rhino. People have been killing this beautiful animal to make medicine for hundreds of years—and now there are approximately only 60 left, living in the Ujong Kulon National Park in Java, Indonesia.

And the worst story of all. Due to loss of habitat in their native forests of the southeastern United States, scientists believe that there are very few ivory-billed woodpeckers in the world, maybe even none. How awful is that?

Come on, people! Wake up! Let's finally learn from this and try to save what is left of our rich and varied wildlife—before it's too late. It's now or never ...

▶ 2.19 Notice /f/, /v/, and /b/.

Are we failing to communicate? Have we forgotten what first inspired our love of nature? All the evidence shows that the single most important factor behind taking action is our childhood experience. The wellspring of our commitment comes from the emotional high we reach when in contact with nature. But how can this wonder be harnessed to change our behavior? Showing the loss of animals in faraway places may pull a few heartstrings—even attract donations. But does it really change our behavior? What if we were able to communicate to people the wonder of nature that surrounds them and promote education that leads to awareness of threatened species and the habitats they live in? In all parts of the world, we're beginning to see that public awareness does lead to change, where people can see the benefits from making their own contribution. It's not the depressing accounts of the wildlife we are losing that moves us. It's awe and wonder, enhanced by understanding, that can inspire us to take action. It's love, not loss.

▶ 2.20

1 Notice /w/ and /l/.

P = Phil L = Laura

P ... threatened species. Anyway, so Claire and I went on the Internet, accessed WWF.com, and we adopted a whale.

L Phil, why would you want to adopt a whale?

P Well, we paid 50 bucks and they ...

L Oh, Phil! Seriously. What is the point of spending money on an animal you will never see? Life's too short. Live a little.

P Honestly, Laura, don't you think ...

2 Notice /ʌ/ and /ʊ/.

W ... so, anyway, guess what. I've just created this brand-new blog to try to raise public awareness and I've been getting a lot of hits ...

M Oh yeah? Let's have a look. Hmm ... Wow, Brenda, you've put a huge effort into this. It looks really good. Keep up the good work.

W Thanks a lot! Yeah, I'm really pleased with it. I know it isn't much, but I need to follow my heart. The gorillas' lives are on the line here. And you know what ...

3 Notice the connecting /w/.

M1 ... and that's why, as I told you, we need to attract as many donations as we can.

M2 Uhmm ... And how exactly are you planning to do that?

M1 Well, I don't know. I've been thinking of going door to door.

M2 Door to door! Wow, you are determined! Good for you. Don't give up!

4 Notice the **connections**.

M Honey, I have a little surprise for you.

W What?

M Look over there.

W Oh my God, don't tell me it's that new electric car you've been going on and on about.

M Yep. Bought it this morning. Wanna go for a ride?

W Honey, what's the use of buying that when you know nothing's gonna change? Look around you! This must be the only electric car in the neighborhood.

5 Notice /ʃ/ and /s/.

W1 ... so, since then, no more plastic bags. Ever. I've been using my own reusable bags whenever I go shopping.

W2 Every time? Way to go, Janet! I wish I had that kind of self-discipline.

164

Audioscript

Review 1

R1.2 Notice the intonation ↗ on the short questions.

OK, now put each noun and adjective together. OK? ↗ So you should have three combinations, for example, an imaginative panda, an easy going chicken, or an outgoing whale. Right, so let's find out what this means. Ready? ↗ The first combination is how you see yourself. Your self-image—OK? ↗ The second combination is how other people see you. Yeah, that's what they think of you. And, wait for it, the third combination is the truth, it's how you really are. That's you! Surprised? ↗ Or do you agree?

R1.3 Notice /θ/ and /ð/.

Amazing Facts!

Fact one: Are you afraid to swim in the ocean? Sharks kill 8 to 12 people a year around the world, but really they should be scared of us. Scientists estimate that humans kill 100 million sharks annually.

Fact two: In 1990, 43% of the global population lived in poverty. By 2010, only 21% were living on less than $1.25 a day. The United Nations hopes to end extreme poverty by the year 2030. Let's hope they can!

Fact three: Edison Peña is one of the 33 miners who were stuck in a Chilean mine for 69 days in 2010. Edison ran 6 miles a day when he was in the mine and one month after escaping he ran the 42 kilometer New York marathon in just 5 hours and 40 minutes.

Unit 3

3.3 Notice the short (/) and long (//) pauses.

While people in Hong Kong are very familiar with western culture, / there are still unique social etiquettes that tourists should observe. // When greeting someone in Hong Kong, / a handshake is common, / but do it with a slight bow. // Kissing on the cheek and hugging is not practiced. // It is OK to gently push your way through the crowd as Hong Kong is so densely packed; // in fact, / if someone says they're sorry / while navigating the crowd, / it's considered impolite. // When giving gifts, / always give them with two hands. // Do not give clocks as the Chinese associate clocks with death. // And / gifts are never opened in front of the person that gave them. // When eating with others, / it's important to be aware of important table etiquette. // As a courtesy, / fill the tea cups of others / before pouring your own cup, / even if their cups are not empty. // When you need a refill, // keep the lid of the teapot half open, / and the waiter will get the hint. // Blowing on the soup is considered OK / to cool down the soup. // After you're done, / don't leave your chopsticks standing straight up, / as this signifies death. / Leave them flat on the table. // Tipping is customary, / a service tip of 10% is expected, // and tip the server directly, / as leaving a tip on the table is considered impolite. // Now you know a little bit more about Hong Kong. // This is Rosanna Wilcox, / informing you about Hong Kong.

3.7 Notice the silent final letters.

Raul I was studying full-time, had a part-time job to help with the student debt, I wasn't eating or sleeping properly, and my nonstop lifestyle was driving me crazy. I couldn't find that work-life balance. One day, I was studying in the middle of the night with the radio on and a classical tune came on that I used to play when I was a kid. It reminded me how much I missed playing the piano! The next morning, I sat down at my piano for the first time in years and started to play. I felt the stress just drain away from me. It's amazing how something so simple can have such a positive effect. Now, although I'm still just as busy, it doesn't really bother me as much. I always make time to sit down each day and play for ten minutes. Everything else melts away and I feel much better after. You should try it!

Tomiko I was getting up, drinking two cups of coffee, and grabbing an energy bar. Lunch was at my desk every day; a sandwich eaten in two minutes flat while working. I'd grab a takeout on the way home from work and in between there were more energy drinks and quick snacks. Food just didn't seem important, but I felt terrible and my energy levels were low. Things had to change! Now, I find it annoying if I don't have time to eat properly. I make sure that at least one meal a day is prepared with care. I plan what I'm going to eat, I go to the local farm shop and take time to enjoy the sights and sounds. I've made food more like a hobby. It takes more time, but I don't mind that. My health has improved and I'm hoping to start growing my own soon. I'm actually going on a beginner's gardening course this weekend.

André I first moved here five years ago for work. I didn't know anyone and I'd never lived alone before. Loneliness became a real problem for me. I couldn't stand coming home to an empty apartment every day. I could call my family and friends, of course, but it's not the same. I was walking home one day when this little cat started to follow me. She came right to the door and was still there a couple of hours later. Eventually, I let her in and that was it! We've been best friends ever since. It's just so nice to have someone to come home to in the evening. Even though I know she can't understand me, I still talk to her. It's just nice to have the company, you know. I still find the city a bit lonely at times, but I'm OK with it.

3.9 Notice how the similar sounds link.

Story 1
R = Rachel J = Juan

R You look a little bit depressed, Juan. What's wrong?

J Yeah, well, last Thursday I had a job interview—the third in a week.

R You poor thing!

J You see, I've been trying to find a job as an architect for months, without success, of course, but I was really optimistic about that particular interview. Anyway, the big day finally came, and, hmm, guess what—there was a massive, massive traffic jam on the main avenue.

R Oh, no!

J Yep, but, you know, I wasn't too worried, since I'd woken up at six and left home at seven ... you know, just to be on the safe side.

R Right. What time was the interview?

J Eight thirty.

R Seems more than enough, doesn't it?

J Well, that's what I thought. At seven thirty, though, I was still stuck in exactly the same place, so I turned on the local traffic radio to see what was going on.

R And ...?

J Apparently, a bus had gone through a red light and crashed into three cars. On the day of my interview!

R Oh, no! Did you make it in time for the interview?

J Hmm ... Guess what time I got there. Eight fifty!

R You're joking! Gee! And how did it turn out?

J Surprise, surprise ... I didn't get the job I'd been dreaming of since I graduated! Darn it!

R Well, I'm sure something better will come along ... and next time be sure to rent a helicopter on the day of the interview.

J Ha, ha, very funny.

Story 2
S = Sandra E = Ethan

S [singing]

E I didn't know you liked Taylor Swift.

S Oh, I'm a huge fan. I'm crazy about her.

E Really? Have you ever seen her live?

S Yep. Well, sort of.

E Uh? What do you mean?

S Well, when I heard she was coming to Rio, I bought two tickets right away. Incredibly expensive, but I didn't care. Anyway, I spent the next two months anxiously waiting for the big day—the day I'd been waiting for since I was sixteen.

E Wow!

S On the day of the show, I left work two hours early and set off for São Paulo with a friend. She had arranged to pick me up in her car.

E OK, go on ...

S Well, we'd been driving for a little while when the car started making a weird noise. Then smoke started coming out from under the hood, so both of us started to freak out.

E No wonder! That sounds a bit scary.

S Yeah, I know ... We had to pull over. People were honking like crazy, but there was nothing we could do—the car broke down and we had to wait for road side assistance.

E So what happened in the end?

S Well, a mechanic arrived and told us we hadn't checked the oil. He fixed the car and we set off again. By the time we finally got to the stadium, she'd been singing for well over an hour. Thank goodness the security guards let us in.

E So you only caught—what—the last ten minutes of the show?

S Only the last few songs! But that was the best half hour of my life. I swear.

3.12 Notice the intonation in questions. ↗↘

1

A Excuse me ...

B Hang on a second, Julie. Yes? ↗

A Oh, hi ... uh ... Meditation 102 is about to begin.

B Yeah, I know. I'm in that group. Can't wait!

A Well, you see, we like to keep the school as quiet as possible, so ... uh ... I was wondering ... could you continue your conversation outside?

B Oh, I'm sorry. Was I speaking too loud? ↗

A I'm afraid so.

B I'm sorry. I didn't realize that. Julie, gotta go, I'll catch up with you later.

2

C Excuse me ... Excuse me, miss.

D Yes?

C Are you shopping with us? ↗

D Well, no, not now. Why?

C Uh ... I'm afraid you can't park here.

D What do you mean I can't park here? ↘ Says who? ↘

C Just look at the sign over there.

D Oh, come on. Be reasonable. The parking lot's nearly empty and I ... and I just need to cash a check at the bank. Can I park here for just 10 minutes? ↗

165

C I'm afraid not.
D But I'm starving. I can bring you a muffin on my way back, how about that? ↗
C I'm sorry, miss. Our parking area's for patrons only. There's another parking lot right across the street and ...
D Well, I want to speak to the manager ...

3

E How may I help you, sir? ↘
F What do you mean "how may I help you"? ↘ Can't you see I'm going for my morning run? ↗
E I'm afraid this is private property sir. You can't go beyond this point.
F Since when? ↗
E Since yesterday. Mr. Jobs just bought this whole area. You see the gate? ↗
F Well, I've been jogging here since 1999, so this is my area, too. They can't just close it off like that.
E Sir, I'm afraid I'm going to have to ask you to step back.

Unit 4

▶ 4.3 Notice the sentence stress and
weak forms.

A I **can't** really **remember** the **last** time I had a **chance** to go in the **backyard** and just **run around**.
B School's just **so** much **pressure** that every day I **wake** up **dread**ing it.
C I'm **afraid** that our **children** are going to **sue** us for **steal**ing their **childhoods**.
D I would **spend six** hours a **night** on my **homework**.
E You **have** to get into the **top schools**.
F You **have** to **take tests** and do **interviews**.
G It's gone **way** to the **extreme**.
H We're **all caught up** in it.
I In **America**, if you don't **earn** a lot of **money**, **something** went **wrong**.
J The **pressure** comes from the **colleges**, from the **parents**, from the **government**, but it **has** to **stop**.
K You **have** to **do well now**, so you can get **into** a **good college**.
L **Every**one ex**pects** us to be **super**heroes.
M You have a **fear** from the **parents** that my **kid** needs to be able to get a **job**.
N **How** do you **expect** us to do **well** when you **can't** even **make mistakes**?
O **You're** de**di**cating your **whole** life to your **grades**.
P You **have** to be **smart** and you have to be in**volved** in the **arts**.
Q I have **soccer** practice **every day**.
R **Plus** the **homework** on **top** of **that**.
S Pro**duce**, produce, produce ...
T It's im**poss**ible.
U I couldn't cope.

▶ 4.5 1 Notice the weak form of /ə/.

I = interviewer   J = Justin

I Right, so you're basically saying that you hate the work you do.
J Well, I'm not sure about "hate."
I But you dislike engineering?
J Yeah ... I guess. I'm good at it, though.
I Oh, yeah?
J People at work say I'm really good at what I do, and ... they must be right.
I So ... Why exactly are you looking for a career change?
J 'Cause ... 'cause that's not where my heart is. I love music. Always have, always will.
I So, how come you majored in engineering, Justin?
J Well, Dad's an engineer and I'm an only child ... Do the math.

I And you've never considered getting a degree in music, arts, or something?
J Nope. Dad wanted me to follow in his footsteps, but I shouldn't have listened to him.
I Well, you're still young, you know. Have you thought about starting over?
J Nah. I'm way too old now. I should have gone to music school years ago.
I Well, I disagree. You see ...

2

I = interviewer   Z = Zoe

I ... so, Zoe, you've come for some advice about your major, is that correct?
Z Uh-huh.
I Freshman?
Z Nope. I'm a sophomore.
I What seems to be the problem?
Z Well, I've been thinking of dropping out.
I Oh really? Why's that?
Z Well, basically, journalism's not my thing. I should have chosen another major.
I Right, but ... how can you be so sure that you've picked the wrong career?
Z Well, for starters, I can't stand writing and ...
I Oh ...
Z Yep. My writing really sucks. I can barely put two words together.
I I hear you, but ... um ... Did you enjoy writing at all when you were in high school? I mean, there's got to be a reason why you picked journalism.
Z Well, the truth is, I didn't want to lose touch with Kylie, Bonnie, Maria, and Tom.
I Excuse me?
Z My best friends. They all wanted to study journalism, so I ... hmmm ... I thought I'd learn how to like it eventually. Guess I was wrong ... Look, I know it was a stupid decision and I should have thought about it more carefully, but my question to you now is: Is it too late to switch majors?
I Hmm. Yes and no. You see ...

3

I = interviewer   G = George

I ... so what is it that you do exactly, George?
G I'm a ... Roger, get out of here. I told you to wait outside, didn't I? Just go! Bad dog.
I You were saying ...
G I'm a dog walker.
I Uh-huh.
G The money's not bad and I ... I like dogs. But I'm 41 and ... you know, my wife thinks there is no future in it.
I Did you attend university at all?
G One year. Then I dropped out. You see, I really enjoyed college, but I just hated university, I didn't like being away from my family. But now I guess I'm paying the price. Every day I wake up and ask myself: Should I have persevered a little more?
I Well, yeah ... probably. But have you considered going back?
G Hmm ... Well, the thing is ...

▶ 4.8 Notice the short (/) and long (//) pauses.

1 One of my main goals is to get onto the property ladder as soon as possible. // Most people think I'm too young to be thinking about this kind of investment. At 22, / they think I should be going out partying and enjoying myself, / not working hard, / saving, / and putting all my money into real estate. // I'm still with my parents at the moment. // They are very supportive. // If I

didn't live at home, / I wouldn't be able to save anything. // My big dream / is to own lots of different apartments. // I'll buy them cheap, / do them up, and then sell them or rent them out. // If I work hard and save my money, / I'll see the benefits later. // My friends all think I'm a bit crazy, / but I'll be able to retire much earlier than them! //

2 I've always had itchy feet. // I never want to stay in one place. // There is a whole world out there to explore! // Imagine all of those different cultures and people and food // ... I have a big map on my wall at home and I put a pin in it every time I go somewhere new. // There aren't enough pins in there at the moment. // I've been to a few places in Europe, / but that's it so far. // My main wish is to reach all seven continents. // If there were nine or ten continents, / I would still want to visit each one! // I want to go in a hot air balloon over Cappadocia, / fly in a helicopter over the Grand Canyon, / dive on the Great Barrier Reef. // I know, I know, / all of this costs a lot of money. // If I save enough this year, / I'll go backpacking around Southeast Asia. // I can't wait! // So many places, / so little time! //

3 Earning this would mean everything to me. // It's taken me six years to get this far. // It means dedication, / perseverance. // You can't just give up. // In martial arts you have to be completely committed and dedicated to your sport. // Reaching that level is extremely difficult. // You have to go to every single class, / get beaten, / sweat, / cry. // All of this and still go to work or school! // If I pass this level, / I'll prove to myself that I can do anything I want. / To be honest, / if I didn't train in martial arts, // I wouldn't be the person I am now. / I feel more confident than ever before. / My ultimate aim is to become an instructor and have my own training school. //

▶ 4.12 Notice the connections and /t/, /d/, and /ɪd/.

1 His parents suspected he had a learning [beep] (disability).
2 He has trouble sleeping because he [beep] (constantly) sees numbers in his head.
3 By the age of three, Jacob could [beep] (easily) solve complex equations.
4 Jacob dropped out of [beep] (elementary) school.
5 At age eight, it was clear that his mathematical ability was [beep] (unusually) high.
6 He joined Purdue University and [beep] (eventually) became a paid researcher.

▶ 4.13 1 (with addition in 4.14) Notice the intonation of *What* and *Really*. ↗↘

I = Iris   F = Fiona

I Hi, sorry I'm late. I missed the five o'clock bus.
F What happened to your car?
I Oh, you don't wanna know.
F What? ↗
I I drove into a tree.
F What? ↗
I Yep. A little dog ran out in front of me and I had to swerve quickly to avoid hitting it!
F Oh my goodness! Well, look, at least you didn't get hurt. It could have been worse.

2

J = Josh   B = Belinda

J Oh, no! Oh, no! Not again.
B What? ↘
J Seven hours of work gone to waste.
B What? ↗

166

Audioscript

J Oh, you don't wanna know.
B Know what? ↗
J PC crashed again.
B Don't tell me you had no backup. Josh, this is the third time this year! You should have known better.

3

G = Gina J = Jay

G I thought this was a new car.
J It is.
G Oh ... uh ... so ...
J Worst thing I've ever bought.
G Oh, no. Really? ↗
J Yeah, this is the second time it's broken down. And don't get me started on the price I paid.
G Oh Jay, what a shame! You loved your last one like this. Well, what's done is done. You can always get rid of this one and get yourself a new model.

4

D = David C = Carla A = Anna

D God, I hate this one.
C What? ↗ No, you don't.
D What do you mean? Look at this painting. My four-year-old could have done better.
C David, shut up.
A No, go on. I'm listening.
D You know what I hate about it?
A What? ↘
D The use of colors. The whole thing's so primitive, you know? How can they call this art?
C Listen, what my friend means is that ...
A Can you excuse me for a moment? There's somebody I've got to speak to.
C David, are you out of your mind? She's the artist!
D What? ↗ Oh, no!
C What were you thinking?

Review 2

▶ R2.2 Notice /w/ and /j/.

M Well, they arrived at the festival, but it had been canceled.
W Yeah. I think it had been raining.
M Yeah. It looks like it. And then they all stayed in one tent.
W Uh-huh. The wind had taken the other tent.
M Unlucky, huh? And what's this picture? They look cold.
W Yeah, right. I guess they had been expecting hot weather because they are wearing T-shirts.

Unit 5

▶ 5.2 Notice /m/, /n/, and /ŋ/ endings and their spellings.

P = presenter N = Natalie

P Hello and welcome to "Money-wise", your weekly consumer program. This week we are talking to Natalie Dupont, a social media marketing expert. Welcome, Natalie.
N Thank you.
P On this program we're talking about the phenomenon of "shopping haul" videos. Natalie, can you explain for us?
N Of course. YouTube "shopping haul" videos is a huge new trend. A "haul" is a video of a vlogger unpacking and describing items they have bought.
P OK, and why do people watch these?
N For shopaholics, these videos are entertaining. It's strangely satisfying to see how people spend their money. There are millions of hauls posted on social media, and many companies have been using this user-generated content to

advertise their product. However, there is now a revolution. Vloggers are moving away from these materialistic videos and posting "anti-haul" videos.
P What is an "anti-haul" video?
N Basically, they encourage viewers to buy less. In the video they post, the vlogger gives a list of products they don't plan to buy because they think the products are useless or overpriced.
P So, where did this trend for "anti-haul" videos come from?
N Well, Beauty Vlogger Kimberly Clark started doing this in 2015. In her video, which has had over 100,000 views, Clark says we should "put the brakes on consumerism" and "stop shopping". She shows the viewer 14 products they don't need and shouldn't waste their money on. Clark's fans begged her to post more videos like this. This inspired other YouTube vloggers to post similar "anti-hauls" and there are now more than 850,000 online.
P Really interesting. Why have they become so popular?
N Because they talk to hardworking, underpaid shoppers. We have too many options and not enough money! Perhaps it's this generation. Millenials and Generation Z have grown up in a financial crisis. Students are in debt, there are fewer jobs. I think these videos speak to that generation. Research shows that Millennials would much rather buy experiences than stuff.
P So, I guess the message is that you don't need most of the stuff marketed to you. Perhaps consumerism is finally going out of fashion!
N Exactly!

▶ 5.3 Notice /ə/ and sentence stress.

I started getting into debt when I was 18. I was at college, like you, so I took out student loans and signed up for credit cards.

I was enjoying student life! Who doesn't, right?! I would go on shopping sprees, buying clothes and music. I paid the minimum back on my credit card per month and the repayments were huge! There was 25% interest on top, so it quickly got out of control. I was overspending without even thinking about it, but what was I supposed to do? Stay home all the time? I just thought, "If I get a good job later, I'll pay it all back. No problem!"

Five years later, I graduated and I was $12,000 in debt. I had wasted a lot of money! I got my first job with a salary of about $2,000 per month, but my rent was more than 50% of that! I had to use the credit cards to keep my head above water. I managed to pay back a bit every month, but not enough. I was permanently in my overdraft. I never had any money and I kept pretending it wasn't happening. I think if I'd listened to advice at this point, I wouldn't have gotten into the mess I did.

When I turned 25, I was in more than $20,000 worth of debt. I was working hard and all the money was going to pay off the loans and credit cards. Think about that. One day, I went to the ATM and I couldn't withdraw anything. It was a wake-up call. I realized I couldn't keep living a lifestyle I couldn't afford. I had completely run out of money.

I couldn't tell my parents. They would have gone crazy! I had to change and get myself out of debt. This is how I did it: I took out one large loan to pay off all the credit cards and then started to pay off the loan. I cut up the credit cards, so I couldn't spend much. I set up a direct debit, so money automatically transferred from my account to pay off the loan every month. Every time I spent money

on something nice, I "matched" it by paying the same amount off on my loan. This was one of the best tips I heard, because it made me think about how much I was spending.

If I could give you one piece of advice, I'd say, be realistic about your lifestyle. Yes, I was young, free, and single, but I couldn't afford to live the life I wanted. I set myself a goal to get out of debt by my 30th birthday and I did it! It was tough, but I did it. I haven't used a credit card for a long time, but I think I'm ready to start using one sensibly now. If I had known then what I know now, I would have been much more careful.

▶ 5.8 Notice the connections and /t/, /d/, and /ɪd/ endings.

You might be surprised to learn crowdfunding has been around for a very long time. But where did it all start?

An early example is the Statue of Liberty. The statue was a gift from the people of France to the United States in 1886. But after the American Committee ran out of money to pay for the site where the statue would go, publisher Joseph Pulitzer started a campaign in his newspaper to raise the money they needed. In five months, over $100,000 was raised by 160,000 donors including children, street cleaners, and politicians.

Even before this, people used crowdfunding to raise money. In 1783, Mozart hoped to perform three piano concertos in Vienna. He published invitations offering copies of the composition in return for money to help put on the concert.

The basic concept of crowdfunding is still very much the same these days, but the introduction of the Internet and crowd funding websites such as Kickstarter means that people around the world can easily connect with each other and donate to projects.

Internet crowdfunding first became popular in the art and music industry. In 1997, the rock group Marillion funded a tour through online donations from fans. They have since also funded albums this way. Their fans must really love their music!

Probably the biggest crowdfunding success is Pebble Technology. Pebble raised an incredible thirty million dollars and broke the record for the fastest ever campaign to be fully funded. Supporters received a Pebble watch, one of the first smart watches on the market.

So, what is the future of crowdfunding? Critics complain that businesses now use it to market their new products to more people and it's not just used by new start-up companies. But crowdfunding is now so popular that sixteen point two billion dollars was raised in 2016. When you look at the statistics and the success stories, no matter what the critics say, it can't be bad for young entrepreneurs! Got a business idea? It could work for you!

▶ 5.11 Notice the intonation. ↗↘

A = Alberto L = Laura E = Ernie
Mrs. A = Mrs. Andrews
T = Tony W = woman S = Susie M = man

1

A What would you like for dinner, Rico? Tuna or chicken? ↘ Oops, we're out of tuna, Rico. Sorry. You poor baby!

2

L Help! Somebody help! Oh my God. Not now. I'm late for work. Can anybody hear me? ↗ Excuse me ... hi ... I'm stuck between the fourth and the fifth floor. Could you send someone, please? ↗ Quick!

167

3

E I swear I did it, Mrs. Andrews, I swear, but Bart ate it. I tried to stop him, but I couldn't. It won't happen again, I swear.

Mrs. A. "The dog ate my homework." Yeah, right. Pretty lame, Ernie. Pretty lame.

4

T [breathing]

W OK, great. Breathe in as you move your left leg, and breathe out as you move your right leg to the left. Is everybody OK? ↗ Now, feel the vital energy flowing to your arms and hands.

5

S OK ... done that. What should I do now? ↘ Really? Well, if you say so ... OK, I've closed the window, but I don't understand ... How will that help? ↘

M Ma'am, I asked you to close the computer window—your browser, you know—not your living room window.

S My computer has no windows. Or doors. What are you talking about?

⏵5.13 Notice the intonation ↗↘of the echo questions.

M You know, I just can't believe you bought that stuff.

W I bought it on impulse. It was pure madness, I know.

M You bet. It can't work the way they advertised it would! Was it expensive?

W Expensive? ↗ It cost a fortune. I felt really guilty afterward, of course.

M Buyer's remorse, huh?

W Yeah, at the time it seemed like a wonderful product, but ... it was such a disappointment.

M Well, what would you expect from these awful infomercials?

W I know, yeah ... And I think this stuff is actually quite dangerous.

M Dangerous? ↗

W Mmm, it smelled awful. Like really strong chemicals.

M Goodness knows what it did to your skin.

W And that's not all! They go on and on in the infomercial about how "natural" it is. Well, if you like looking like an orange ...!

M Oh dear. Was it really that bad?

W Yes, it was and I used it before going to Jessica's wedding, so not only did I smell weird, but I was bright orange!

M But, uh, why on earth did you want to look tanned anyway, Liz? You have gorgeous skin.

W I do? ↗ Thanks! I guess it's just so fashionable these days, I wanted to give it a go.

⏵5.16 Notice /dʒ/, /tʃ/, and the consonant clusters.

1 Choosing

C = customer, SC = store clerk

SC Hello. Do you see anything you like?

C Oh, hi. Yeah, I like these shoes. Can I try them on?

SC What size do you take?

C Do you have a size ten in stock?

SC A ten? Uh—I'm sorry ma'am, we're sold out.

C Ah, that's such a shame! It seems impossible to find larger sizes. Can you email me when you have some in stock?

2 Paying

SC Next, please ... Hello. Just the jeans and these two T-shirts?

C Yes ... No, sorry, this dress, too.

SC OK, that looks very nice.

C Oh, it's for my girlfriend.

SC Very nice. So that's $174.70. Cash or charge?

C Uh, charge.

SC OK. Insert your card, please.

C Uh-huh.

SC Ah. I'm afraid your card has been declined. Um, do you have another card?

C Declined! I don't understand. It's a new card, and I know I'm not over my limit. There must be a problem with your card machine.

3 Complaining

C Hello, hello. Yes, I'd like to return this phone. I bought it here the other day and it's damaged.

SC I see. Uh ... What seems to be the problem?

C Well, I bought it on ... Thursday, and when I got it home, I took it out of the box and ... well, you can see. The screen has a scratch on it.

SC Oh, oh yes. Well, uh, unfortunately, we can't give you a refund, but we'd be happy to exchange it for another one.

C Oh, that's great. Thank you so much.

SC Sure. Uh, I just need to see your receipt.

C Yes, of course. Uh, it's in here somewhere. Here it is.

Unit 6

⏵6.1 Notice the schwa /ə/ in the non-content words (for, to, a, the, of).

1 Ads for a movie, showing extracts of it are trailers.

2 Critics' opinions are reviews.

3 To pay regularly to receive something is to subscribe.

4 To really like something is to be into something.

5 All the episodes in one year of a series is a season.

6 On-screen translation of speech are subtitles.

7 Foreign movies spoken in the viewer's native language are dubbed.

8 When you are unable to stop doing something, you are addicted to it.

⏵6.3 Notice the sentence stress and weak forms.

D = daughter F = father

D Hey, did **you** have a TV when you were a **kid**, Dad?

F **Yeah, believe** it or **not. TV** has been **around** pretty much forever. But it's **changed** a **lot** in **my lifetime.**

D **What? TV's** just **TV**, isn't **it?**

F **No way!** The **first TV** I **remember** was in **black** and **white**, and it was **massive**. TVs **now**, well, you can **put** them on the **wall** and they **take** up **no** space. **When I** was a kid, they were like a piece of **furniture.**

D Huh?

F And the **way you** guys watch TV is **very** different from **my generation.**

D I don't **get** it. What do you **mean?**

F Just **think**. When **I** was a kid, we watched TV **together** in the **evening** as a **family.**

D **Watch** TV with your **parents? Yuck!**

F **Yeah, really,** and there was **no** choosing. **We** watched what **Mom** and **Dad** wanted to **watch! Now,** you all just **download** or **stream** everything—**sitcoms, movies, news programs**— and watch **what** you want, **when** you want.

D Live music, soaps, yeah, **that's** true, I guess. Uh, I **mean**, I hardly **ever** watch TV in **real** time. Only big **sports** events.

F Or in the **car** on long **journeys** ... You never **speak** to us! Yeah, and TV is just about **everywhere** now—on **tablets, computers, smart phones**— you name it.

D Sure ...

F Hm, and even **watching** TV has changed.

D How? We still use our eyes ...

F Yeah, right, but instead of **chatting** to **friends** or **family** in the same room, everybody uses their **smart phones** to chat with their "**cyber buddies**," you know, somewhere else.

D Oh, **come** on Dad! That's **social** TV! Twitter is the **best** place to talk about TV now.

F Uh-huh. But there's **one** thing I'm sure of. The word "**viewer**" will never mean the same **again.**

⏵6.4 Notice /æ/, /ɒ/, and /eɪ/.

C = Clara E = Emilia

C So, have you been watching anything good recently?

E Yes! I'm really into *Stranger Things* at the moment. Have you seen it?

C No, not yet. Everyone is raving about it, but, I don't know ... it just sounds ... well ... *strange* ...

E Well, that's kind of the point. Oh, you've got to watch it. It's amazing!

C So, what's so good about it, then? What's it about?

E It's hard to explain. It's about this group of kids who discover lots of weird paranormal activity going on in their town.

C It's about kids? Isn't it really scary, though?

E It is pretty spooky, yeah, but that's the interesting thing about it. You know, it was rejected between 15 and 20 times by different TV companies before Netflix decided to make it. Apparently, other TV executives didn't like the fact that it was a story about children, but wasn't for kids' TV.

C I guess that is pretty unusual. Does it work?

E Totally! That's the best thing about it! The children's performances are amazing, and I got hooked on the spooky storyline immediately.

C I guess the industry didn't get the concept of a TV show starring kids that was actually for adults!

E That's it exactly. It's so unusual. And, of course, it gave Winona Ryder her big comeback. She plays a mother whose son has gone missing and she's going to do everything in her power to get him back. She's fantastic in it!

C Well, you've certainly sold it to me! I think I'll start watching tonight.

E Great ... I can't wait for the third season. You'll love the pilot episode when ...

C Stop! No spoilers!

⏵6.7 Notice the pauses. //

DJ ... and, remember, today's prize is two front row tickets for Sia's October show. Wow! This week we've been talking about moviemakers who have changed American cinema. And we have Gloria on the line. Gloria, how's it going?

W I'm good, thanks.

DJ The first question is about Ryan Coogler, // who many people consider to be one of the finest new moviemakers around.

W Oh my gosh, I love Ryan Coogler! I think he's the best.

DJ So, here's our first question ... Are you ready?

W I guess ...

DJ Which box office smash did Coogler direct in 2018?

W That's easy. *Black Panther*!

DJ Correct! This movie made Coogler the youngest ever Marvel moviemaker.

W Oh, wow! What an achievement.

DJ Second question ... In 2013, Coogler directed a movie, which was called *Creed. Creed*, // which also starred Sylvester Stallone, // was a spin-off from a classic series of movies, *Rocky*. What are these movies about?

168

Audioscript

W Can you give me a clue?

DJ Well, // it's a kind of sport that involves two people and a ring.

W Oh, of course! I know, I know. Boxing?

DJ Did you say boxing?

W Yep.

DJ You're absolutely right. The movie, // which won Stallone a Golden Globe, // was highly-acclaimed by critics. I loved it! ... Anyway, here's our third question. Which famous person tweeted this after watching *Black Panther*: "I loved this movie and I know it will inspire people of all backgrounds to dig deep and find the courage to be heroes of their own stories."?

W Who said that? Oh ... That's a tough one.

DJ OK, Gloria. Time's up.

W Well, I guess another director said it. Erm ... Steven Spielberg?

DJ Good guess, but I'm afraid not. It was // Barack Obama.

W Wow! Imagine an ex-president saying that about your work!

DJ Pretty cool, huh? OK. Question 4 is actually about Steven Spielberg! Are you ready? What did ...

▶ 6.9

1 Notice /k/.

A And it's just such a powerful movie, you know, like how science could destroy us eventually. I really think it could be true. I think the whole trilogy is amazing.

B Yeah, some of the experiments they do on animals now, it's pretty sad. But didn't they use animals for the movie, too? I mean, that's bad as well, right?

A No, no animals. They are all actors. The cast members who play apes have to wear this special suit when they shoot the movie. It captures all the movements of the actor and then they can add everything else with computers. It's very clever. Imagine working as an actor, wearing that special suit and acting in front of a green screen all day!

B No way! So the actors actually move like apes? They look so real! Man, he should get an Oscar for that role! Acting like a chimpanzee! That is real acting!

2 Notice /eɪ/.

C Bah! I've got that song in my head again!

D Huh, I hate it when that happens. But that is a great song!

C I know, there's a reason it was so popular. I saw a clip of the video on a TV show last night about the power of the Internet. It's had billions of views. It was such a cool video and the song is so catchy!

D Huh, really? I didn't see that. But yeah, the video was great, wasn't it? And they made a few different versions of it. A Portuguese one ...

C Yeah, and of course the Justin Bieber version.

D I know! I wish I could sing in Spanish like him. They're all good, but I like the original.

C Of course!

3 Notice /ʒ/, /dʒ/, and /g/.

E Hey, I've got this movie from iTunes, do you wanna watch it with me?

F Uh ... What's it about? It's not filled with explosions like that last one you got, is it?

E Well, probably. It's about a bunch of superheroes defending the universe, so I guess there's going to be quite a lot of explosions!

F Oh, come on! You know I'm not into action movies. I like something with a bit of intelligence, you know?

E Duh, always the same. Why can't you just relax and enjoy the fun? All the big Hollywood names star in it!

F Why can't we watch my choice this time? What about that one with the woman who works as a cleaner in a government lab ... with the fish guy ... what's it called?

E *The Shape of Water*?! No, I'm not watching that ...

▶ 6.10 Notice the **sentence stress** and weak forms.

Here are some **tips** and **tricks** to **making** a **short video**. **Plan** your **shoot**. **What** is your video **about**? Sketch **out** your **idea**. **Think** about what your **topic** will **be** and **how** many **people** will be **in** it. **What** do you **want** the **final** video to **look like**?

Technologies: Decide what **media** you will be **using**: **digital camera, camcorder, webcam,** or **mobile phone**.

Capture your **clips: Press** the **record** button a **few seconds** before the **actual shoot**. The **professionals** always say "**Keep** it **steady.**" If possible, use a **tripod**. **Take** lots of **shoots** and **still images**— they **might** come in **handy**. **Try** not to **cut off** the **top** of the **subject's head**.

Lighting: Shoot in a **well-lit area**. Make **sure** there is **not** a **bright light** like the sun **behind** the **subject**. **Before** your final **recording**, do a **test** shoot to **check** the **lighting**.

Length of **shoot: Plan** your **script beforehand**. **Don't** talk about **one** topic for too long, as this may **lose** the viewers' **interest**. **Keep** the **video short** and simple.

Sound and **audio**: It's **best** to **use** an **external microphone**. **Always** be **conscious** of background **noise**. Always do a **sound** check **before** the actual **shoot**.

Copyright: If you are **shooting outside**, make sure you don't capture **anyone** on camera **without** their permission. It can be **difficult** to use **images** from the **Internet**, so be **adventurous** and take your **own**. **Always** gather **written** permission from your **subjects**.

Accessibility: To **make** your video **accessible** to **all**: Prepare **transcripts**, use **subtitles**, record a **voiceover** if you are **making** a video of **still images**. And **remember**, have **fun** making your **video**.

▶ 6.11 Notice /ɪ/ and /iː/.

S = Sue J = Joe

S I can't get enough of Ellen. I think she's awesome.

J So do I. I'm a huge fan. She's a terrific host.

S Yeah, I can still remember the Sia interview a while ago.

J Oh, yeah? Mmm ... Sia's not my thing. I like a song or two, but that's about it.

S Really? I think she's amazing. She's written some fantastic songs. She's written a lot of songs which have been huge hits for other singers, too.

J Like what?

S Oh, you name it! She wrote *Titanium* ... *Diamonds* by Rihanna.

J What? Get out of here! She wrote those?

S Yes! Everyone knows that ... Anyway, I'll never forget that interview ...

J Why? What happened?

S This is how it goes ... First Ellen asks her to explain why she doesn't like showing her face.

J Oh, I bet *nobody* ever asks her that!

S Ha, ha. Yeah. But Sia is so natural and so funny. She says that she hides her face so she can go to the grocery store or use a public restroom without being recognized.

J Like nobody would recognize her with that wig on!

S No, silly – she only wears the wig when she's performing! Anyway, then Ellen starts saying that they've made a deal that when Sia performs on the show, she'll take her wig off so everyone can see what she looks like. And she agreed to it!

J Really, you're kidding, right?

S Yeah, this was in the days when nobody knew what she looked like. So all the people around me start getting really excited and ...

J What do you mean the people around you?

S I was actually in the audience. I got two tickets for my birthday.

J No way! You were actually in the audience? You never told me that!

▶ 6.12 Notice the intonation. ↗↘

J No way! ↘ You were actually in the audience? ↗ You never told me that! ↗

S It's true! ↘ So, as I was saying .... ↘ They make this big deal over pulling the wig off ... ↘ and everyone's going crazy and then ... ↗

J What? ↗

S Nothing. ↘ It was all a dumb joke. ↘ She wasn't really going to reveal herself at all. ↗

J Are you serious? ↗ You mean they were just pretending? ↗ What a disappointment! ↘

S I know. ↘ Talk about an anti-climax! ↘ But, I guess it would spoil her image. ↘ Anyway, she performed live in the studio and I got to see that, which was amazing! ↗ She performed with the dancer, Maddie Ziegler, who's often in her videos and she hid behind this crazy long dress thing. ↘ Typical Sia. ↘

J My goodness! ↗ Yes, Maddie Ziegler is so talented. ↘ What a show. ↗ It must have been great to see her live. I wish I could have been there. ↘

S It was. ↘ I'm so glad I got tickets. ↘

▶ 6.17 Notice the **reductions**.

1 A Wanna come on over for spaghetti tonight? I'm cooking!

   B No way! You're making spaghetti?

   A Well, there's always a first time.

2 C I'm sick and tired of this SUV. Gonna buy a smaller car.

   D Get out of here! You want to buy a smaller car?

   C Yeah. What's wrong?

3 E Janet's turning 18 next week. Gonna get her a puppy.

   F What? You're going to get Janet a dog for her birthday?

   E Uh-uh.

4 G Love this chocolate diet! I've lost ten pounds in two weeks.

   H No way! You've lost ten pounds in two weeks eating chocolate?

   G Yeah. Isn't it amazing?

Review 3

▶ R3.3 Notice the **disappearing consonants**.

1 I'm dead serious. Savejohnsmith.com is my last hope.

2 There must be a problem with your card machine.

3 Although it's supposed to be for kids, I loved it!

4 They ran out of money to pay for the statue.

5 "Shopping haul" videos are a huge trend.

169

Unit 7

⏵ 7.4 (with addition in 7.6) Notice the intonation / emotion on *right*.

1 Notice stress and /ə/

A **God**, it seems that for **every** five letters I type, **one** comes out **wrong**.

B American keyboard layout, **right**?

A Well, the salesman said some of the keys were different, but it was **basically** the same thing, blah, blah, blah. Yeah, **right**! But how was I to know? He said I would learn fast. Guess he was wrong.

2 Notice stress and /ə/.

C Oh, **Dad**, you're wearing the **watch** I got you. **How** do you **like** it?

D **Well**, I'd like it **better** if it **worked** properly. I missed **two** meetings last week. Do you have the warranty?

C Warranty? **No**, he didn't **give** me one.

D **What**? No **warranty**? **Where** did you **get** it?

C **Well**, there was a guy in the **market** selling this **watch** really **cheap**. He **said** that it worked **just** as well as the **famous** brand.

D In the **market**! So, this **isn't a** Rolex?

C Uh ... **no** ... Maybe **not**. Oh no, **look**, it says **Polex**. He told me he was there every week and he could get me video games, too. Maybe we can ask him for a refund?

3 Notice /aʊ/.

E Oh, my ...!

F What in the name of ...

E Oh no ... There goes my Christmas present.

F But how ... how ... did it happen? You didn't ... you didn't put it up yourself, right? Right?

E Uh ... Well, the delivery guy told me I could mount it on the wall myself. How was I to know?

F But you're not a pro! You're a doctor! Doctors don't install TV sets. What were you thinking?

E But ... Look, he said it was easy and it would only take ten minutes!

4 Notice /e/ and /eɪ/.

G Paula, we're OK, right? I mean, it's just that ... Well, you haven't returned any of my calls.

H Sorry, didn't get your messages—yours or anybody's. My phone's dead.

G Dead?

H I bought it from this site and it came straight from the States. Turns out I can't make or receive calls. Some sort of network problem ... Which is odd, because on the site it said I'd be able to use it in any country ... Guess they were lying. But how was I to know?

G Can't you get a refund or something?

H Oh yeah—easily. They told me that lots of people had complained and so on.

5 Notice /ʌ/ and /ə/.

I One of these days I swear I will throw this tablet right out of the window.

J Oh, come on! It's not so bad!

I You're kidding, right? The screen sucks and the software's full of bugs. To think I could've gotten a laptop! I bought it on ... on impulse, I guess. The store manager said it had just arrived and, you know, I couldn't resist it. But how was I to know?

J Well, try to control yourself next time.

I I know ... But she said that these tablets usually sold pretty quickly, so ...

J You were afraid they would sell out?

I Bingo.

⏵ 7.7

1 Notice /a/ and /uː/.
M = mother W = William

M William Bonney Junior! What is this?

W It's my school report, Mom.

M I know what it is! But you told me you'd done well this year. You wait till your father sees this.

2 Notice /g/ and /k/.
V = Vanessa C = Chris

V Hi Chris. So good that you could come. Come in, come in.

C Hi Vanessa, yeah, it's gonna be a great party. And this must be Pickles. Who's a cute little dog, then? Huh?

V Pickles. Pickles, no! Bad dog, bad dog.

C Ow! Get it off! Get it off! Vanessa! I thought you said your dog was friendly.

3 Notice the contractions and the connections.
G = Geri J = Josh

G Hi Josh, uh, nice shirt.

J Geri, what is this? James Bond night?

G Josh, it's_a cocktail party, you_are supposed to look smart.

J But ... but you told me the party was_informal_and ...

G No, I said "a few friends_and drinks," I didn't say "wear your beach clothes."

4 Notice /iː/ and /ɪ/.
A = Andy Z = Zoey

A Please leave your message after the beep.

Z Andy! Where are you? I'm in the line and the movie is going to start soon. Andy, you said that you wouldn't arrive late.

⏵ 7.9 Notice the final /k/.
P = Presenter PB = Paul Le Bernard

P Good evening and welcome to *Tech Talk*, your weekly discussion program on what's new in tech. I'm joined in the studio this week by the editor of *Technology World* magazine, Paul Le Bernard. This week we are discussing young tech innovators. From medical breakthroughs, energy technologies, or engineering electronic devices. First, Paul, what makes someone an innovator?

PB Personally, I think innovators are persistent and inquisitive and they are easily inspired by what they see around them. Take our first example this week, Brazilian tech innovator, Neide Sellin. She's an ex-computer science teacher and she's spent most of her career inventing new technology to help improve the quality of life for people with disabilities.

P I see. We'd love to hear more. Can you tell us what her latest development is?

PB Well, do you have any idea how many Brazilian people have vision problems?

P No, I don't.

PB 6.5 million people. Do you know how many guide dogs there are in Brazil?

P Absolutely no idea.

PB There are only 100 guide dogs! The problem is that buying, training, and looking after a guide dog can cost thousands of dollars. This is impossible for many blind people.

P And this is where Neide Sellin comes in?

PB Exactly. Neide has invented a robot guide dog called Lysa. Her invention has five sensors and two engines. It can tell the user about risks and obstacles via recorded voice messages. With this device, blind users can be guided around indoor areas such as shopping malls and schools. By 2020, Neide hopes Lysa will be used outside, too.

P It sounds amazing, but I wonder if this is really a more affordable solution. Do you have any idea how much it costs?

PB Well, Lysa still costs around $3,000, but this is far cheaper than a real guide dog. At the moment, the device is available to private and public companies, such as airports and hospitals. Neide eventually hopes to improve the dog with artificial intelligence and GPS. Her greatest ambition is to offer dignity and independence to the 253 million blind and visually-impaired people around the world.

P Well, that certainly sounds very inspiring. Let's move on to our next young innovator ...

⏵ 7.11 Notice spellings of /n/, /t/, and /d/ endings.
A = Ann B = Bruce

A Cool phone, dude.

B Thanks. Mom was like, "What's wrong with the one we gave you last year?" and I was like, "Mom, that model is so last year," so she got me this one for Christmas.

A You like it?

B Are you kidding? I love it—especially Justin.

A Justin?

B Yep—my, what do they call it—personal assistant.

A Oh, speech recognition. Sweet. Does it, uh, tell the time, check the weather, and stuff?

B Yeah, and much more. This morning I told Justin I was bored—which I was—and I thought he was going to, like, ask me to repeat the command and whatever, and, guess what, he asked if he bored me.

A Get out! No way! Man, this is, like, so cool.

B Then I asked him if he was hungry and he, uh, he was like, "I'm a cell phone, not a person." Freaking unbelievable.

A Mine has voice recognition, too, but it's not so smart, you know? It'll, like, make calls, set the alarm clock ... and stuff. The other day I asked her to text someone and it took her, like, three minutes to figure out what to do.

B Her?

A Mine's not a dude—it's called Alice.

⏵ 7.12 Notice the weak h in *he* and *him*.

A Dude, I so want to try Justin.

B Here, have fun.

A Sweet ... Justin, where am I?

J I'm sorry, I don't know your name.

A And you said he was smart, right? I asked where, not who.

B He is smart, I'm telling you. Give it another shot.

A OK. Uh ... Justin, will the weather get worse?

J It looks like rain tonight. Here's the forecast for the next two days ...

A Wow ... Pretty awesome, dude. Justin ...

J Yes?

A Do you love me?

B AHAHAH—never tried to ask him that.

J I'm not ready for that kind of commitment yet.

B Isn't he amazing?

A Oh my God, I love him, I love him! Mmm ... What can I ask him now ... Justin, please call me an ambulance.

J OK. From now on I will call you Anne Ambulance.

A What? No way! Uh ... Justin, make me a coffee.

J Ahem, I'm just a phone.

B Don't you just love him?

A But was it, like, a joke? Or did he misunderstand me?

B I think he was kidding.

170

Audioscript

▶7.16 Notice Mark's hesitation / repetitions and Nick's listening sounds.

M = Mark   N = Nick

M What I don't understand is how, how is it that, on the 2001 NAEP history exam, 52% of high school seniors chose Nazi Germany, Imperial Japan, or Fascist Italy as our ally. Not the Soviet Union.

N Hi, I'm Nick Gillespie with Reason TV. I'm here today with Mark Bauerlein, author of *The Dumbest Generation*. A provocative new book that says "the digital age stupefies young Americans and jeopardizes our future." In fact, there's even a, uh, second uh, subtitle, which says "don't trust anyone under thirty." Mark, what's the premise of the book?

M Digital culture … uh, means, means this to most teenagers. It doesn't open them up to the great big world … of ideas and artworks and, and, and documents and politics and foreign affairs—which is all out there on the Internet, the potential is there. Instead, it gives them what a … teenagers really care about: other teenagers.

N Mmm hmm.

M Access to one another. They're not going to the Smithsonian Institution website. When Nielsen Ratings examined the most popular websites for young adults, nine out the top ten, teenagers, nine out of the top ten were for social networking.

N Mmm.

M 55% of high school students spend less than one hour a week reading and studying for class. They spend nine hours a week social networking.

N Sure.

M And this, this is what brought me into this, this work. Studies of leisure habits by, by young adults. And one thing we can say is … that … the leisure reading people do, young people do, the visits to museums that they do.

N Mmm hmm.

M The library visits that they do, those have gone down. And that's, that's just natural, because the menu of leisure options for young, for teenagers and young adults, has gotten bigger. Reading is, is, is … has a smaller portion on the menu … uh, that they have. And when you go into the average fifteen-year old's bedroom now, it's a multimedia center. Yeah, there're a few books up there on the shelf. There's the laptop, the cell phone, video game console, Blackberry, iPod, and all those diversions give them something a lot more compelling … than the story of Anthony and Cleopatra and Caesar!

N Mhm.

▶7.17 Notice the stress, pauses, and /ɔɪ/.

H = host   T = Tom   B = Barbara

H … which means, that, / yeah, the website was most probably hacked. // Speaking of the Internet, / I just got my hands on a book by a guy called Mark Bauerlein and … // well, the book's called *The Dumbest Generation* and basically it says that Internet is making young people … // **stupid**.

T Well, he has a point.

B Seriously, Tom?

T Yeah. I mean, / we can't deny that teens are buying fewer books and generally …

H How old are you, Tom?

T 32 … / We're not reading as much as people in their 40s or 50s, you know? // I mean, / bookstores are going out of business week after week. I find that …

B Well, it depends on what you mean by **reading**. // It's … / It's not that teens are reading less, / it's just that we're reading on our tablets … or e-readers, smart phones, or whatever. // For example, I'm 19 / and I've got hundreds of digital titles downloaded.

H But how many of those have you actually **read**?

T That's a good point.

B I don't know, but, / you see, / the point is … reading has been on the decline for …

T Barbara, / but don't you think …

B Hold on a second, let me finish. // Listen, / people have been reading less for **at least** 30 years, / long before the Internet ever existed. / So, / really, // we can't blame the Internet, can we?

H Well, you may agree or disagree, but he makes some valid points, / don't you think? // Young people have access to more information than we ever did, but, / honestly, how much are they actually / **learning**? I mean, I was talking to my son the other day and he thought Rome was a country … / **a country**! / And he's a pretty smart boy, you know?

B My point **exactly**! / The book says teens are getting dumber … / I totally disagree. // If anything, / people's IQs have gone up, / **not** down, / over the past 90 years or so.

T Mmm … / That may be true, but don't you think there's something wrong here? / **Rome** / — a **country**? / Come on! // And you know what, / I also think the, uh … / young people are starting to avoid face-to-face contact because of the Internet …

B Yeah, / I couldn't agree more.

T I mean, / most of my friends spend hours and hours locked in their rooms, / chatting on Facebook. // I mean, this can't …

Unit 8

▶8.2 Notice /ɪ/ and /iː/.

Sure, we all want to look better. Some people try makeup or even plastic surgery. Others choose Photoshop. Graphic designer and Photoshop expert James Fridman is well-known for taking people's Twitter requests for image alterations. James reads people's requests for changes to their pictures and does exactly what they ask him to do. Unfortunately for them, James does literally whatever he is asked. Most of his images are silly and fun. People ask James to remove photobombers, make them look smaller or bigger, or add something to the picture. But Fridman does not encourage people to retouch their images to meet today's often unrealistic beauty standards. He now has thousands of online followers because of the creative way he doctors the "vain" photos shared on social media.

One heart-warming example of James's work is a photo sent to him by a young woman who was suffering from an eating disorder and low self-esteem. She asked James to photoshop her to make her look beautiful. He responded by making no change to the image and telling her that nothing could make her more beautiful than she already was.

▶8.3 Notice /ð/, /θ/, and /v/.

J = Jon   E = Eliza

J I used to love Michael Jackson. *Smooth Criminal* had the coolest video ever!

E I know! I loved it, too. Remember that thing he did when he leaned right over. I used to try to do it and fall down … a lot! How on earth did he do that?

J He must have had wires attached to his jacket. It's the only explanation, surely!

E Well … maybe it was something to do with his shoes.

J Yes, I suppose, he might have put magnets on them and on the floor.

E Magnets?! To hold up the weight of a man, they must have been very strong!

J True, but it's possible, isn't it? Or maybe he really could lean that far!

E He was good, but not that good! He can't have been able to do that. It's impossible.

J I bet Michael Jackson could!

E Or, I guess his clothes were specially engineered.

J Yeah, he may have had special pants made!

▶8.4 Notice /ʌ/, /uː/, and /ʊ/.

Fans all over the world tried to copy Michael Jackson's smooth moves. However, there was one move in particular that left everyone wondering just how he did it: that famous lean from *Smooth Criminal*. Jackson and his dancers leaned forward at an angle of 45 degrees with their feet flat on the floor and then returned to an upright position. So just how did they manage to defy gravity like that?

The truth is that Jackson had a special shoe designed. The shoe had a triangular opening in the heel which attached to a metal hook which emerged from the floor at exactly the right moment. This anchored the dancers to the floor and stopped them from falling over.

This clever shoe did the job perfectly apart from one mistake in 1996. Jackson's heel came loose from the hook during a concert and he fell flat. Luckily, the star wasn't injured, and the shoe was redesigned to make sure it didn't happen again. The shoe was sold for $600,000 after Jackson's death and is now in the Hard Rock Café in Moscow.

▶8.7 Notice /tʃ/, /ʃ/, /ʒ/, and /kt/.

What David Blaine is actually performing is an optical illusion called Balducci levitation. This method involves the illusionist positioning themselves approximately three metres away from their audience and at a 45 degree angle. The audience should be a small one so that they are always in this limited field of vision. The audience will only see the back of one foot and most of the other foot. It's also important to wear long trousers which obstruct the view of the illusionist's feet and increases the effectiveness of the trick. The performer, of course, uses various methods to misdirect and distract the audience. Then they simply stand on the toes of one foot and raise the other foot. To the audience it looks like they are really levitating.

David Copperfield had a performance area of a stage with two towers and an arch to support a huge curtain. The TV cameras and the audience could only see the statue through the arch. The curtains were closed and Copperfield distracted the audience with enthusiastic chatter. While this was happening, the stage was actually slowly rotated! When the curtains opened again, the Statue of Liberty had disappeared! In fact, it was simply concealed behind one of the towers and the audience didn't realize they had been moved. The lights on the stage were also so bright that the audience would have been partially blinded anyway!

171

◗8.9 Notice s = /s/ or /z/.

B = Brandon C = Courtney

C No way! You're kidding! You mean just like the one on *My Super Sweet 16*?

B Yeah, but, like, a thousand times better ... Mom was like, "Sweetheart, why don't we have an ice-skating party?", and I was like, "Mom, that is so last year."

C Yeah, totally.

B So ... We're having a movie party.

C Yay! Awesome!

B There'll be a massive outdoor screen by the pool and ... Well, you'll see. It'll be, like, the most fun you've ever had ... Ever. I hope it doesn't rain.

C Brandon, this is so exciting! What will you be wearing?

B Dad bought me this pathetic grey suit and tie ...

C Yuck!

B Yeah, I know! So I told him, "Dad! Hello? This is a movie party, not a fairy tale!"

C Duh!

B And I wanna look just like Alden Ehrenreich.

C Who?!

B You know, the actor who plays Han Solo in the *Star Wars Story* movie.

C Oh yeah, he always looks great!

◗8.10 Notice s = /s/ or /z/.

B And I wanna look just like Alden Ehrenreich.

C Who?!

B You know, the actor who plays Han Solo in the *Star Wars Story* movie.

C Oh yeah, he always looks great!

B So Dad hired—wait for it—a fashion designer and we're going to have a new suit made.

C Specially for you?

B Of course.

C That is so cool! And your hair looks awesome! Tell me, did you have it dyed?

B Yeah. I spent, like, four hours at the salon and I got my nails done, too ... Look!

C Oh, yeah! They look so good. So ... is everything ready?

B No! Can you believe it? My parents are, like, so incompetent. I mean, the pool's dirty and Dad hasn't gotten it cleaned yet. Hello? Does he expect me to do it? And Mom can't cook, so we still need to have the cake made. This is all so stressful! I'm exhausted!

C Who wouldn't be?

B And, get ready for this, I signed all the two hundred invitations myself. It took me, like, one hour.

C Humph! Like you had nothing better to do.

◗8.13 Notice the three-syllable words.

I love this bedroom. The double bed looks so comfortable. I like the color scheme. The dresser, mirror, and closet are the same color. It looks very fresh. The pillows and the comforter match, too. I also like the color of the walls and how it complements the color of the furniture. There are lots of cool accessories, too, and I love the light and the colorful bird hanging from the ceiling. They add a modern touch. Yes, I really like this bedroom.

◗8.14 Notice the intonation. ↗↘

B = Barry M = Mick

B Hey, you've gotta come and see what we've done in here.

M Done? Hmm, you haven't done anything crazy, have you? ↗

B No, of course not! Come and have a look.

M Oh, wow! When did you do all this? It looks fantastic!

B I've been doing it evenings and weekends for the last few weeks. This room really needed some attention. It's great, isn't it? ↘

M Well, what a surprise for Tom! He'll love it, won't he? ↘

B I hope so!

◗8.15 Notice the intonation. ↗↘

M I can't believe it! You didn't do it all yourself, did you? ↗

B No. I got some of the guys to come over and help me last weekend. We gave the walls a fresh coat of paint, painted some of the furniture. I had the bookcase on the wall made by a friend of mine. I remember Tom saw one like that in a magazine and really liked it.

M It's very cool. That rug wasn't there before, was it? ↘

B No, that's new.

M Tom's been talking about doing this for ages. You know he's going to be over the moon, don't you? ↘

B Let's hope so! I wanted to surprise him when he got out of the hospital.

◗8.17 Notice the intonation. ↗↘

B = Barry T = Tom

B Hey, look who's here! Welcome home!

T Hi, Barry. Man, it's good to be back.

B But you said you'd be discharged tomorrow, didn't you? ↗

T Yeah ... but they let me out early, thank goodness, so here I am.

B So, how are things?

T Good. I'm feeling a lot better and it's so good to be home. The hospital bed was just ... What in the name of ...?

B Surprise!

T Oh, wow! What have you done?!

B You've been thinking about doing this, haven't you? ↘

T Yes, but I wasn't expecting this? You aren't serious, are you? ↗ I don't know what to say.

B I knew you'd love it. Just say "Thank you".

T Thank you so much. That's the rug I saw in the department store, isn't it? ↘

B Sure is!

T Thank you, Barry. This is awesome!

◗8.18 Notice /ʌ/, /oʊ/, and /ɒ/.

... and we will cover that in the next couple of days. So today, as part of our "image is everything" series, we're going to be looking at the reasons behind three different companies—global companies—altering their logos and how their target markets liked—or didn't like—the new versions. And trust me, some of the stories are fascinating. Our very first story involved the international ...

◗8.19 Notice the **sentence stress** and weak forms.

So, as most of you probably know, Instagram's former logo was considered one of the most recognizable tech logos of all time. The retro brown and cream camera with a rainbow stripe that reminded us of instant Polaroid cameras was iconic, but one day, [beep – 1] for some reason, they sadly decided to change the logo! Users were not impressed and took to the Internet to share their opinions. The main complaint from original users was that it seemed no time or effort had been spent on the new logo. No one really got it, and it didn't make sense. However, [beep – 2] Instagram was trying to attract new users— you know people who might've never visited the site before, and wanted the new logo to reflect how the app had transformed since its creation. The new purple, orange, and pink icon is more colorful, sleek, and modern, but was it a good idea? Hmm [beep – 3], I'm not convinced it works.

Now, take a look at the second slide ... As some of you may know, in 2011, Starbucks celebrated its, uh, its 40th anniversary. To mark the occasion, they must've thought: "Hey, let's create a new logo and drop the words 'Starbucks Coffee.'" Well, unfortunately, [beep – 4] most Starbucks customers were not crazy about the new logo ... They preferred the old one and didn't quite understand why Starbucks took their name off. Well, personally, [beep – 5] I find the new green logo simple and elegant. You see, Starbucks and its logo are well-known all over the world, and the green circle ... well, the green circle speaks for itself. In other words, [beep – 6] the logo doesn't need to tell the world that it's Starbucks Coffee—everybody knows that.

◗8.20 Notice /ə/ and /ɜː/.

Now, moving on to our third story ... and the last one today ... Gap released their new logo ... yeah, this beauty ... a few years ago. They must've tried to create something modern and contemporary, but, boy, were they wrong. The dark blue square of the original logo certainly looked very traditional, didn't it? It was used for more than two decades, and most people loved it. Then the new one comes along and, guess what, everybody ... hates it. In a matter of hours, there are thousands—I mean thousands—of negative comments on Facebook and Twitter. A few weeks later, Gap discards the new logo, returns to the old one, and fires the president. How about that? Honestly, I think they were right to go back to the old one. Moral of the story? Well, if it ain't broke, don't fix it!

◗8.22 Notice /ʌ/, /ʊ/, and /ɔː/.

G = Guilherme F = Fabi

G I love this class. It's really interesting.

F Yeah, it's really good, isn't it? I wish we'd had Professor Ford last year.

G Yeah. She's awesome.

F That Instagram logo is interesting, isn't it?

G Honestly, I don't like the new one. I really don't.

F Hmm ... I kind of like it ... It feels, I don't know, different ... What about Starbucks? Which one do you like better?

G I don't know ... Both are OK, I guess, but I think I like the old one better than the new one.

F Really? Oh, come on! It feels so ... old, with the name and all ... Well, I don't really like either of them ... I'm tired of the green mermaid.

G Now, maybe I'm crazy, but remember the Gap logo?

F Uh-huh.

G I actually prefer the second one to the first.

F You mean the one that looks like it was drawn by a child?

G Exactly!

F You know what? Me, too. They shouldn't have gone back to the old one.

Review 4

◗R4.1 Notice the spellings of the repeated sounds.

1 I asked, then I parked, and then the problems started.

2 We accuse you of causing the accident. No excuses!

3 Should they accelerate, accommodate, or experiment?

Unit 9

◗9.3 Notice /ʃ/, /θ/, and /ð/.

1 ... And I mean, it's just not fair. You're simply downloading a song! This is not theft! You're not

172

Audioscript

a thief! Why should you go to prison? For using something that's out there for the whole world to use? Just last month they arrested this 19-year-old who'd been downloading CSI episodes. That's so unfair! That's why I really think songs, books, and music should be completely free. Also …

2 So this one's kind of hard to answer, but, uh … Gee, I don't know, maybe … armed robbery … I've lived in this neighborhood for, what, two years and I've never actually seen a robber. So, yeah, I mean, I never even think about it. I feel pretty safe here, actually. By the way, this is really for a school project, right? I mean, you're not going to share this on the Internet or anything, are you?

3 … Uh, yeah. Burglary. Our next-door neighbors went away for the weekend and someone broke into their house. I was watching TV, you know, and I saw the whole thing. The burglar was a woman in her 40s—yeah, a woman, a blonde woman wearing a mask. I called the cops, but when they got there, she'd already left, you know? So, I wonder …

4 Yeah, and call me a pessimist, but, really, I don't see any way out. People are turning to drugs for all sorts of reasons – it's never for just one thing. What has the government been doing to change things? No one knows for sure. And I … well, I think drug dealing is likely to get worse as the years go by. And you know what? The new legislation next year will probably make no difference. I mean, sending drug dealers to prison isn't enough. You see … Excuse me …

5 … Yeah. Well, not only me, but every mother in my neighborhood. I mean, my husband and I are doing OK: brand new car, nice house, we've just had a new pool built … So, you know, all eyes are on us. So, uh … I keep telling my kids to, you know, just run if someone they don't know gets too close … Run as fast as they can, no matter who—anyone can be a potential kidnapper, you know? Or, even worse, a murderer. So, yeah, that's something that worries me. A lot. Oh, and here's something else …

⊙9.7 Notice /w/ and / w̄ / when two vowels connect.

1 Thirty-two-year-old Shena Hardin was caught on camera driving on a sidewalk in order to go around a school bus that was dropping off children. She was taken to court and the judge sentenced her to an embarrassing punishment. She was told to stand at a busy intersection holding a sign which read, "Only an idiot would drive on a sidewalk to avoid a school bus." Just to add to her humiliation, the event was live-streamed by television crews. Hardin also had her license suspended and was ordered to pay $250 in court costs.

2 It was an ordinary morning in San Francisco's District Court, and then, without warning, someone's cell phone rang and broke the silence. Judge Robert Rather didn't like what he heard: "Whose phone is ringing? Bring it to me now!" Nobody did. "Everyone will be arrested unless I get that phone now!" Again, no one confessed at all. Judge Rather wasn't kidding: all 42 people present were charged with disturbing the peace and sent to jail. After suffering in prison for a couple of hours, they were released, of course. But the judge was permanently removed from office for abusing judicial power. In a recent interview, he said he had been under a lot of stress.

⊙9.10 Notice /aɪ/.

Cybercrime. This is a term we are used to hearing in the news almost every day. In fact, experts predict that by 2025 cyberattacks will have become—are you ready for this—the world's top threat. Cybercrime covers a wide range of different offences. Cybercriminals can delete or change computer records, create fraudulent documents, and sell classified information. And there's nothing to stop them from one day saying: "I have an idea. Why don't we overheat some nuclear reactors?" With us on set this morning, we have Deniz Kaya, author, consultant, and technology guru. He'll be telling us if we should take these warnings seriously. But first, the shocking news about the tragic …

⊙9.11 Notice /ə/.

H = host D = Deniz

H Joining us now is Deniz Kaya, senior editor of *Technology Today* and author of *Dark Times Ahead*. Deniz, thanks for being here.
D Thanks for having me.
H So … is it that bad?
D No.
H Oh yeah?
D It's catastrophic. And it'll get much worse.
H Really?
D I'm afraid so.

⊙9.12 Notice /j/ and /w/.

D For starters, there's a new generation of hackers out there, and some are as young as, what, 12, 13.
H No way!
D Yeah, and they're only kids, you know? But at some point you have to stop and ask yourself— what's gonna happen to these kids? Will they have become big-time criminals by the time they're 20, 25?
H Exactly.
D Here's another problem. Malware is getting more and more intelligent …
H Who's malware? A super villain or something?
D No, that's not a person. Malware refers to, uh, to all sorts of viruses out there, you know? And some of them are pretty scary. Did you hear about the Facebook Messenger virus?
H Yeah. The one with the video?
D That's the one. By December, one out of 50 computers in New York will have been infected by that thing. Here's what it does: It sends a message, from a "friend", which says: "OMG! It's you?" and has a link to what looks like YouTube. However, when you follow the link, it downloads malware onto the computer. The same message will then be sent to more victims from your account.
H Wow. That's awful. Do not open links to videos if you're not sure, then!
D Bingo! But you know what really worries me? Cybercriminals will be carrying out more and more attacks wirelessly, and we won't be protected. They will have developed the ability to spread viruses across multiple devices very, very easily. They'll jump from phone to phone … and then from phone to laptop, and then to tablet …
H Over wireless networks …
D Exactly. So you might be walking down the street and … bang! And you know, there's actually some data suggesting that by the end of the decade, cybercriminals will have targeted 20 per cent of all the world's smart phones. And that's an optimistic estimate.
H Wow. But is there anything we can do to protect ourselves?
D Yep. There's all sorts of trouble you can avoid by taking a few simple precautions.

⊙9.13 Notice /p/, /v/, and /b/.

H So you've told us about the dangers we'll be facing in the future. Can you offer us some advice on what we can do about it?
D Of course! The first thing is passwords! I know it's much easier to use the same password for all your accounts, but you're putting yourself at risk. Use a unique password for everything. Each one should have at least eight characters and be a combination of letters, symbols, and numbers. Also be very aware of what you click on. It's so easy to get caught out by just clicking on a link from someone you don't know. The consequences can be dramatic. Just don't do it. If you are attacked, you might lose all of your files. To prevent this, make sure you regularly back up your files. If you are targeted, you will have already stored your information elsewhere. Another important point is to always install the latest updates. Don't ignore the messages your computer sends you. By updating, your software will be easier to use.
H Yes, essential rules we all need to follow. Deniz, thank you very much for your input today. Coming up …

⊙9.15 Notice the intonation. ↗↘

1

H = husband W = wife B = burglar

H Oh, it's good to be home, isn't it? ↗
W Sure is. ↘ I know that late flight was cheaper, ↘ but, boy, I'm exhausted! ↘
H: Me, too. ↘ I can't wait to crawl into …What the …?! ↗ What's going on?! ↗ Who are you?! ↗
B What, wait, hang on …
W Oh my goodness! ↗ I'm calling the police! ↗
B No, wait …

2

F = father D = daughter

F Do you have any idea what time it is? ↗ Your mother and I were worried sick ab … Wait a second … Are those my car keys? ↗
D What?
F Jennifer, what are you doing with my keys? ↘
D Dad, uh, it's not what you're thinking.
F Oh, that's good news. ↘ 'Cause I was starting to think my teenage daughter had stolen the family car. ↗
D It's not what it seems. I swear. I was, uh, I was …

3

F = flight attendant P = passenger

F Excuse me sir, we're about to take off. ↘ I'm gonna have to ask you to put your bag in the luggage compartment. ↘
P1 Uh, no, it's fine here, thank you. ↘
F Sir, I'm afraid this is …
P2 Hey, is that bag moving? ↗
P1 What? No, it's not. Of course not. ↘
P2 Yes, it is. Something's just moved in that bag. ↘
P1 Hold on, I can explain. ↘
F Sir, I'm gonna have to ask you to …

⊙9.16 Notice the sentence stress and weak forms.

1

W The **police** will be **here** any **minute**!
B **Wait** a minute. This is **not** what it **looks** like!
H **Stay** where you **are**.
B Just **hear** me **out**! Please! I just … I got **kicked** out of my a**ccommo**dation and I **saw** the **house** was **empty** and … I **haven't** taken **anything**, I **promise**.
W **No**! We **don't** want to **hear** it! Just **keep** quiet until the **police get here**.

173

2

F Jennifer, what are you doing with my keys?

D Dad, uh, it's not what you're thinking.

F Oh, that's good news. 'Cause I was starting to think my teenage daughter had stolen the family car.

D It's not what it seems. I swear. I was, uh, I was just checking out your MP3 collection.

F Yes, of course you were. I mean, that's just the kind of music you're into, isn't it?

D No, but, but Dad ... You don't understand.

F No ifs and buts, Jennifer. I don't want to get a phone call from the police. You stay out of my car unless you're with me. Do you hear me?

D Yes, Dad, but ...

F No!

3

P2 Yes, it is. Something's just moved in that bag.

P1 Hold on, I can explain.

F Sir, I'm going to have to ask you to get off the plane.

P1 Lucy's just six months old, she's not dangerous at all. Look!

P2 Oh well, that makes me feel much better. Thank you.

F Now sir, please stand up and come with me.

P1 OK, OK. But really, she wouldn't hurt anybody, I promise.

Unit 10

▶10.3 Notice /j/ and /dʒ/.

C = Carlos G = Gloria

G Hey, what are you doing home so soon?

C Good to see you, too! What are you doing?

G Some silly quiz ...

C Cool as a cucumber, occasionally moody, or chronically short-tempered. Let's hear your answers then. This should be interesting ...

G Hey, what's that supposed to mean? I have my ups and downs, but I'm pretty stable.

C Well, yes, you do, but you're trying to work it out. How's the yoga class going by the way?

G Really well. I think it's really helping. You know, little by little, I'm learning how to relax.

C That's good. Let's have a look at the first question ... Do you ever wake up feeling grumpy? Yeah, I'd have to agree with that. You definitely do!

G I know, I know, I'm grumpy in the morning, but I'm sick and tired of waking up early, Carlos! Five thirty feels like the middle of the night still!

C I guess, it's easy for me to say. I don't even dare to talk to you before 7 a.m.

G It's probably wise. I just ... I need some peace and quiet in the morning, that's all.

C What about this one: Do you ever get fed up with activities and people you actually like ... What do you mean "no"? You're fed up with your job!

G Well, yeah, but the question is about stuff I like. And I don't like working in retail.

C But you did when you started, right?

G Well, yeah, I did, but not anymore. "How can I help you today? That looks great on you. Have a nice day." Blah, blah, blah, blah, blah. I just ... I hate doing the same things again and again ...

C ... and again and again. Yeah, I get it. You need variety.

G Yeah. Sooner or later, I'll need to start looking for a new job.

C Five ... Do you ever swear when other drivers do something stupid? Yep, that's right. You do.

G How would you know that?

C I've been told.

G What?

C It's a small neighborhood, Gloria.

G Well, but you can't blame me, can you? I mean, you know what it's like to drive in L.A.!

C Do you ever yell at people for no serious reason? "No." You're kidding, right?

G Carlos, when did I ever yell at someone? Tell me!

C Whoa, whoa. OK, forget I said anything. You're really, really calm!

▶10.5 Notice the connections.

... and that just_about does_it for_us tonight. But before we go, here's the moment you've_all been waiting for: People's top pet peeves. Yes, we_asked_ and you voted! So, here_are the results.
At number 10, with 871 votes, people who suddenly_open the door without knocking first. Yep—we've_all done that before, haven't we?
Number 9, when people keep_interrupting you when you talk. Well, that's just rude.
Number 8, people who keep using the word "like" all the time. Yeah, that_is_annoying.
Number 7, with_a_little_over 1,000 votes, bad phone habits, like not returning texts_or phone calls.
At number 6, with 1,234, people who honk, instead_ of ringing the bell, when they come to pick_you_up— especially late_at night. Hate that, too.
Number 5, people who promise to call you and then they don't.
Number 4—oh, I hate this_one—people who_are too lazy to put their trash_in the trash can. I mean ...it's right there.
Number 3, with_exactly 1,700 votes, when someone uses_a finger to pick their teeth. Well, that's just gross. Don't do_it.
The next one kind_of surprised me—I didn't_expect to see_it near the top with_as many as 1,809 votes, number 2 being the first_one to_arrive_at a party— Well, I guess it_is pretty embarrassing, isn't it?
And finally, at number 1, something I think many_of_ us hate, it's people who_are addicted to playing with their phones. What do you think? Let_us know on ...

▶10.6 Notice /juː/ and /uː/.

C = coach Mi = Mia J = Jim V = Vince Ju = Julia

C ... the last time we met. So, anyway, let's give a warm welcome to anyone who's joining our anger management group for the first time—and that's, well, everybody except Julia. So, first of all, Mia, hi. Welcome aboard.

Mi Hi.

C So, Mia, why are you here?

Mi My name's Mia and my employers have told me I have to sort my issues out. They say I'm too demanding and impatient with my staff. They are probably right. If things aren't done the way I want them or immediately ... like, if I call and leave a message, and I don't hear from them in an hour, I get really mad and yell at them. You know, I really want to change, 'cause I'm afraid of losing my job.

C OK, Mia. Listen, I want to thank you for being so honest—that's the spirit! Jim, would you like to introduce yourself?

J OK, I guess.

C Go on ...

J Ah, yeah, well ... my girlfriend ... she thinks I'm, like, too possessive. You know, I just want to know where she is and, like, what she's doing.

C OK, is that it?

J Well, I don't like it when she talks to other people——she's constantly on the phone with her friends and on Snapchat and stuff——I mean, all the time——and it makes me jealous, you know, and then she accuses me of being aggressive. So, that's why I'm here.

C I see. Interesting. Thank you, Jim. OK ... Uh, next on the list is ... Vince. Hi. Why don't you tell us what brought you here?

V Well, actually, I'm afraid it's people like Jim that brought me here.

C What do you mean?

V I don't mean to be arrogant, but ... I'm sick and tired of hearing that kind of English. Didn't you learn anything at school?

J Excuse me? What are you talking about?

V "Like, like, like." How old are you? Like, 14?

J Wow! OK. Well, I am sorry! I apologize for upsetting your sensitive ears.

V So you should be! You know, there's just no excuse for bad grammar.

J Well, I guess we know why you're here now, don't we?

C OK, guys. I think we can talk about this reasonably.

Ju Reasonably? Do you think yelling at someone for the way they speak is reasonable?

V Hey! What's it got to do with you?

Ju Hey, didn't your mother ever teach you any manners?

C Julia! Vince! Everybody, calm down. Remember, there are ways of dealing with this ... carefully, step by step. We are responsible for controlling our anger. In fact, let's use this as a good example. Let's look at some strategies to help us face these feelings and ...

▶10.9 Notice /s/, /z/, and /ʃ/.

1

B = bride G = groom

B I cannot believe that you said that. To my mother, Jose, my mother.

G Well, she just wouldn't stop talking about your ex-boyfriend, you have to admit it!

B Jose! Stop it! You should apologize for saying that or we're never going to ...

G Oh, or what? I'm sick and tired of hearing how wonderful Chris is! I don't think I'm being unreasonable.

2

G = grandmother Gd = granddaughter

G Oh ... but ... what happens if I press the wrong button by accident? I'm afraid of losing everything.

Gd Oh, don't worry, you won't. Look, there's an easy way of saving this. I promise. Just click on the file here and save here.

G Is that really all I have to do? That's easy, isn't it?

Gd Of course! I told you it was. Now you have a go.

G OK, so I just click here and then ...

▶10.11 Notice the sentence stress.

Good morning everyone, and welcome to Assertiveness Training. I hope you're ready to learn some life-changing lessons! What is assertiveness? Any ideas? No? OK, assertiveness is a way of communicating your needs and wants but without hurting other people.

It's difficult to tell the difference between assertiveness and aggression. Aggression is about getting what you want without caring how you affect others.

Now, there are many benefits of being assertive. Assertive people are better managers. They get the job done but treat colleagues respectfully. They're good at negotiating because they can understand the opponent's argument and can reach a compromise more easily. They are also less stressed because they are more self-confident. Sounds good, doesn't it?

Audioscript

So, how do we **become** more **assertive**? **First,** you have to **believe** in **yourself**. **Believe** that you de**serve** respect. **Next,** i**dent**ify what you **need** and **say** that in a **clear** and **confident** way. You **shouldn't** ex**pect** others to **know what** you **want**! **Accept** that you **cannot control** other **people**. If **someone** re**acts badly** to you, this is **not your fault** (but **remember** to be **respectful**). **Don't return** their **anger** and re**sentment**. **Stay calm**. You can **control your own actions**. If **you** are **not** off**ending** others, you have the **right to do** as **you wish**.

Next, say what **you're thinking** even if it's **difficult**. However, say it con**struct**ively and **with sensitivity**. You can **confront people** who **disagree** with you but **stay in control** and **be positive**.

Accept criticism as well as compliments. It's **important** to take **feedback** even when it's **negative**. If you **don't agree, that's fine** and **you can say so** without **being de**fen**sive**.

A very **useful tip** next. **Remember saying yes** to every little thing you've been asked to do over the years? Well, **stop** it. You need to **stop agreeing** to everything and **learn** to **say no** more often. **Understand** your **limits. Stop** to **think** about **how much** you can **manage realistically**.

Change your **language. Instead** of saying "I **could**, or **would**", say "I **will**". **Try** using more "**I**" **statements**: say "I **want**, I **feel**, I **need**" rather than "You **don't**, you **should**, you **never**", etc. This can be **very e**ffec**tive**.

And **finally**, something **simple. Listen. Listen** and try to **understand** the other person's **opinion**. Try **not** to **interrupt**.

So, let's **try putting** some of this **into practice**. I'd **like** to **try** some **roleplay**. Let's **get** into **groups** of …

⊙ 10.13 Notice /ʃ/, /ð/, /θ/, and /f/.

Any true relation**sh**ip between friends or signi**f**i**c**ant others **sh**ould be one between e**q**uals: you give and take e**q**ually. One person's needs aren't met over ano**th**er's. Friends and partners are supposed to give you energy and li**f**t you up when you're down, and want **th**e best for you. But sometimes we get into relation**sh**ips that drain energy from us. **Th**ese are toxic relationships and they can ne**g**atively a**ff**ect all aspects of our lives. On **th**is week's *WellCast*, we're going to tell you how you can tell if you're **e**ven in a toxic relation**sh**ip. And then we're going to help you ex**t**ricate yourself from that un**h**eal**th**y situation, *pronto!*

⊙ 10.14 Notice the short (/) and long (//) pauses.

Step 1: // Diag**n**ose the relationship. // How do you know if a friend or partner is bringing you down? // Well, / in much the same way that you know you're coming down with a cold. // Toxic relationships come with symp**t**oms. // When you're around this person, / how do you feel? // Here are a few other questions you should ask yourself if you're thinking you might be in a toxic situation: // Does my friend put me down all the time? // Are they jealous when I spend time with others? // Do they con**st**antly bring up parts of me that they want to change? // Do they take more than they give? // Am I only doing the things that they want to do? //

Step 2: // Recognize your role / in the relationship. // As Eleanor Roosevelt once said, / "Nobody can make you feel in**f**erior without your consent." / All right, look, you know we got that from *Princess Diaries*, **ob**viously. Moving on. // Listen, you have autonomy in every relationship in your life. // If a friend or partner is stealing your sun**sh**ine, / you need to figure out what you're doing to allow them to do this. // Are you being a **d**oormat? // Are you

putting this person's e**m**otional needs ahead of your own health? //

Step 3: // Start to build **boun**daries for this relationship. // Does your friend invite themselves over at all hours of the night? // Are they constantly bossing you around? // Are they always borrowing money from you? // Once you know the boundary that you want to set, / stick to it! / Draw your line in the sand. //

Step 4: // Recognize that you can't change other people, / but you can stop being a doormat. // If you've de**t**ermined that a friendship or relationship is toxic, / you know that you have to change the nature of that relationship. // Start by spending less time with that person / and do your best to de**t**ach yourself e**m**o**t**ionally. // Setting boundaries will hopefully help you begin to phase this relationship out. //

Step 5: // Get a second o**p**inion. // Especially if you're emotionally **vul**nerable, / the best thing you can do is surround yourself with people who love you / and who want you to be happy and healthy. // Use them as a lifeline during this time. //

Step 6: // Above all else, / look out for yourself. // Studies have shown that people with low self-e**st**eem / are far more likely to find themselves in toxic relationships. // You will never be treated with love and respect / unless you ab**s**o**l**utely believe that you de**s**erve these things. // Remember: you teach people how to treat you. / So do yourself the favor of loving yourself!

⊙ 10.16 Notice the connections that produce /w/ and /j/ sounds.

Welcome t**o** *English for all*, the podcast for students who want t**o** improve their English—fast! Last week, w**e** asked you to tell us about your strengths and weak**n**esses, your successes and your fru**str**ations. So, today we've chosen three messages to read on th**e** air. The first one—where is it? Oh, here—was written by Bruna, a listener from Colombia—hi, Bruna—who says she's good at grammar, but finds it hard t**o** e**x**press herself fluently. Listen, your English sounds fantastic and, you know, maybe you're much more fluent than you think. Anyway, here's what I think you should do: Try to focus on expressing your ideas fluently instead of speaking 100% correctly all the time. 'Cause, you see, the more you stop to think about what you're going to say next, the more you hes**i**tate. And remember: People will still understand yo**u** if you make a few mistakes. And here's another suggestion: Have you thought about asking a friend to practice with you for a few hours a week? You probably have at least one or two friends who speak some English, right? So think about it: You can have fun and improve your English at the same time without having to, I don't know, live a**broad** or anything. Thanks for writing, Bruna, and good luck.

Our second message comes from South Korea. Our listener says he has trouble understanding spoken English … Yeah, that's a common problem. Byung-Sang, listen, I have two su**gg**estions. First, listen t**o a**s much English as you can outside the classroom. For example, a good way of practicing is watching Internet videos on sites like YouTube, Dailymotion, and so on, at least every other day, for about an hour or so. Re**l**i**g**iously. Turn the su**bt**itles on and off sometimes, too. But be sure to choose a va**ri**ety of videos—both more and less ch**all**enging, OK? And who knows, you might even learn a new expression or two! And here's the second suggestion: If you want to improve your listening, you should con**s**i**d**er giving pronunciation a little more attention. Yeah, I'm serious. Research has shown that students with good pronunciation tend to be much better listeners. How about that?

And our final message comes from Omar—where's he from?—oh, Turkey, wow. Omar says he's not comfortable reading quickly, for, uh, for general comprehension. Omar, listen, reading too slowly is not always a good idea. For example, if you take an international exam, you'll need to be able to read fast, without a dictionary. So here's what I think you should do: Next time yo**u a**pproach a text, read it once quickly first. Then, if necessary, read it again, more carefully, looking for information you need. But try t**o** avoid reading slowly all the time. And about your vocabulary question, here's something that might help: learn words together. For example, how about learning "make an effort" instead of "effort"? Or "take a course" rather than only "course"? Our brains like these kinds of associations, you know? Well, that does it for us tonight. In the next e**p**isode, we'll be talking about …

Review 5

⊙ R5.1 Notice /r/ and /h/.

1

R = Ron H = Hanna

R   Hey Hanna, what a**r**e you **r**eading?

H   Oh, hi **R**on. Oh, this? It's a book **R**alph lent me. He said it was **r**eally good, but I just can't get into it.

R   Huh, so, what's it about?

H   Well, uh, that's just it. **R**alph said it was a **r**eally inte**r**esting de**t**ec**t**ive story … but the**r**e's no crime, not much sto**r**yline, nothing **r**eally. I just can't figu**r**e it out.

R   Hmmm … Well, maybe it'll tu**r**n out better than you think. You know, keep **r**eading!

2

L = Lenny S = Sue

S   Lenny? Have you changed something … You**r** ha**i**r or something?

L   Nope, not my ha**i**r. But I'm on this diet **r**ight now. I've lost a little weight.

S   Ah! That must be it! Yeah, you look **r**eally good!

L   Oh, thanks Sue. You know, it's p**r**etty ha**r**d to stick to it, the**r**e a**r**e so many things I can't eat, but, you know, it **r**eally lifts me up when I hea**r** things like that. So, thank you.

S   No p**r**oblem! Yeah, stick to it Lenny, don't give up!

3

J = Jackie B = Beth

J   What is it, Beth? You look kind of mi**s**erable. You'**r**e not coming down with anything, a**r**e you?

B   Oh, I don't think so … No, it's this work. I've got so much to do and so little time. I just don't know what to do. It's **r**eally b**r**inging me down.

J   Oh Beth, you poo**r** thing. Look, tell me it's none of my business, I don't want to boss you a**r**ound o**r** anything, but you **r**eally need to look out for yourself. Take a b**r**eak or something, you know?

B   Yeah, Jackie, maybe you'**r**e **r**ight. But then when will I finish this work?

⊙ R5.2 Notice the /t/, /d/, and /ɪd/ endings.

William Watts was a thief. One day he was stealing some jewels from a shop and set off the alarm. The police arriv**ed** at the shop before William had finish**ed**, so he quickly jump**ed** out of the window and ran away. Unfortunately for William, he turn**ed** the wrong way and saw the police station in front of him. He stopp**ed** running and tri**ed** to act naturally, but he was arrest**ed**. He was taken to court and convict**ed** of burglary. When the judge read the sentence, William start**ed** to cry.

175

Richmond

58 St Aldates
Oxford
OX1 1ST
United Kingdom

ISBN: 978-84-668-2611-2
Sixth reprint: 2024
CP: 896069
© Richmond / Santillana Global S.L. 2019

All rights reserved. No part of this book may be reproduced, stored in a retrieval system or transmitted in any form by any means, electronic, mechanical, photocopying, recording or otherwise, without the prior permission in writing of the Publisher.

Publishing Director: Deborah Tricker
Publishers: Luke Baxter, Laura Miranda
Media Publisher: Luke Baxter
Content Developers: Paul Seligson, Deborah Goldblatt
Editor: Shona Rodger
Proofreaders: Lily Khambata, Rachael Williamson, Daniel Deacon
Design Manager: Lorna Heaslip
Cover Design: Lorna Heaslip
Design & Layout: emc Design Ltd
Photo Researcher: Magdalena Mayo, Helen Reilly
Audio Production: John Marshall Media Inc.
***ID Café* Production:** Mannic Media

We would like to thank all those who have given their kind permission to reproduce material for this book:

Illustrators: Bill Brown, Alexandre Matos, Beach-o-matic, Laurent Cardon, Guillaume Gennet, Phil Hackett, Alvaro Nuñez, Leonardo Teixeira, Rico

Photos:
123RF/mopic, Getty Images Sales Spain; A. G. E. FOTOSTOCK/ Lubitz + Dorner; ALAMY/Everett Collection Inc, David Cattanach, Jim Newberry, Maciej Bledowski, Eddie Gerald, TP, Marmaduke St. John, PJF Military Collection, age fotostock, Marek Poplawski, Jemastock, Andrea Raffin, Jim O Donnell, Ian Allenden, WENN UK, runsilent, Jochen Tack, Elnur Amikishiyev, aberystwyth, B Christopher, ABC/Everett Collection Inc, Jess Kraft/ Panther Media GmbH, Mim Friday, Astronaut Images, dbimages, dpa picture alliance, Cyberstock, Steve Sant, Terry Harris, ZUMA Press, Inc, Domiciano Pablo Romero Franco, Moviestore collection Ltd, Fernando Quevedo de Oliveira, Mpi04/Media Punch/Alamy Live News, Irina Fischer, Collection Christophel, Ink Drop, M4Os Photos, WENN Ltd, Panther Media GmbH; CARTOONSTOCK/Way, Roy Delgado, Ian Baker, Zuvela.O, Bucella, Mike Baldwin; GETTY IMAGES SALES SPAIN/Hero Images, Andriano_cz, Littlebloke, Soren Hald, Thinkstock, Kadmy, NikFromNis, wwing, Bulgac, Gipi23, Jodiecoston, Champc, BartCo, Kike Calvo, Joe_Potato, Brosa, ASIFE, Vladimir Vladimirov, shootdiem, ZIG8, Fuse, ViewApart, BSIP, StockFood, Andreas Schlegel, Steve Hix, Tzogia Kappatou, Stephan Hoerold, Sirawit99, Purestock, Altrendo Images, Martin-dm, Dulezidar, comptine, Paul Zimmerman, Neustockimages, S-cphoto, RapidEye, Sally Anscombe, Jhorrocks, Daniel Schoenen, Moodboard, Lily Roadstones, ShutterOK, Kyle Lee/EyeEm, Catherine Ledner, TIMOTHY A. CLARY, Stockbyte, Monika Proc/EyeEm, Wavebreak, Weedezign, Westend61, Witthaya Pradongsin, Aiqingwang, Andy Sacks, Dave Reede, Portland Press Herald, Juanmonino, Alessandro De Carli/EyeEm, Fotog, NNehring, Peter Cade, Petrunjela, Tom Hoenig, Ktsimage, CaseyHillPhoto, Shironosov, AndreyPopov, AntonioGuillem, Austinadams, Imagno, Karwai Tang,

Kondor83, Leungchopan, Hanohiki, Elena Pueyo, Phaelnogueira, Filmwork, Nick Clements, Barcroft, Monty Rakusen, Lisa Stirling, marcduf, Wrangel, Johner Images, TVP Inc, RoNeDya, Jason LaVeris, JGI/Tom Grill, Rmnunes, MixMike, Alex Lapuerta, Llgorko, Tim Robberts, Steve Cicero, Jpa1999, South_agency, Alex Robinson, Ariel Skelley, Doug McKinlay, SergeyNivens, Humonia, Jeffrey Mayer, Joel Carillet, PeopleImages, Jupiterimages, Keith Brofsky, Klaus Vedfelt, Mike Coppola, Beinder, Marcelo Horm, Paul Bradbury, Luis Alvarez, Stuart Pearce, Studio-Annika, Wundervisuals, Andresr, KateSmirnova, Cecilie_Arcurs, GoodLifeStudio, Johnny Louis, Manuel ROMARIS, Martin Barraud, Mischa Keijser, da-kuk, Image Source, Paulprescott72, Philipp Nemenz, FreezingRain, Silverlining56, Zero Creatives, AleksandarNakic, Rayman, David Forman, Desiree Navarro, Igor Vershinsky, Alvis Upitis, Photos. com Plus, Priscilla Gragg, Simona Flamigni, Pumba1, Yuri_Arcurs, Yagi-Studio, PIKSEL, T3 Magazine, Alexander Spatari, Corbis Historical, Fancy/Veer/Corbis, Phil Walter, laszlo_szelenczey, Andrew Bret Wallis, Michael Heim/EyeEm, Hill Street Studios, Lee Whitehead/EyeEm, Pascal Le Segretain, Richard Theis/EyeEm, Mmac72, Nancy Honey, Andrey Vodilin/EyeEm, Ben Pipe Photography, GIUGLIO Gil/Hemis.Fr, Jose Luis Pelaez Inc, Monkeybusinessimages, Jean Baptiste Lacroix, Mint Images, Gareth Cattermole/TAS18, Narin Deniz Erkan/EyeEm, PhotoAlto/ Odilon Dimier, Lowryn, Kittiyut Phomphibul/EyeEm, Mark Edward Atkinson/Tracey Lee, Manuel-F-O; ISTOCKPHOTO/Getty Images Sales Spain; SHUTTERSTOCK/Lucasfilm/Bad Robot/Walt Disney Studios/Kobal, 20th Century Fox/Paramount/Kobal, Red Umbrella and Donkey, Patrimonio designs Ltd, KA Photography/KEVM111, Ultimate Prods./Kobal, Lewis Tse Pui Lung, Gurgen Bakhshetyan, Moviestore Ltd, Netflix/Kobal, Moviestore collection Ltd, Intararit, Artazum, Ollyy; Tom Fishburne/Marketoonist.com; copyright Vixisystem; Penguin Random House; Arnos Design Ltd; www. govloop.com; copyright PLelQ; www.italki.com; Faber & Faber; SPLASH NEWS; telfie.com; player.me; Starbucks; copyright Kengaru; geobeats; iTunes; IUCN; Gap; ARCHIVO SANTILLANA

Videos:
Andrew Thompson; Colin Beaven; IUCN; geobeats; Vicki Abeles; NIACE; Reason TV; watchwellcast

The Publisher has made every effort to trace the owner of copyright material; however, the Publisher will correct any involuntary omission at the earliest opportunity.

Printed in Brazil by Forma Certa

Lote. 800419